WE ARE STAYING

Eighty Years
in the Life of
a Family, a
Store, and a
Neighborhood

Jen Rubin

CARB
HOUSE

Alan Rubin (*for all the stories*)

and

Leon Rubin (*for having the dream and the chutzpah in the first place*)

Cover design: Diana Boger

ISBN: 978-1-7323000-0-2

Published by Carb House Press
carbhousepress@gmail.com

Praise for this book

"The best political stories are the human ones, and Jen Rubin recognizes this. We Are Staying is a remarkably powerful, poignantly told story of a family, a business, a neighborhood and a city. But what makes this book so brilliant, and so necessary, is the skill with which Rubin places this very personal story in the broader context of our struggles to understand one another and the common ground where we make our shared lives. Anyone who cares about sustainable development, urban policy, the history and the future of New York City and of a country that suffers from so much division, yet has the potential still to unite, will cherish this book."

—John Nichols, The Nation

"Jen Rubin's *We Are Staying* is about an America and a New York that is rapidly disappearing. It is a wonderful, true story of three generations of love, struggle, loss, courage, grit, and above all, family."

—Kevin Baker, author of *America the Ingenious*

"Jen Rubin's West Side neighborhood has been mine too for almost 50 years. She outlines the tale of a successful family, storefront business with panache, and it includes the New York story of beginning, striving, and belonging, and of heart, soul, and compassion for customers and workers. Just be sure you don't miss it."

—Gale A. Brewer, Manhattan Borough President

"Jen Rubin is a beautiful storyteller...both on stage and on the page!"

—Jenifer Hixson, The Moth

Contents

Prologue

"You gotta get a gimmick"

—Stephen Sondheim

FOR EIGHTY YEARS, A store named Radio Clinic stood on the 98th Street
block of Broadway on Manhattan's Upper West Side. My grandfather, Leon
Rubin, opened it in 1934 during the depths of the Depression as a radio repair
shop. To distinguish his shop from his many nearby competitors in those early
days of radio, he sat fixing radios in the storefront window—visible to the public
in his "clinic"—wearing a white doctor's lab coat. The business grew over the
decades to sell radios, televisions, appliances big and small, electronics, video
games, and air conditioners, lots and lots of air conditioners.

Radio Clinic laid strong roots in the community and remained a positive
anchor no matter what economic or social force was bearing down on the neighborhood. During its 80 years on the block, the Great Depression, World War II,
urban renewal policies, and gentrification all had an impact. Grandpa brought
his son and son-in-law, (my father Alan Rubin and my uncle Bill Grossman),
into the business in 1966, a time when the Upper West Side, like the city as a
whole, was in economic decline. Radio Clinic became my dad's to run alone a
decade after that. Dad barely had a week alone running the business before the
store was completely ransacked in the New York City Blackout of 1977. A resil-
ient and street-smart character, Dad was never stronger than he was during and

7

in the aftermath of the blackout. When others closed up shop and neighbors feared the neighborhood's further decline, he hung a sign on the window the day after the blackout that read, defiantly, "We Are Staying."

He stayed and he stayed and he stayed, until, finally, he could stay no longer. This is his, and Radio Clinic's, story.

1

The Blackout

That period was also punctuated by the blackout of 1977—
a brief, cautionary incident that has perhaps been too easily forgotten...
When morning came, they learned that many neighborhood businesses,
and the neighbors that ran them, had been wiped out.

—Peter Salwen, Upper West Side Story

Where were you when the lights went out in New York City
(I wanna know, I wanna know)

—The Trammps

IN THE SUMMER OF '76, I was the kid every kid wanted to be. I was paid a dollar an hour to play video games. Standing in the glass vestibule of Radio Clinic, I demonstrated to the world the latest in modern technology: the Atari arcade video game. I mainly played Stunt Cycle, a game modeled after Evil Knievel's infamous King's Island jump where he cleared fourteen Greyhound buses. The game allowed you to turn the throttle on your handlebar controller and to try to equal his stunt on the screen.

Arcade video games were new in 1976. Dad knew there was no better way to sell these video games than to have a 10-year-old kid play them in the window. The store was located on New York City's Upper West Side and I drew the attention of the thousands of people who passed by the store each day.

Standing in the front vestibule, using the plastic steering wheel on the arcade console, I carried on a family tradition of gimmicks that started in 1934 when my grandpa put on his white doctor's smock.

Leon opened Radio Clinic when the streets of New York were packed tight with what we now call "start-ups." Grandpa fled the Cossacks and Bolsheviks in Russia in 1920 after his father was killed in the Pale of Settlement (the geographic area where Russian Jews lived), and he and his family settled in New York City when he was twelve. He learned to repair radios, and he turned that skill into a business when he opened Radio Clinic. In the 1930s it was easy for European immigrants to get a lease and start a business. If you had an idea or a skill, money for the first month's rent, and courage to strike out on your own, Broadway was yours.

With more than 500 stores on Broadway between 80th and 100th Streets, Grandpa wasn't the only immigrant pursuing the American dream in the 1930s. Each block was filled with small shops fixing appliances, mending clothes, or selling hats, flowers, fish, or stationery. The Upper West Side was then a comfortable middle class neighborhood, and residents shopped where they lived. My dad worked at Radio Clinic as a kid, studied metallurgical engineering in college, had a brief career as a metallurgical engineer, and when he was thirty joined his father and brother-in-law in the electronics business.

The following summer, I had hoped to reprise my role as a paid video game operator, but a massive heat wave made that impossible. For my family, a brutally hot summer was typically good news. Dad lived in dread of temperate summers. During hot summers, air conditioner sales could make up as much as a third or more of Radio Clinic's annual sales. Every sweltering day in the summer of 1977 brought new customers into the store. As a kid, I could not in good conscience complain about hot sticky days, since they kept braces on my teeth. But this time it was not good news for Radio Clinic as New York City buckled under its longest and hottest heat wave in recent memory.

While in the grip of this prolonged heat, New York City's 8 million residents were doing what they could to keep cool. The evening of July 13, 1977, was no different than the days before it. Some people were coming home that night from beaches or public swimming pools. Some cooled off in the fire hydrants or escaped to air-conditioned restaurants and movie theaters. Others tried to ignore the heat by playing basketball in the park or attending a street party. Those without extra money to get air conditioning or the stamina to ignore the heat fled their sweltering apartments and joined neighbors on their stoops in search of a hint of a breeze. Others drank cold beers on street corners. Anyone with a window air conditioner turned it on high and went about their nighttime business. If the air conditioner was purchased on the Upper West Side, odds are good it came from Radio Clinic.

At 9:36 p.m., the air conditioners and fans that were cooling millions of New Yorkers abruptly turned off. A lightning bolt at 8:37 p.m. led to a cascading power failure that within an hour plunged New York City into darkness. The power stayed out for 25 hours.

Dad was in a meeting on the Upper East Side when the power went out across the city. His first thought was of Radio Clinic's basement freight elevator. Without electricity, the pump that kept the elevator from flooding wouldn't work, and it would become close to impossible to move heavy air conditioners and other appliances from the basement warehouse up to the showroom floor. When customers came into a store during a heat wave to buy an air conditioner, they were desperate and wanted one immediately, or they would go elsewhere. Radio Clinic, like many small businesses, lived on a profit margin so small that a hiccup in daily operations could be ruinous. A broken elevator could lead to lost air conditioner sales, and Dad was worried that this could lead to his default on a payment to a creditor, which in turn could impact future loans from creditors, subsequent inventory, and sales. So, he immediately drove his car through the darkened Central Park to the Upper West Side to avert a crisis for the next business day.

But saving the elevator turned out to be the least of his worries. As Dad drove from the East Side to the West Side of the city, Radio Clinic was looted. Sergeant Freud, of New York's 24th precinct, was in one of only eight squad cars charged with patrolling a vast, 125-block area of the Upper West Side that night. Just minutes into the blackout, he saw a group of 60 to 70 men prying open the metal gates safeguarding Radio Clinic. Sergeant Freud stood on top of his police car with a loud speaker, attempting to address the men crashing in the doors. "I'm asking you to disperse," he called to the men. "Go to your homes. This is your community." In a sign of what the night would bring, the men answered the Sergeant's appeal by throwing a barrage of bottles and a trash can in his direction. When he attempted to radio headquarters for backup, he wasn't able to get through, so he quickly left.

Like most New York City merchants, my dad was confident that Radio Clinic was sufficiently secured by the heavy metal gate that extended from the top of the storefront to the sidewalk. Each day after closing the store he or an employee lowered the gate to the sidewalk using a thick metal pulley, and then secured the gate by inserting a padlock into the two slide bolts at the bottom of the gate. But Dad hadn't envisioned dozens of people working together using crowbars and hammers to free the gate from its padlocks and bolts. Once he got to the Upper West Side, he parked his car in front of Citibank on the corner of Broadway and 96th, and walked towards 98th Street. In a few minutes, he would learn that the metal gate had not been sufficient and that a battle for Radio Clinic had already been waged and lost.

From the grassy median on Broadway and 98th, he saw a large crowd in front of his store. People had already used crowbars to pull the steel security gate up to waist level, crawled under, broken the door, and entered the store. Crawling under the gate was the only way in and out of the store. Dad watched as people formed an assembly line to move the merchandise from the store, under the gate and out onto the street. Dad recognized several of the men doing the stealing, since they often leaned against Radio Clinic's side gate while drinking. He watched in increasing agitation as dozens of people looted his store until he couldn't take another second. He walked over to a small group of people carrying boxes of appliances and yelled, "Get out of here!" When the crowd angrily responded, "You get out of here," Dad backed away. Understanding how greatly outnumbered he was and not wanting to get hurt, Dad reluctantly left and ran to 96th Street, a major thoroughfare, where the police were directing traffic.

Since the power had been out for less than 30 minutes, Dad thought the police could contain the situation. Radio Clinic's large glass display windows were not broken, and he hoped the damage could be minimized. It looked to him like his store was the only store on the block being looted. Several officers left the 96th Street intersection and went with him to 98th Street to see what they could do to help protect Radio Clinic. As soon as the police got to the store, the people doing the looting scattered. But within minutes of the police returning to 96th Street, a crowd of people returned to Radio Clinic and resumed stealing whatever they could find. Dad repeated the process and ran back to 96th Street to bring a few police officers back to the store. Again the crowd scattered when they saw the police. Again the police returned to 96th Street and again the crowd returned to loot the store once the coast was clear. My dad, the police, and the people doing the looting did this dance for several more rounds until the officers told him they didn't have the manpower to stay and safeguard the store. Without police protection, Dad stood alone on the sidewalk as he watched Radio Clinic's destruction.

There was a non-stop flow of people coming and going from Radio Clinic, carrying off the merchandise. Watching as the metal gates were further pried away from the store, Dad could hear the dozens of people inside the store. He didn't know if the looters had found a ladder to reach the top shelves filled with small appliances or located the door to the warehouse where the major appliances were stored. Dad was furious as he stood on the sidewalk, furious with the people looting his business, but particularly furious at the city for abandoning Radio Clinic. Angry that there were only a handful of police officers to deal with both the traffic and the looting of neighborhood businesses, he wondered if the city diverted police from nearby precincts to protect the big businesses in Midtown. Then he heard the inevitable shattering of the vestibule glass window, letting him know that all the merchandise that had been displayed in the vestibule would soon be gone.

Outsized optimism, not anger, had long been the driving force for my dad. The sound of breaking glass calmed his anger and steadied his thinking. It planted a germ of an idea in his head that remained lodged there. He had never liked the glass vestibule where his father had so picturesquely fixed radios and where I used to play video games. It took up too much floor space, and in a cramped Manhattan store, floor space is valuable. For the past year, he had argued with his business partner that they should just get rid of it. With the glass vestibule destroyed, it occurred to him he could redo the storefront however he wanted. Even as he watched the further destruction of Radio Clinic, a part of his brain was thinking about how to rebuild and improve the store.

It was now 11 p.m., almost one-and-a-half hours into the blackout. The owner of the pizzeria next door guarded his store with a gun and shot several times into the air to scare off looters. He asked Dad if he needed a gun, since he had a second one. Dad said, "no way", since he thought using a gun would only increase the chances of getting shot himself. Watching the steady stream of people carry off his merchandise wasn't doing him any good. Since he couldn't stop them on his own, they were unstoppable. He was ready to find a phone to call my mom, Sandi Rubin, to let her know he was ok. The owner of Riverside Pizza had already called her and given her the unsettling news about Radio Clinic. When the Riverside Pizza owner first got to 98th Street he didn't see my dad and wanted to let him know what was happening on the block. He called my parents' house in suburban Suffern and informed Mom that Radio Clinic was being looted and that he had heard gunshots. Once he learned about this conversation, Dad was anxious to assure Mom that he hadn't been shot and let her know what was happening, so he walked to the nearest payphone to make a call. But by this point in the blackout, it was not possible to make a call outside of the city. After a few tries he gave up and instead called his Uncle Jack in Queens, explained the situation, and asked him to relay the news to Mom. Then he left 98th Street and walked two blocks north to the 24th Police Precinct.

The first thing Dad noticed at the police precinct was that their emergency generator wasn't working. It was fairly dark inside and they were using flashlights and candles. Many of the flashlights needed batteries but the precinct didn't have a surplus of batteries. He told them where they could find batteries in the back office of Radio Clinic. Having worked in the neighborhood since he was a kid, Dad knew the local police. Many were angry that local businesses were being destroyed, and a few officers told him they would "make it rough on the bastards for you." Dad noticed that more people were arrested than the precinct had room for in their holding cell.

Feeling uncomfortable in the police headquarters, Dad decided it was time to head home, see his family, try to sleep, and return to Radio Clinic in the morning to assess the damage. He again called his Uncle Jack and asked him to relay this update to my mom. During the hour he sat in the precinct, the looting continued to escalate throughout the city. A few cops insisted on driving him to his car since the streets were dangerous. But the four-block drive in the under-cover police car felt more dangerous to Dad than if he had walked. The crowds of people were so thick at this point that police were using cars to chase them off the sidewalks. Sitting in the passenger seat, Dad thought that the police were actually trying to run over some of the looters. It was a horrible ending to a horrible night.

I never saw my dad that night. My 14-year-old brother and I learned about the blackout when the power first went off since it affected the TV coverage of the Mets game we were in the middle of watching. It was hours past my bedtime when Dad came home, and I was still asleep when he left in the morning. When I woke up, I didn't know anything was wrong with Radio Clinic and went next door to hang out with my friends. Later that day, I learned what was happening in the city and sat in my living room with my mom and brother watching the looting on television. It was unreal to know Dad was in the thick of such a volatile news story. I was a generally anxious child and kept a hand-sized rock between my mattress and box spring because you never know if you might be attacked while sleeping. I convinced myself that my plan to grab the rock, smash it against the picture above my bed to break the glass and in a moment of confusion take a glass shard and stab my attacker, would be sufficient to save me. To calm myself I also made up stories or rearranged facts. That afternoon, watching the television news, I was certain the tenants above Radio Clinic had poured water out of their windows to scare away the looters. I was comforted to know there were people looking out for my dad. Years later, I was surprised to learn the story wasn't true: I had made it up.

As an eleven-year-old, I missed many of the subtleties of what was happening, but the night after the looting when Dad returned home was the first time I saw him cry. And in the immediate aftermath of the looting, the tension level rat-cheted up considerably in my house. I had an eleven-year-old's unshakable belief in my dad. As I absorbed his stories about the looting and his scramble to save the store in the weeks and months to come, I conjured up an image of the bibli-cal David and Goliath story. I saw Dad as Davey, the kid with the slingshot and a pouch full of stones, raising his weapon against the better-armed giant. I did not cast the looters as the giant, but instead awarded that role to the city of New York. I cannot claim an early awareness that portraying the poorest and most disenfranchised people of New York as the nine-foot giant with full body armor would be a gross miscasting. I had been raised on anecdotes of city government not helping small businesses in general, and Radio Clinic in specific, but bending over backwards to help big businesses. I shared my dad's belief in the virtue of small businesses and the immorality of any institution that harmed them. As I got older, I didn't need to look too hard to have this essential truth confirmed for me again and again. The United States has an ignoble history of protecting the interests of big money and leaving the rest of us to fend for ourselves. I have always been a sucker for a good story and my dad, slingshot metaphorically in hand trying to save the family business, was a good one.

When Dad went back to the city the next morning, 11 hours into the 25-hour blackout, the streets were quiet and his store empty—of merchandise as well as looters. In the daylight, he could see that Radio Clinic was not the only store that had been looted. He was friendly with the owner of a bicycle store on 96th Street, just off Broadway, and he too faced an empty store. Dad returned to the 24th precinct and asked two officers to accompany him back to the store. One stood watch outside, and the other checked inside the store by flashlight to see if anyone was still inside. The store, while picked clean, was safe to enter. Radio Clinic, in a deteriorated section of upper Broadway, with its stereo equipment, televisions, Boomboxes, and air conditioners, had been an irresistible target.

Standing in a nearly dark store, Dad surveyed the wreckage. The glass vestibule in the front was destroyed, and the side windows were smashed. Except for the high shelving units filled with boxes of toasters and tape recorders, the main floor was stripped bare of all merchandise. However, the air conditioners were still in the basement warehouse. The warehouse was a bit of a marvel with 30 feet high ceilings, which allowed for a great deal of stacked merchandise. In addition to the freight elevator, a long, steep sailor's staircase led to the basement through a trapdoor in the floor of the back office. The only way to get down the stairs safely was backwards, gripping the metal handrails. I thought these stairs were treacherous and didn't work up the courage to use them until I was ten. A long board was attached to the stairs and folded over half the staircase so you could slide boxes of merchandise up the steps as you climbed. The looters had found the trapdoor, ladder and a warehouse filled with major appliances. But they couldn't climb the stairs while carrying the large heavy boxes, even if they used the long board, so they had no choice but to leave boxes of air conditioners and televisions in a heap by the foot of the ladder. The lack of an easy way out of the warehouse made all the difference. There was a tiny silver lining to this week. Even though Radio Clinic was decimated and almost everything was stolen off the commercial floor, the store still had a stockpile of air conditioners during a week where New Yorkers were desperate for them.

With the power still out and the subways not running, most employees couldn't get to work on Thursday. Dad, long past shock and already in triage mode, knew he had to take advantage of the heat wave. If the weather forecast was correct, the heat would continue unabated for the rest of the week and he couldn't squander a single air conditioner sale. Radio Clinic had a second store on 83rd Street that my grandpa opened in the 1940s and it had not been looted. Dad anticipated this store would have a crush of customers wanting to buy air conditioners. Plus the five crews that delivered and installed air conditioners during the summer had a full schedule for the rest of the week. The dilemma was how to get the air conditioners to them. All of Radio Clinic's air conditioners were stored in the 98th Street warehouse, and without a working freight elevator, the merchandise was essentially stuck in the basement. He needed to get the air conditioners up to the delivery trucks on the street and into the store. Dad couldn't do this alone. So, for the next two days, several employees and my 14-year-old brother helped him clear the store of glass and debris and created space for the air conditioners. I am not sure why I wasn't part of the clean-up crew; since sweeping up broken glass was the kind of no-skill task I specialized in when I worked at the store. But that Thursday and Friday, the men slowly brought air conditioners and fans into the store. They placed a couple at a time on a dolly and wheeled them out the back door of the warehouse, which led into the hallway of the apartment building, past the laundry room, out of the side door of the building, up a steep ramp in an alley alongside the building, up to the sidewalk on 98th Street, and then around the corner to Broadway, then into the store.

By the time the electricity was turned back on, the city suffered $350 million in damages. The economic impact on the city was devastating and wide-ranging. Eighty-two sanitation trucks and 4,000 workers were needed to deal with the garbage and spoiled food. More than 1,500 stores were looted and more than 1,000 were set on fire. In all, the Upper West Side hadn't been as badly affected as the South Bronx and parts of Brooklyn, but 61 stores were looted in the two-mile stretch between 63rd and 100th Streets. Of these 61 stores, 39 were on Broadway, 16 on Amsterdam Avenue and 6 on Columbus Avenue. Thirty of the 39 stores looted on Broadway were in the 90th to 110th Street stretch of real estate that Radio Clinic called home.

Some local business owners didn't want to start over after the blackout. They planned to leave the neighborhood. So, while Dad and his employees were cleaning and re-stocking, neighborhood residents streamed in, wondering if Radio Clinic planned to remain. Dad was working furiously to get the store ready to reopen, and he didn't have the time to stop and talk to everyone who wanted to know what he planned to do. The glass was broken on the street side window, but the Broadway window was intact. He took a blank white poster used for promotions and with a thick black felt marker wrote, "WE ARE STAYING." Then he taped the poster to the window. He wasn't just telling people what he thought they wanted to hear; he loved the neighborhood and thought it was a great place to do business. Radio Clinic's customers were a mix of theatrical people, blue-collar workers, business people, service industry workers, people receiving public assistance, and housewives. He knew the customers and he knew their kids. As a native New Yorker, Dad knew that New York City might seem like a big, cold place, but every neighborhood was its own small town.

New York City had long been known for its cycles of decay and renewal, but by any measure, 1977 was part of a particularly dramatic cycle. While New York remained a powerful draw for countless people to pursue their dreams and opportunities, it was also in an economic free fall. Steep budget cuts were made at terrible human cost, reducing essential city services such as police, garbage collection and basic maintenance. Municipal employees fought back with a wildcat garbage strike in 1975 and the police union threatened to pass out 'Fear City' flyers to scare tourists away from New York. In parts of the Upper West Side, the city landscape itself felt inhospitable with abandoned buildings, unreliable subway service, unsafe parks, garbage-strewn streets, and rising crime. It is hard to overstate how out of control life felt to many New Yorkers at that time. They feared that the social order, and perhaps the city itself, was in irreversible decline.

After he put the sign up, people came in to thank him. They were relieved that this longstanding business did not see the looting as proof that the neighborhood was too deteriorated to remain. People came in offering my dad flowers and hugs. Some said they were considering leaving the neighborhood but were reassured by Radio Clinic's decision to stay. One longtime customer said, "We were thinking of moving, but if you are staying then we are staying." Another, after hearing the news that the store was staying, said, "What would we have done without you in the neighborhood?" Dad was amazed at the effect that sign had on people.

This was the moment that initially got me interested in this book project. Why did my dad decide so definitively to keep the store open and why did it matter so much to people outside our family? Radio Clinic was one store in a city with thousands upon thousands of stores. And a modestly successful one at that. It didn't provide the type of service people get emotionally attached to such as a hair stylist who can do wonders with hair. It was not a particularly beautiful place. The store didn't have the homey feel of a neighborhood bar. Yet customers were coming into the store with flowers and happy to the point of tears that the store was staying open. In 1977, on the Upper West Side, it felt like it mattered whether one small business remained opened or closed its doors.

For the residents of the Upper West Side, the looting looked a bit like the end of civilization. It left many people shaken. They knew that once a community goes far enough downhill, a vicious cycle of disinvestment begins. Every vacant storefront meant a lower commercial tax base, which hurt the schools and general infrastructure. The lower portion of the Upper West Side had experience a revival in the years before 1977, but that wasn't true north of 96th Street, where Radio Clinic resided. Middle-class New Yorkers did not want to be left in a dying neighborhood, and many had the resources to leave if that seemed like the best course of action.

Dad was under no illusions about the neighborhood. He knew Radio Clinic shared the block with boarded-up stores, vacant buildings, residential apartments and established businesses. He didn't keep Radio Clinic open to avoid adding another vacant storefront to the block or with the lofty intention of anchoring the neighborhood. It was far simpler than that. Forty-three years earlier his dad, who had run for his life from Russia, put his stake down on this block and slowly built up the business. When Grandpa became ill with cancer, he passed the business on to his son and son-in-law. This was the family's business, and my dad wasn't budging.

2

From Russia with Love

Immigrants (We Get The Job Done)

—Lin Manuel Miranda

TO **UNDERSTAND THE STORY** of Radio Clinic, you need to understand that it originated as an immigrant story. Like countless Russian Jews in the first half of the twentieth century, my grandfather and his family fled religious persecution and took their chances in a new country halfway across the globe. Like the thousands of people that immigrated and migrated to New York City each year, Grandpa arrived without a lot of resources, eager to make his mark in this new country.

My family has always been devoted to its oral traditions. While we do not have a Rubin family handbook formally mandating that the stories of one generation will be told repeatedly until the next generation absorbs these stories as their own, it has been our informal operating procedure. Although Grandpa and his family fled Russia long before I was born, I know this story. In 1920, Jews couldn't get permission to leave Russia, so my grandfather and his family needed to sneak out. They sold most of their possessions to raise money for their escape. As a result, they had enough money to bribe whomever needed bribing to get them across the border. On a cold November morning, Grandpa, then a twelve-year-old boy, his three sisters, their mother, and a family they knew from their synagogue left Berdichev on a horse-pulled sleigh.

When I was in 6th grade, the big school project was to research a country for several months and then write a final report about it. In addition to research in the library, I interviewed my Great Uncle Jack, grandmother, and parents to get greater detail for my report on Russia. It was the first time I appreciated that actual people were swept up in the historical events that my textbooks dryly described. Hearing their Russia stories was thrilling to me. I was a very ordinary person living a very ordinary life in suburban New York. Yet people I knew, people I was related to!, were swept up in large historical forces they couldn't control. So were Rick and

Leon's father, Aaron

Isla from the film, *Casablanca*, and other heroes and heroines from my favorite books and movies. I traced my grandfather's journey on contemporary and historical maps, but it was hard to keep straight which town was in which country, as the borders changed several times in 1920 and the lines on the map kept shifting. I do know, however, that their journey started in Berdichev, and ended in New York City.

My grandfather Leon was born in Berdichev, in 1908, when the city was still part of the Russian Empire. His father managed a tannery, and before that his grandfather managed it. Grandpa and his siblings were educated and lived in a nice home. He dreamed of being a chess master. They were thoroughly assimilated and spoke Russian, not Yiddish, the everyday language of Jews. But their middle-class life didn't protect them from the *pogroms:* the organized and collective violence against Jews. Most Jewish families were forced to flee the pogroms with minimal possessions in search of another Russian "shtetl" to seek safety outside the country. My great grandfather was murdered in 1919, two years after the Russian revolution by Cossacks. As Grandpa told my older cousin when my cousin interviewed him for a school project, "For the Jews, it was irrelevant whether the Czar's army, the Mensheviks, the Bolsheviks, the Polish Republic, or the Ukraine People's Republic Army seized power. As different armies marched through the city, each one would rob, kill, and rape the Jews."

Not surprisingly, my great-grandmother decided this was no place to live with her children. Like most people fleeing their country, my grandfather and his family relied on luck as much as careful planning and cautious routes. The Russian and Polish woods offered secure cover, but it was still a risky journey.

Their first stop after leaving Berdichev was a small city in Belarus. On the first day, they were robbed of some of their money by a traveling army, but no one was hurt, so they continued on. Next, they traveled to the Polish border and were stopped in a small border town. This town consisted of one house for the military and one house for the peasants who lived there. The military officers denied my grandfather's family entry and lectured them on how Jews should behave. "You should be smarter than that," Grandpa heard them say. "You don't travel by day when people can see you. You should travel at night. Pay us off and then we will let you through." But before they could hand over a bribe, they were arrested and placed in the building that housed many peasants. After a few more days, they attempted to cross the border again. This time their bribe worked and the soldiers allowed them through.

It wasn't easy or comfortable to ride for long periods of time on a crowded sled. The nights were long, as they traveled through the snow-covered wilderness, and everyone took turns sleeping. A few days into the journey, Grandpa woke up abruptly and found himself lying alone in the snow. He had fallen off the sleigh during the night. It was nowhere to be seen. After a few moments of confusion, he got up, brushed the snow off his face and looked for the hoof marks in the snow. Once he was sure which direction the horse and sled was heading, he started walking alongside its tracks. Meanwhile, his family noticed he was missing, turned around the sleigh and carefully backtracked to find him.

This was the story that most captivated my sixth-grade self. It was one of the stories I have told my children for them to use when they were doing their family history type school projects. As a child, I spent many hours lying in my bed thinking about it. There was never quite enough detail for me in this family legend. I wanted to know more. What was going through his head? Did he wake up as soon as he landed in the snow? Or did he lie there for a while, covered in snow? Did he have a few moments of panic before he clearheadedly looked for the hoof marks of the horses and the sleigh tracks in the snow and started walking? And more importantly to me, would I have been able to do the same. I spent many nights as a kid sleeping in my cramped closet to make sure I would be able to hide like Anne Frank did, if the need ever arose. It calmed me and helped me sleep if I felt prepared for some horrible thing happening. But I wasn't sure how to practice falling off a winter sled in the middle of the woods at night. After a few hours of walking, Grandpa and his family found each other. He was pulled back on the sled and the journey continued.

Once they got to Grodno, Poland, they took a train to Warsaw. The fact that they had some money and were educated was invaluable at this point in the journey. They worked with the Hebrew Immigrant Aid Society, an organization founded in 1881 that helped Jews with papers and legal procedures, and decided to sail from Antwerp, Belgium, to Canada. It was a safer bet to get a

Canadian visa and then take a train to New York, since, unlike at Ellis Island, papers were rarely checked at the Canadian/US border.

Standing on the deck of the ship that brought him from Belgium to Canada, my twelve-year-old grandpa heard many exciting rumors about what life was like in New York City. On the ship, he tasted his first banana and other delicacies, which according to the rumor mill, were commonplace in the United States. A skilled chess player, he hustled some money playing as many as ten chess games at one time. He was hopeful about another rumor, that he could make some money playing at chess tables in public parks throughout the city. He was still incredulous about how quickly his life had changed in the past year. Just a year before he witnessed his father's murder by a Cossack for the crime of being Jewish while walking home. For the following nine months, his mom planned and sold off possessions so she could get her family out of Russia. And now, after three months of harrowing travel, he was on a ship, on his way to North America. Getting into the United States has always been a big hurdle for any immigrant to clear. Starting with the Naturalization Act of 1790, restricting citizenship to "free white persons of good character," the United States has long been concerned about who could enter the country and become a citizen. Like other immigrant groups before them (and after), in 1920 recent arrivals were blamed for escalating poverty, disease, and crime. To limit immigration, the U.S. government, comprised mainly of politicians descended from immigrants, began imposing literacy tests and quotas.

Since there was minimal risk of being denied entrance to Canada, Grandpa and his family docked in Canada, entered the United States illegally on a Pullman train to New York City, and began their new lives. In 1867 the Pullman trains, with their sleeper berths, had changed train travel. Porters were hired to fold up the berths by day and fold down the berths by night. George Pullman hired recently freed slaves to be the first porters. When my grandfather traveled in 1920, African Americans still worked as porters (this was just 5 years before the porters organized The Brotherhood of Sleeping Car Porters, the first labor union led by African Americans, to fight for better working conditions and fair wages). My grandfather didn't know any of that. He was struck by one simple thing when he saw the porters; he had never seen a black person before. There were no black people in Berdichev at the start of the 20th century. He did not see movies in Berdichev. Televisions hadn't yet been invented. It is hard to know what you don't know. Seeing the porters gave my young grandfather an inkling that life in New York City would be very different than life in Berdichev. The Pullman train was the perfect introduction to the life my grandfather would soon be living in the ethnically diverse Bronx.

The geographic facts of the island of Manhattan are fixed: 13.4 miles at its longest, 2.3 miles at its widest, and a total of 23 square miles of land. Cattle ranches in Montana are larger than this island crammed tight with people. In 1920 more than five and a half million people lived in New York City. Nearly 40 percent of them were foreign-born, and roughly 480,000 of them came from Russia. Sorting through the census data, it was impossible for me to see my family's journey to the United States as anything other than utterly ordinary. I imagine most people that live in the United States, that are descendants of immigrants, hold tight to their ancestors specific immigration story. I know I do. It is hard not to—the elements of these stories are often quite harrowing and dramatic. The murders. The hiding and fleeing. The desperation. The leaving family members behind not knowing if you will ever see them again. The gun toting smugglers and the falling off the sled in the snow. But New York City was crammed with people from all over the world that came there desperate to survive and hopeful this country would allow, if not them, then their children, to thrive. By the time Grandpa settled himself on that ship, the Rubin family was just one of the more than one and half million Jews that had fled the pogroms and economic discrimination of Eastern Europe to settle in New York City.

1920 was a good year to arrive in New York City. The Yankees had just bought Babe Ruth from the Red Sox and during that year he hit 54 home runs and drove in 137 runs. The police department hired Lawon Bruce, the first black policewoman, a sign that the demographics of the city were shifting. Thanks to the state legislature, the city was able to exempt new housing from property taxes for the next twelve years, which stimulated new housing construction. And, in recognition of the booming population, the first traffic light was placed at 42nd Street and Fifth Avenue. Standing on the ship deck, watching the Atlantic Ocean, Grandpa was right to be optimistic about his future in New York. By the time he turned eighteen, he would have a high school degree, speak fluent English, and be employed.

My grandfather has always loomed large in our family stories. He was the one whose father was shot and killed and risked his own life to bury his dad. He was the one who escaped with his life from Russia. He was the one that made the daunting leap from one continent to another. He was the one that built up the family business from nothing. My dad's admiration for him is evident in every conversation about my grandpa. In writing a book about Radio Clinic, I needed to include its founder in a meaningful way, but my memories of him are negligible, since he died when I was young. What I know about him I know mostly from my dad, but I wasn't sure how reliable he was as a source about his father. Dad tends to view the people he loves the most through rose colored glasses, and his descriptions about his dad have always leaned toward hero worship. But my mom, never one to sugar coat anything, felt the same way about him. Her opinion, that Grandpa was one of the best men she knew, carried weight.

From the day his family settled in the Bronx, my grandfather was eager to assimilate. His older brother Jack had arrived in New York City a year earlier and already spoke decent English. Jack had arrived penniless after Romanian smugglers robbed him at gunpoint while in a small boat in the Black Sea. He hoped to attend college to increase his career options, but first needed to pass an English exam. To support himself he worked twelve hours a day, six days a week at a drug store and didn't have time to take English classes. Instead he bought the New York Times for two cents a day and wrote out twenty words every day to slowly learn the new language.

As a somewhat lackadaisical student, I was repeatedly told two school stories about my grandparents. My maternal grandmother, living in a poor Russian village whose family could only afford to educate the oldest son, wrestled her brother to the ground each day until he showed her what he learned in school. I couldn't miss the implied lesson about the thirst for knowledge that once ran through the women in our family. And my paternal grandfather ignored embarrassment so he could learn English as quickly as possible.

When Grandpa initially moved to the Bronx he followed the advice of other Russian Jews in his new neighborhood and enrolled in a school that was comprised of Russian Jewish students with classes taught in Russian. But within days he realized he didn't want to be in this school. Impressed by the progress his brother had made and how quickly he was moving toward his goals, Grandpa wanted to more fully immerse himself with English speakers. (Within a year of living in New York, Jack passed the English test, qualified for Fordham College and was an experienced guide for my grandfather, shepherding him through the challenges of immigrant life.) After less than a week at this private school for Russians, Grandpa transferred to the local public school. Instead of entering seventh grade with his peers, his lack of English placed him in the third grade, and as he studied hard, every month or so the school moved him up a grade until his English was finally good enough to join students his own age. Surely if my 12-year-old grandfather could perch his body on the small chairs in the primary grade classrooms, I could put a little more muscle into my math homework.

The stories I heard about Grandpa always revolved about him being creative, innovative, a good salesman, and a good person. As a teenager, to earn spending money, he brought his chess hustling skills to the Bronx public parks. For his first real job, he worked as a soda jerk in a neighborhood drugstore, where he quickly learned he had a knack for sales. Making fountain drinks (milkshakes, egg creams, and malteds) was the main job of a soda jerk. To increase profits, the pharmacist asked his soda jerks to sell the malteds with an egg added, so he could charge more for the drink. After a few weeks the pharmacist pulled Grandpa aside and asked him how he was able to consistently sell the malted with eggs, since no other soda jerk had managed it. He told him, "It's

Leon, his mother Ginde, Esther.

simple. The other guys are asking customers if they want an egg in their malted. I ask them a different question. I ask customers if they want one or two eggs in their malted and so far everyone's decided on one." Growing up, Dad heard this story (and its lesson) many times from his father; to be a good salesman you need to make every sale simple.

During his free time Grandpa liked to tinker. He took machinery apart to understand how it worked. The apartment he lived in with his family was sweltering in the summer. Air conditioners would not be available for home use until the 1930s and wouldn't become popular until after WWII. Store-bought mechanical fans had been popular for a couple of decades, but my grandfather decided it would be more fun to rig one up on his own. On steamy days, he and his siblings would position a bicycle upside down and take turns spinning the wheel, while the others lay down under the wheel to catch the breeze.

As a young man, he focused his tinkering skills on radios. Grandpa taught himself how to build a radio from scratch, and then he figured out how to repair radios. Concentrating on radios was a wise choice since radios were rapidly becoming a very popular product. While new and uncommon in 1924, by the close of the 1930s more than 28 million households owned a radio. My grandfather tinkered his way into a solid profession.

Wanting to further develop his skills and understanding of how machines worked, my grandfather decided to study engineering. He set his sights on Cooper Union College, since it offered a world-class engineering program and was tuition free. Peter Cooper, a self-educated industrialist, envisioned a top-notch college that would be as "free as air and water," with no color or gender bar. Studying electrical engineering for three years at Cooper Union in

Greenwich Village, Grandpa dropped out when he married Esther Lifschitz in 1930 and started repairing radios at Ludwig Baumann Department store. For their honeymoon, they went to Niagara Falls and wanted to take the Maiden Mist boat ride under the falls. Realizing that because he wasn't in the United States legally he needed to stay on the U.S. side and couldn't take the boat ride, Grandpa decided he had to get his papers in order. A few months later he snuck back into Canada with his papers, and re-entered the United States legally.

Working at Ludwig Baumann, a prestigious department store, was an important opportunity for my grandfather. He had a chance to learn from more experienced technicians and had access to high-end equipment. Radio repairs were done inside a copper mesh cage to keep out stray radio signals. Grandpa was often at odds with the other technicians who wanted him to slow down, since he repaired four times as many radios per day than they did. But Grandpa was young and ambitious and did not want to slow down.

After a year at Ludwig Baumann, Grandpa chafed at being a small cog in a large operation. He wanted to be his own boss and left to put out his radio repair shingle. For the next few years he and my grandmother lived with her family in the Bronx to save money. He rented some space in a cramped storefront a few blocks from his in-laws to start his radio repair business. But he saw this as a stepping stone to one day owning his own store. From his first day on the Atlantic Ocean heading to the United States, my grandfather had been dreaming about his life in New York. Now he was 25 and had lived as much of his life in the United States as he had in Russia. He told his wife, "I as a foreigner had the same opportunity as anyone American. I went to school for free. I graduated high school for free. After high school I had no problem finding a job. I went to college at night and had the same opportunity as any American." The more he thought about it the more it appealed to him. Running his own business. Being his own boss. Making as much money as he could by his own ability. Besides he was an American now, and nothing seemed more American to him than striking out on his own.

3

A Dream, Some Chutzpah, and the First Month's Rent

...(Broadway) is the street of people who have come up in the world;
fat with prosperity and good living. The people are fatter, freer in manner,
more prone to smile; the women just as expensively dressed and furred as those
of the bold bloc, but in a more flamboyant style. Jews predominate. The sidewalks
are thronged all day with people buying. The stores are not great in size but display
all the luxuries of the six continents and seven seas, particularly in things to eat:
caviar, truffles, salmon out of season, peaches in the winter and so on.

—Hulbert Footner, New York: City of Cities, 1937

THREE HUNDRED DOLLARS. That is how much money Grandpa needed in 1934 to open his own business. He just needed enough money for the first month's rent. Landlords didn't ask him for a security deposit, and the only personal guarantee he would need to provide was his signature affirming that he could pay the monthly rent. My grandfather had complete confidence in his ability to be a successful merchant. He was only missing one necessary ingredient to be the success he envisioned: $300.

He first turned to his brother Jack to invest some money in the business and be his business partner. Jack did not like retail and much preferred his life as a pharmaceutical salesman. But he offered to loan his brother some of the money when he was ready to sign a lease. Without a business partner, my grandfather didn't feel ready, so he remained in that cramped space in the Bronx and waited for the right opportunity. The Bronx was a comfortable neighborhood for him to do business. New York City had long been a melting pot, but people still liked to live in neighborhoods that in some way resembled their families' homeland. Each ethnic group settled in particular neighborhoods with grocery stores, restaurants, and other shops that felt like home. In the 1920s, many Jews from Eastern Europe settled in the Bronx, where they comprised almost half the population. Grandpa became friendly with Harry Baum, another young man who repaired radios in the Bronx. The two men, who each had a small but steady stream of business, decided to go into business together. They figured that if they pooled their resources they would have enough money to put down the first month's rent and open a store.

Grandpa and Harry decided to open their shop in Manhattan, not the Bronx, since it seemed like a more lucrative location. A New York City travel guide of the day agreed, referring to Manhattan as the "loudest, busiest, most up and bustling borough of the five." Of the roughly 7 million people living in the city, almost 2 million lived in Manhattan, even though geographically, Manhattan took up only 22 of the city's 305 square miles. More specifically they were interested in renting a storefront on Manhattan's Upper West Side. With its expansive public parks, beautiful residential buildings and easy access to public transportation, the area had an infrastructure that was unparalleled in the city. Covering about two square miles, this neighborhood was roughly 200 blocks, starting at 59th Street and stopping at 110th Street. Developed in the second half of the nineteenth century, Riverside Park provided its western border and slightly more than half a mile east, Central Park provided its eastern one.

Before I started this book project, I didn't know that Grandpa had a business partner for 32 years. My dad assumed I knew this so it didn't come up in our first round of interviews. Early in the project I contacted the editor of the West Side Rag, the neighborhood's online newspaper, to do a little blurb about my book project and ask people with Radio Clinic memories to contact me. I was surprised to hear from Harry's granddaughter who explained her connection to the store. She connected me with her dad, Matt Baum, Harry's son, who like my dad spent a lot of time in the store as a kid. I contacted Matt, who agreed to meet up with me and Dad to talk about his memories of Radio Clinic. The three of us met at the Metro Diner, two blocks from Radio Clinic, for what turned out to be my favorite interview of this project. For several hours, the two men reminisced about their fathers, the odd jobs they had at the store when they were kids, and what Radio Clinic was like in the 1950s.

After leaving the Metro Diner, Dad walked me up and down Broadway to introduce me to other long-time merchants in the neighborhood. It struck me that this was the same exact walk Grandpa and Harry took while scouting out a good location for their business. And while the businesses on the ground floor of each building were different today than in 1934, the buildings were not. To me, these buildings built at the start of the twentieth century seemed liked time capsules. Ever since an elementary school time capsule project, I loved the idea that an ordinary object like my pet rock, when discovered a few generations later, could be exotic and fascinating. This is how I felt about these 100-year-old buildings. Each building carried history within its walls, if the floors could talk about what type of stores they once housed, they could tell the story of a continually changing city.

After walking Broadway with Dad, I went to the public library to see what kind of resources it had that could stand in for talking floors and walls. I spent hours looking through the microfiche of New York City's phonebooks, and from this treasure trove I traced the commercial history from 1929 until 1993 (the microfiche records stopped at 1993) of each building between 80th and 100th Streets on Broadway. Looking through the evolution of stores in each building and on each block underscored to me that each building in and of itself is an ordinary building. But when you follow the history of what each building has contained over a 70 year period, it becomes something else. It seemed to me that if you put a team of archeologists on any New York City street, once they start peeling away the present, they would find evidence of, if not exactly past civilizations, a past way of life.

I imagined these two men, more than 80 years ago, walking each avenue and block of the Upper West Side to get a feel for the neighborhood and find the best spot to open their business. On Amsterdam and Columbus Avenues they would have walked past crowded tenement apartments and dodged the falling soot from the elevated steam trains whose tracks ran thirty feet above the sidewalk. They might have admired the luxury apartment buildings on Central Park West and Riverside Drive and seen the white-capped maids pushing babies in strollers and chauffeurs shining cars on these blocks. But it had to be clear to them that Broadway was the avenue of commerce, with dozens of stores on each block. Thousands of people were walking on Broadway with them and many stopped inside the stores. They must have taken stock of Sherry & Barron's Hat Shop, Annabelle's Dress Shop, Dubro's Perfumes, Harman Dress Shop, Fernandez & Diaz Cigars, Broadway Appetizers and Nut shop, Apfelbaum Furrier, Schlumbohm Confectionery, Lincoln Haberdashery, and countless other stores near 98th Street, and liked what they saw.

From the phone records, I know that as they walked the 20 blocks they saw more than 500 stores. It would have made sense for them to conclude that the wealthy residents shopped in the neighborhood and not midtown department stores since the area supported 19 furriers. Plus, there were plenty of millineries, restaurants and taverns, pharmacists, barbers and hair dressers, corsetiere shops, gown makers, food markets, tailors, dairies, florists, fruit markets, theaters, and haberdasheries. All kind of repair shops dotted these blocks, and nine of them repaired radios. So many businesses could be sustained because most stores did only one thing. You went to the fruit market to buy fruit, the butcher to get meat, the tailor to repair your jacket. Neighborhood residents could walk just a few blocks to get their basic household needs and still support countless businesses. They correctly figured that another radio repair shop would fit right in.

The Upper West Side hadn't always been a prime location to open a store. The amenities and bricks and mortar infrastructure that impressed my grandfather and Harry in 1934 had only been around for a few decades. Development of the west side of Manhattan had been more sluggish than its east side counterpart during the nineteenth century. The area initially lacked any rapid transportation and was miles north of where most jobs were located, making it a difficult place to live for people that needed to work each day. Elegant mansions on large plots of property were scattered throughout the area, but these were country homes for the city's most wealthy inhabitants whose main residences were much further downtown. Rock outcrops, hills, and other natural obstructions made it hard to build roads and contributed to the area's lack of development. But this was New York City and there has always been a fortune to be made on real estate. Builders and real estate investors did what they do best; they figured out a way to tame nature and to exert their influence with City Hall. In 1878 the West Side Association (a gathering of property owners, investors, and real estate people) met to figure out how to develop the West Side. Their main concern was how to move large numbers of people from where they lived to where they worked. Without fast public transportation, promoters of the area believed it would remain "a howling wilderness of vacant lots and rocks and morasses."

From these 1878 meetings where city leaders strategized how to get people to live in the Upper West Side until today, the area underwent a series of transformations. Each transformation was the byproduct of policy decisions that were discussed at meetings like the ones hosted by the West Side Association. Sweeping changes to a neighborhood don't just happen out of nowhere. You can draw a fairly straight line from meetings of powerful real estate developers and the Upper West Side's dramatic changes from an area where no one lived in the late 1800s, to a middle-class enclave in the 1930s, to an area with deep pockets of poverty and the highest concentration of mentally ill people newly released from state mental hospitals in the 1970s, to the gentrified neighborhood of today. I knew from the beginning of this project, that I would center the book around the 1977 blackout and looting. My dad putting up the 'we are staying' sign was arguably the defining moment in Radio Clinic's story and an important moment for him personally. But why that sign reverberated so powerfully through the neighborhood in 1977 was in part the story of the Upper

West Side. Some of the sediment I had to dig through to understand the not-so-distant past, were the policy decisions that caused the neighborhood to go so far downhill from the day in 1934 that Radio Clinic opened to the day Dad taped up his sign.

In the waning days of the nineteenth century, city officials were also interested in making it easier for people to live in Upper Manhattan, so they could depopulate the overcrowded lower Manhattan. Its severe overcrowding was a growing health hazard, so the city invested in the elevated train system that connected the southern and northern parts of the city. This transportation was a marvel, an elevated train that operated thirty feet above the sidewalk with solid iron beams holding the weight of the tracks and the trains. By the 1890s the elevated Ninth Avenue Line (now known as Columbus Avenue), had stations roughly every ten blocks as it traveled up the avenue, making it easy to commute to and from each Upper West Side neighborhood.

The first ethnic group to move en masse to the Upper West Side were Irish immigrants. They moved to the area to build the elevated railroads and the tenement buildings on Amsterdam and Columbus Avenue that soon provided their housing. More and more people moved to the Upper West Side, providing work for the laborers who continued to build row houses and tenements. A *New York Times* article from 1886 titled, "Settling the West Side," reported that, "On the first day of the present month there were, according to the reports of inspectors to the Building Bureau, 866 buildings erecting on the west side of New York from 59th to 155th streets, while 34 had just been completed." By the start of the twentieth century, Broadway was no longer a country highway lined with liveries, saloons, and churches, but had become an urban neighborhood.

As useful as the elevated railroad was to the area, the opening of the underground subway system in 1904 was even more important. The new subway traveled nine miles under Broadway and stopped at twenty-eight stations, which positioned Broadway perfectly to become the main artery of the neighborhood. Cutting the travel time from the Upper West Side to downtown to twenty minutes, it was a catalyst for a building boom on upper Broadway that changed where middle-class New Yorkers lived. Without the IRT subway line my grandfather, and Harry would not have ventured south to 98th Street and Broadway and instead would have opened their business in the Bronx.

This type of public investment in infrastructure was exactly what the gathering of property owners, investors, and real estate people were hoping for from the city. From 1900, when the subway was initially planned until it was completed four years later, 94 apartment houses and apartment hotels were built in the area. Many of these buildings were lavish residential hotels inspired by Parisian styles with as many as thirty rooms for some apartments. Real estate developers, wanting to lure wealthy New Yorkers to these Upper West Side residential hotels, loaded their buildings with amenities. Individual apartments were quite fancy with formal dining rooms and high ceilings. At the time, it was considered impolite for a luxurious building to have something as common as a store on its main floor; instead, the large central lobbies were grand public spaces for dining, a library, or ballroom. A particularly ornate hotel had a Turkish bath and a fountain with seals in its lobby.

After World War I, people moved in large numbers to the city, causing a severe housing shortage. The city again put some muscle into solving this problem when the Board of Estimates created a tax abatement program so any housing development started between 1920 and 1922 was exempt from paying taxes until 1932. Due to its success, the date for accessing this abatement was pushed back several times. Between 1920 and 1930, 93 new apartment houses were built on the Upper West Side. By 1930, so much housing had been constructed citywide for middle class tenants that real estate taxes provided about 80 percent of New York City's revenue.

With subway stops located at 79th, 86th, 91st, 96th and 103rd Streets, there was steady foot traffic on the avenue. Hundreds of thousands of people walked these streets on their way to and from the subway stations, and many of them wanted to shop on Broadway. Soon stores opened in the lobbies of the residential hotels that once housed ballrooms and grand lobbies. By 1934, small businesses lined Broadway.

Scouting the area, Grandpa and Harry would have also noticed that the Upper West Side was also a place with lively recreational activities. Baseball games, croquet, lawn tennis, and horse and goat rides were all happening at Central Park. Although Riverside Park was a bit of a mess with its rotting piers, that didn't stop local youth from stripping down and swimming in the Hudson. Navy sailors, whose ships were anchored in the Hudson, walked to the Upper West Side to flirt with the "Riverside Girls." At the southern tip of the neighborhood, people traveled to the St. Nicholas Arena to watch boxing. At the northern tip of the neighborhood, people played mini golf on Riverside Drive. All of these activities were good news for merchants, increasing the number of people out and about on the streets.

Convinced by the opportunities in the area, Grandpa and Harry signed a lease for 2580 Broadway. If location is everything, then the two men made a smart decision. Positioned between 97th and 98th Streets, Radio Clinic was two blocks north of one subway stop, five blocks south of another one, and two avenues from an elevated railroad station. They benefitted from sharing the block with many popular stores such as Milady Hat Shop, Irving's Dairy and Appetizing Store, Hudson Fruit and Produce Market, and Nedick's Orange Juice shop. Just one block away, the Riviera Theater and Japanese Garden Theater, part of the vaudeville subway circuit, added flair to the block. Neighborhood children lined Broadway on weekend evenings to watch people in their formal wear go out to dinner and the theater.

I read through dozens of New York travel guides, business reports and census reports, trying to get a better sense of what New York City, and more specifically the Upper West Side, was like when they opened Radio Clinic in the 1930s. Each resource detailed the magnitude of New York City's growth in the early part of the 20th century. Reading data point after data point, the growth seemed staggering to me. Hundreds of new immigrants arrived in New York each day. A quarter of a million people visited the city each day. The city's ports handled forty percent of all foreign trade. By 1930, New York City had close to 120,000 street lamps. There were more than 29,500 manufacturing plants, employing 560,000 workers and producing 60% of all the clothes manufactured in the country. The city supported over 120,000 retail dealers and the retail business was estimated at over $3 billion annually. My favorite piece of information was from the New York Chamber of Commerce, reporting that in 1939 the city had over 103,000 stores or one store for every 66 people. By the time they opened Radio Clinic, more than one and a half million people lived in Manhattan and the transit system carried many more passengers than that. Thousands of people either climbed down steps from the elevated train or climbed up the steps from the underground train and streamed onto Broadway each day. And that was just the people that lived in Manhattan, plenty of others traveled to the area. More than two million commuters traveled into the city each day using one of the 20 bridges, 18 tunnels or 17 ferries.

Grandpa and Harry saw that the Upper West Side was a business area on the rise, and they wanted their store to be a part of it. They had confidence in the Broadway Association and the West End Avenue Association, both actively trying to make upper Broadway as desirable a place to shop as Fifth Avenue on the east side. While the neighborhood had several radio repair competitors, Grandpa wasn't worried. They had settled on Radio Clinic for the name of the business and had some creative ideas to draw interest in the store. The two men didn't have quite enough money to rent their own storefront, so they shared 2580 Broadway with Blau Brothers Dairy, an inexpensive kosher luncheonette. From the day his store first opened, Grandpa knew he chose wisely in staking his future on this block. I imagine him standing on the sidewalk, watching the people come and go and taking in his surroundings. Even though the country was in the grips of a depression, he had to be pleased by what he saw. Broadway was bustling.

4

The Golden Age of Radio

New York has tomorrow morning's newspapers on sale tonight; and
every time the clock ticks a single tick, somebody, somewhere within its
portals, is trying to call somebody on the telephone; is buying someone else
a drink, waiting to be married, murdered, hired, fired, flirted with or slapped...
Here the skyscraper of today is the dust pile of tomorrow; architecture grows
old over night; styles change in a single round of the clock...

—The John Day Guides, All About New York, by Rian James, 1931

Radio was a novelty. Most people were intimidated by it. You know,
the idea of information coming through the air, through the ether, was
something that was one step away from Black Magic. Within a few years
people regarded it as the greatest thing since flushed toilets.

—Bill Schneck, son of Harry L. Schneck, who started the first
radio store on Radio Row, The Sonic Memorial Project

O NE WAS ONLY HALF a block away. Another was two blocks north. Yet
another was ten blocks to the south. All told, there were nine radio service
shops West Siders could take their radio to for repairs on upper Broadway in
the 1930s. Radio Clinic shared the block with the more established Davega City
Radio Inc., located in a prime spot on the southwest corner. A corner store was
a better location because it provided windows on two sides, offered more space

to display radios and had additional basement space for storage. Plus, Davega City Radio had also been selling sporting goods for years and had another store on 86th Street, giving it better name recognition. Wanting a way for their fledgling business to stand out, Grandpa and Harry settled on a gimmick to draw in customers. A radio clinic needed a radio doctor. Instead of doing his repair work in the basement or in the back of the store, Grandpa set up his operation table in the glass vestibule of the storefront window. As pedestrians walked by they saw my grandfather, a real-life mannequin.

From the first radio broadcast in 1920, radio's rise in popularity was swift. Radio provided a lifeline to a country struggling through the Depression, with programs that offered much needed amusement to distract people from their hardships and news. By the mid 1930s almost every household had a radio. Rich or poor, people had a radio; anyone who could scrap together the money owned one. Three quarters of these radios were used at least once each day. Reading the Columbia Broadcast Service (CBS) advertising report, *Radio in 1936*, it seemed to me that CBS was slightly incredulous of this fact. In the avalanche of data compiled in this report, the authors marveled that this was "the first time any advertising medium has had to work with a circulation-total of 22,869,000 families." With their eyes on advertising dollars CBS declared that, "whoever uses your product can be reached by radio." This was good news for a radio repair shop. If a radio became inoperable or the sound quality became fuzzy people were quick to get them repaired since they relied on the radio broadcasts. Impersonating a doctor with a screwdriver in hand, my grandfather was ready for them.

Radio repair was a reliable profession. New Yorkers were more likely to own a radio than a telephone. Before the invention of the transistor radio in 1954, radios were made mostly of tubes and weren't very complex devices. If a radio wasn't working, it was much cheaper to repair than to buy a new one. My grandfather and Harry slowly, but surely, built up their business.

Even though there was plenty of commercial life on the Upper West Side, no part of New York City was immune to the Depression. With over a million people out of work, more than 80 bread lines and countless soup kitchens sprung up to feed the many hungry New Yorkers. Many people without housing made their way to the Upper West Side and slept in Central Park under Hoover blankets (used newspapers named derogatorily after then-President Hoover) or in the Hooverville on the Hudson River at 74th Street. Tens of thousands of New Yorkers were evicted because they couldn't pay their rent and that rippled through every area of the city. I spent some time using Ancestry, sifting through the 1930 and 1940 census to get a better picture of who lived near Radio Clinic in its early days and who, most likely, were its customers. The federal census had all sorts of interesting information letting me know the nationality of each person that lived in each apartment unit, their occupations, and if they owned a radio. One housing trend was clear in the 1940 census records, the Depression forced many of the people that lived in large residential apartments to take in lodgers to make ends meet. It was now more common for the inhabitants of a household to read, "head, wife, daughter, cousin, cousin, lodger, lodger, lodger" or "head, brother, son, lodger, lodger" than to solely be people that were related to each other.

Area landlords followed suit, and some converted the grand apartments they owned by breaking them into several low-rent rooming houses. Many landlords offered free first month's rent to draw people to their property. Aspiring writers and actors from across the country moved in and became a strong presence in the neighborhood. Enticed by the low rent, day laborers from every corner of the country moved into these rooming houses. Signaling the beginning of another ethnic shift to the neighborhood, Puerto Rican and Southern Blacks migrating north were part of the day laborers looking for work. From these early days of Radio Clinic Grandpa learned two valuable lessons about owning a business on the Upper West Side. The demographics of who lived in the neighborhood were always rapidly changing, and, if you provide a good service, the customers, no matter who they are, will keep coming.

When Radio Clinic opened, it was primarily a service and repair shop. There really wasn't much of an appliance industry at the time. But neighborhood customers nudged Grandpa and Harry to carry other items, and to process film. So, cords for the radios, batteries, new radios, glassware, toasters and film could soon be found on Radio Clinic's shelves. Radio Clinic wasn't the only repair shop that branched out from its core service business to sell other types of goods. More products were being manufactured and the companies needed stores to carry them. And in the years before WWII, sales representatives form Zenith, Sony and other large manufacturers started coming to the store to sell Grandpa parts for the various radios he serviced and other merchandise. Many of these sales reps were young men who lived in the neighborhood and Grandpa was happy to give them some business. He didn't know it at the time, but in the years to come these relationships would evolve into the most important ones for his business.

This was a peak time for small businesses on the Upper West Side. There were a lot of stores and a lot of people living there. One comprehensive guidebook of that era said, "in the Upper West Side 50,000 families will be reading the newspaper by the sitting room table..." Having five hundred stores within a twenty-minute walk of your home, to buy both the things you needed and the things you simply wanted, was convenient for these 50,000 families. Young people promenaded up and down upper Broadway on weekend evenings. This evening stroll was a popular activity as people made their way to the theaters or just enjoyed being on the street flirting with whoever caught their eye. The shops on the 98th Street block of Broadway had many practical offerings for neighborhood residents who wanted to look their best for these strolls. You could purchase stockings at Thrift Hosiery, hats at Nancy's Hat Shoppe, get your hair done at either Rosedust Beauty Salon or Louis Beauty Salon, shoes resoled at Arch Preserver Shoe Repair, clothes cleaned at Wright Laundry or pressed at Orange Cleaners and Dryers. And if you were hungry, Blau Brothers Dairy, New Yorker Delicatessen, Elkwood Bakeshop, Nedicks, Dave's Dairy, and Chisholm & Chapman Bakers could keep you well fed without leaving the block. And Radio Clinic had something to offer for a night out as well. Grandpa might have sold you film for your camera to capture an image of the evening.

Some of the people walking on Broadway and shopping in the store were famous. Radio Clinic had always had celebrity customers; too many famous people have lived in the Upper West Side for that not to be true. No matter how famous a person is, at some point they need to purchase appliances. My personal favorite was when I got to deliver a fan to Mick Jagger in an apartment he was renting a few blocks from the 83rd Street store. My grandfather's favorite celebrity customer was Babe Ruth. I can't confirm that Humphrey Bogart brought his radio to Radio Clinic to be repaired, but odds are good since he lived on 95th Street, in the Pomander Walk apartments between Broadway and West End Avenue. At the time, the Upper West Side was thick with theaters. The Riverside and the Riviera, two very popular theaters on 96th Street, were part of the Vaudeville Subway Circuit. Bob Hope, Milton Berle, the Marx Brothers, Bette Davis and other Vaudeville luminaries performed in these theaters and odds are also pretty decent that they bought something at Radio Clinic as well.

Although he lived a few miles north of the store, Grandpa liked to roam the neighborhood with his camera. Along with Jack, he was active in a camera club that Stanley Kubrick's father also belonged to. Sometimes young Stanley would tag along with the group and was memorable because he often stopped to set up seemingly strange and obscure shots. Grandpa and Jack had a chance to take photography classes from famous, or soon to be famous photographers, and I have framed photos from both of these men hanging in my house. While he was far removed from his chess training in Russia, Grandpa still liked to play chess. He played chess games by mail with family scattered throughout the city, but these games could take months and weren't as satisfying as a game in real time. While he no longer relied on it for pocket money, he still preferred playing at the concrete chess tables in Riverside Park, trying his skill against whoever was there to challenge him.

During World War II, Dad started working at Radio Clinic. Born in 1935, he was one year younger than Radio Clinic. Growing up on 190th Street and Fort Washington Avenue, he lived just a few miles from the store and spent many

Saturday and summer days there. Small business owners, and I mean truly small businesses not the 500-employee definition that the Small Business Association (SBA) considers a small business, spend an enormous amount of time at their businesses. Typically, they do not have the funds to hire extra employees, do not have a layer of middle management to deal with the daily headaches, and are needed at the store. For Dad, the best way for him to spend time with his dad was at Radio Clinic. Plus, Dad was also a tinkerer who liked to see how things worked. His tinkering led him to an early career as a metallurgical engineer and he still likes to talk about his time working with metallic elements and alloys. As a kid, he was proud that he could be helpful to his dad by doing minor radio repairs. His very first job at the store was using the mimeograph machine in the basement with customer names on a plate to make personalized postcards. He spent hours in the basement, hand-cranking advertising postcards out of the machine for ten cents an hour. While not quite as great as my first job being paid to play video games, he was pleased with it. He also swept the floor, handled customers dropping off film to be developed, or used the cash register to ring up sales.

In elementary school, Dad was a devotee of radio and was happy to spend his Saturdays in a radio repair shop. Like many kids at that time, he was riveted by the World War II news broadcasts and enthralled with the stories broadcast over the family radio. He would rush home from school by 5 p.m. to listen to the 15-minute serials: the Sky King, Captain Midnight, and the Adventures of Superman. His favorite shows were the crime drama, "The FBI in Peace and War," on Saturday evenings, and "Tom Mix Ralston Straight Shooters" and the "Horn and Hardart Children's Hour" on Sunday mornings. He listened to most of these shows on the large radio in the center of the living room with his family. Typically, these radios were built into large wooden cases to accommodate the vacuum tubes and large speakers, and were treated like pieces of furniture. A small Philco radio was what he used at night to listen to the radio under his bed covers when he was supposed to be sleeping. Radio Clinic was closed on Sundays and my dad and grandpa had time to build things together. When my dad was nine, Grandpa brought home a quartz crystal so he could try to build his first radio. Quartz crystals provide an accurate frequency for radio transmitters and radio receivers, so when he hooked the crystal to some wires, Dad could pick up two stations. It had a limited ability and the sound was crackly, but it worked.

Seeing how seriously his son took this quartz crystal project, Grandpa knew his son was ready to learn the basics of radio repair. Fixing a crackling sound was as simple as slowly turning the dial and using a tuner spray to blow the dust off the tuner dial. For the other problems, the handle of a screwdriver was often all Dad needed to assess the degree of damage. If a radio tube crackled when he hit the radio tube with the handle, then it was damaged and needed to be replaced. He also learned the more philosophical "flinch method" from his dad. The "flinch method" was essentially an art form in reading people; understanding the exact spot where pushing people too far and not pushing them at all meet. Grandpa used this method to determine how much repair a customer could afford. He listed everything that was wrong with a radio. At the top of the list were the problems that made a radio inoperable such as bad tubes, resisters or capacitors. At the bottom of the list were the problems that damaged the sound quality or would later become big problems but at that moment were not. Grandpa watched the customer carefully as he read from the top of the list to the bottom. When he saw the customer flinch he stopped reading.

Dad developed confidence in his radio repair skills and sent away for a Heathkit to build an actual radio. Heathkit was a catalogue company designed for hobbyists and Dad loved to look through the catalogues that he got in the mail. Back then, it was not unusual for people who liked technical stuff to build their own radios. It was possible to build a radio from a $20 kit that would cost hundreds of dollars from a manufacturer. The Heathkit radios came with wrinkle paint. Back then many of the wooden radio cases had a textured wrinkle finish. All Dad had to do was spray the can of wrinkle paint on the radio and when it dried it would look the same as a store-bought radio.

Since my grandfather worked from 9-9 during the week and 9-6 on Saturdays, Dad often took the subway after school to hang out with his dad at the store. Grandpa had put together a small darkroom in the warehouse and showed Dad how to use printing paper and the solution to develop photographs. When he saw how enthralled his son was by this process he got him a camera and together the two of them went to the Manhattan MC Club meetings. But mostly Dad worked at the store and ran essential errands for the business. Radio Clinic sold a wide range of radios since their customers differed greatly on what type of radio fit in their budget. Each type of radio required a different type of part. Grandpa kept the store stocked with parts for simple radio repairs for the more commonly owned radios. Single dial station selectors, six tube components and chassis could be found on the shelves. But the store didn't have the shelf space or the money to keep the repair business stocked with components for more complicated parts or for less commonly owned radios. When an unusual part was needed, Grandpa sent Dad one hundred blocks south to Radio Row to buy them.

Radio Row was the hub for New York City's electronics industry from the early 1920s until it was leveled in 1966 to make way for the World Trade Center. It was a thriving business area and considered an electronics paradise. For a 13-block stretch, hundreds of shops, as many as could unreasonably fit on a city block, were filled floor to ceiling with vacuum tubes, condensers, transistors and any surplus part a radio enthusiast might want. This might have been Dad's favorite task, to be paid to roam through Radio Row, which he likened to a fruit market but with electronics.

Radios became even more indispensable during World War II as President Roosevelt's fireside chats kept people informed, so Dad did a lot of runs to Radio Row. During the war, Radio Clinic held firm as a reasonably successful enterprise and Broadway remained a vital shopping district. Virtually every address housed one or more business. There had been only some minor changes to the stores that shared the block with Radio Clinic when it first opened. A restaurant replaced a cigar store. A florist became a stationary store. A millenary and a furrier joined the block. But mostly the stores stayed the same. Radio Clinic still shared a storefront, although now with a cleaners and a barber shop. Blau Brothers was growing and opened a larger store across the street. A New York City market analysis, conducted by the city newspapers in the early 1940s, considered the Upper West Side a top area for shopping. It had "considerable purchasing power...proof of this is shown by the number of retail outlets of all varieties that flourish within its boundaries."

World War II had a big impact on New York City and it was felt by Radio Clinic. It was impossible not to. More than 900,000 New Yorkers served in the military, including both employees and customers of the store. A massive war time production sprung up in New York City to supply the Allies with ships, uniforms and other essential items that needed to be manufactured on an enormous scale. Every corner of the city contributed to the war effort, and the Upper West Side had plenty of resources to offer. Some of the once-grand residential hotels on Broadway had their rooftop cornices removed for the scrap metal drive. The Manhattan Towers Hotel on 76th Street and Broadway was a training center for the air force. Victory gardens were planted in yards of the Riverside Drive mansions. New York's Harbors, some located on the West Side, were the busiest in the world and moved 63 million tons of supplies and more than 3 million men shipped out from there. With some of the ports located on the west side's Hudson River, service men found their way to Radio Clinic.

Radio broadcasts were used to keep people informed about the war efforts and the demand for radio, and repairs, continued to intensify. The government launched patriotic publicity campaigns encouraging people to ration. Buying precious wartime materials, such as rubber, metal, and gasoline was discouraged. But the government wasn't trying to suppress the sale of radios for the war effort; if anything the reverse was true. Radio, the most popular form of entertainment, was crucial for the government to connect with its citizens. Radio broadcasts were used to both keep people informed about the war efforts and as a main vehicle of propaganda, imploring every American to think of themselves as a "fighting unit on the home front."

Small businesses didn't benefit from war supply contracts; those were the domain of large companies. But wartime did provide many business opportunities. The Army had so much equipment it needed to keep maintained to a very specific standard that it often disposed of parts that were still usable. Battery-operated portable radios were common before WWII, and during the war the United States Army relied on them. Army rules required that each radio had to have fresh batteries. Once the batteries outlived the army's use-by date, they were resold to the civilian market. Grandpa and Harry bought these batteries in large quantities and Matt Baum, Harry's son, then stripped the batteries to their basic components, reconfigured them to the standards for the civilian market, and then they were ready for sale.

Several of the young salesmen who had regularly stopped in the store before the war were fighting overseas. But their wives and young families still lived in the neighborhood. One woman brought her radio in for repair and while Grandpa examined it he asked for any news about her husband. He learned where her husband was stationed and the battles he had fought in. She was anxious to get her radio fixed since she felt closer to her husband when she carefully followed the news. Seeing that the radio needed considerable repair and knowing that money was tight with her husband overseas, Grandpa decided to not charge her for the repair. He felt good about this decision and decided not to charge any wives of the neighborhood salesmen who were overseas for repairs or simple purchases. This might have been a well thought-out decision on his part; it might have been a spur of the moment thought or somewhere in between. But regardless, this decision reverberated for decades.

I almost didn't learn about these relationships because it was one of the many things Dad casually referred to within a very detailed description about Zenith and the other large companies he bought merchandise from over the years. Since I knew I wasn't going to write about these companies in any detail, my attention wandered, probably to getting a refill on my drink or some more toast. My dad says so many things in passing and often it was only if I circled back to it—"what did you mean by that"—that I learned something important. But the meaning quickly became clear to me. The friendly relationship Grandpa developed with these young men and their wives would be instrumental in Radio Clinic's post WWII success.

One reason Dad liked telling me this story was to highlight the decency of his dad. Maybe it was as simple as that. But I am always curious about what is underneath the decisions we all make, even if on an unconscious level. Grandpa could simply have been showing his appreciation for the young men fighting to keep the country safe by easing the financial burden on their families. Or he could have been thinking about his oldest brother who remained in Russia and might be one of the thousands of Russian soldiers away from home for years struggling, and dying, on the eastern front. Or sometimes it just feels good to do a simple favor for a person. But whatever his motivation, it turned out to be a strategic move.

After World War II, the electronics industry exploded with a pent-up demand for consumer products. Jobs were more plentiful; wages were higher and people were ready to buy things. It was a great time to own a radio and appliance store. Anyone who had any spending money was spending it. By now Grandpa had some good connections in the electronics industry and helped several of the young neighborhood men newly returned from war, who didn't have a job waiting for them, to find a toehold in the industry. As they got their sales jobs at large manufacturing companies, they remembered my grandfather and gave him preferential treatment. Because of these relationships, Radio Clinic could establish itself as an appliance store with good, and sometimes difficult to get, inventory. The timing was crucial since this was a moment in history when appliances were becoming more integral to daily life.

Manufacturers produce products to be sold at a profit. It is an obvious point, but a point worth making. Until the invention of the Internet, manufacturers had to rely on stores in cities throughout the country to sell their products. It was easiest to distribute their products to large companies, such as Montgomery Ward, since they could handle a large volume of merchandise. Manufacturers offered these large companies much better pricing then the small family owned stores, which meant they could sell an appliance for less money and still make a bigger profit. But thanks to these increasingly well-positioned neighborhood guys, Radio Clinic often got the same low pricing as the big stores. Typically, a small business owner would get three percent of advertising money along with the merchandise he purchased. But Radio Clinic often got more than its share. With a few manufactures they got as much as twenty percent of advertising money, approaching the amount that large stores got. If merchandise was scarce for a new and popular product, these guys made sure Grandpa had access to the in-demand merchandise. The fact that Radio Clinic always had popular appliances and a significant advertising budget at a point in time when customers were deciding what store to rely on for household appliances made an impact on the success of Radio Clinic that lasted for several decades.

New York City was then one of the world's largest manufacturing centers, the nation's largest wholesaling center and the world's biggest port. With more and more people making decent salaries living in every neighborhood of the city, Radio Clinic and other small neighborhood stores had more customers who had money to spend. Young people were marrying and having children at a rapid rate and bought appliances that would make their home life easier. Between 1945 and 1949, 20 million refrigerators and 5.5 million stoves were purchased in the United States. My grandfather was happy to add larger appliances to the types of appliances sold at Radio Clinic, since they typically had a higher profit margin. Refrigerators, stoves, washing machines, and vacuum cleaners could then be purchased at Radio Clinic.

Like countless small business owners before them and countless after, Grandpa and Harry decided to build on their success and open a second store. Both men were happy on the Upper West Side and wanted the second store to also be in the neighborhood. They opened the second store on 83rd Street, a decidedly more affluent section of Broadway. In addition to the usual

Leon Rubin

From Radio Clinic's annual fishing trip, sometime in the 1950's.

assortment of butchers, fruit markets, and clothing stores, Radio Clinic shared the 83rd Street block with a dance studio, a slenderizing salon, and a dentist. The very popular Steinberg's Dairy Restaurant and Zabar's Deli were within two blocks, adding to the number of people walking by the store each day. From the day it opened, the 83rd Street store was, and would remain, the more successful store.

With a second store, and the increase in service and delivery demands that came with more customers, Radio Clinic needed to hire more employees.

Raymond Harding

Charlie Mackoff

Leonzo Simmons

Harry Baum

Grandpa and Harry hired several young men who stayed with the business until they retired. Several of them still worked at the store when I started spending time there thirty years later. By the 1970s, when I was in the store, it was a very ethnically and racially diverse place. Employees were Puerto Rican, African American, and white. But this was New York City and even in the 1970s, the white employees were noticeably ethnic; some were Jewish and others were close enough to their families immigrant experience that they spoke Greek and Italian as easily as they spoke English. Tracing the chronology of the employees that helped build Radio Clinic, I realized how closely its employees mirrored the demographic shift of the city. Hailing from rural North Carolina and Florida, several of the new employees in the late 1940s were part of the large-scale migration of African Americans out of the South that transformed who lived in the city. Pay was better and the opportunities wider for African Americans in Northern cities such as New York, so many left the Jim Crow South in search of work.

My grandfather met Leonzo Simmons in 1946, as he drove the trucks and did repairs at Camp Kittatinny in the Poconos, the summer camp where Dad and his older sister, Gay, went as kids. During my grandfather's visits to the camp, he and Leonzo talked about repair work and at the end of the summer he offered him a job to do deliveries and installations. Grandpa liked Leonzo, trusted his opinions and he quickly became an integral part the business. So much so that when Leonzo recommended three of his friends and family members for work, who had recently moved to New York City from the south, Grandpa readily hired them too. Radio Clinic mirrored national trends here as well. Leonzo and the other black employees primarily did the more physical type of work in the warehouse, and warehouse work—paid less than being a salesman.

By 1950 Radio Clinic had moved out of its cramped spot on 2580 Broadway. It no longer needed to share a crowded storefront with a dairy, cleaners, or any other business. The store moved to a more spacious corner spot on 98th Street, which greatly increased the size of its basement warehouse. The basement was an increasingly valuable part of the business. Radio repairs no longer happened in the store front window, but in the basement. Grandpa was busy running the business and hired others to do the bulk of the repairs. Radio Clinic replaced Davego Radio on the southwest corner—meaning it no longer had competition on the block. The closest businesses were a bakery, butcher shop, fruit market, and luncheonette bringing plenty of street traffic by the store. Moving to this corner spot was a wise move because the years after the war were good years for the city's small business owners. Collectively, small businesses would account for more than half of the domestic output of the 1950s. The future was bright for the business. Radio Clinic had good access to merchandise, a customer base just itching to buy appliances, a second store, new employees, and a great corner location. It was set.

5

The Post
World War II
Bust

Now you can tear a building down. But you can't erase a memory.
These houses may look all run down. But they have a value you can't see.

—Living Colour

IN THE YEARS AFTER the war, Radio Clinic was an informant for the FBI. More specifically, my grandfather was an informant. This came to be from a seemingly uneventful negotiation about the price of a television with a Russian customer that led the FBI to Radio Clinic's doors. In 1946, Stalin declared in a fiery speech that, "communism and capitalism were incompatible," and Russia needed to build up its military. This worried many people in the United States and soon we entered the Cold War with Russia. Grandpa's Cold War role can be traced back to one interaction he had with two Russian men who worked at the Russian Embassy. These men were buying a television and negotiating hard with Grandpa to try to get him to lower the price. They haggled in English with him, not knowing he spoke Russian, and conferred with each other in Russian. They kept telling each other to not agree to a price yet since they were sure they could get him to lower it. Grandpa let this dance go several rounds. After these men convinced themselves to try again, that this time he would lower the price, Grandpa spoke in Russian to tell them that "this price was the best he could do." Realizing they had been out-negotiated and happy to meet a neighborhood Russian businessman, these men sent a great deal of business to

Radio Clinic. Russians from the Embassy, as well as their relatives and friends, all shopped at Radio Clinic. One particularly good day, the representatives of the Bolshoi Ballet came to the store and bought thousands of dollars' worth of merchandise.

With all those Russians coming in and out of the store, the FBI took notice. The American fear of the "Communist Menace" leaned toward the hysterical and informants and information gatherers were the foot soldiers of the Cold War. The FBI worried about Communist expansion and used its informants to spy on Communist groups and flush out possible Russian spies operating in the United States. My grandfather was surprised when an FBI agent asked him to help them identify some Russians they thought might be spies.

While Grandpa didn't have a problem with Russian people, he had no love for the Russian government. The Cossacks murdered his father; he grew up with religious persecution all around him, and when his family fled they needed to leave behind their home and possessions. In his experience in the early years of the Russian Revolution, Jews didn't fare much better than they had under the Czar. When I started this book project, Dad sent me a recording of Grandpa describing his young life in Russia and the details of his escape. One of my older cousins had interviewed and recorded him in the year before he died and it was nice for me to hear his voice and, in a way, have a first-person interview with him. Grandpa had nothing positive to say about the Russian government. "When the Russian government wanted to divert attention from a problem they needed a scapegoat" he said, "And naturally the Jews were the scapegoat."

The United States had been very good to Grandpa and his family, and he valued his new country. He was willing to help. His informant role was straightforward. Whenever his Russian customers dropped off film to be developed, Grandpa notified the FBI. Once developed, the FBI would comb through the photos to determine what Russian people of interest were in New York at any given time. These photos gave them a lens into the supposedly private activities of people they believed to be Russian spies. Grandpa was continually surprised by how valuable the FBI found the photos.

The Russians weren't the only ones buying televisions after World War II. Televisions had become the appliance that people most wanted. In 1941 the first television stations, WCBW, WNBT, and W2XWV, went on the air, reaching the 5,000 residents that owned a television. World War II stopped commercial production, but things changed quickly after the war, and by 1948 more than one million homes in the United States owned a set.

Radio Clinic was well situated to sell televisions since 40 percent of the people that owned televisions within the United States lived in the greater New York area. In the years immediately following the war, televisions were expensive and cumbersome enough that Grandpa only kept one or two at a time in his store. But technology was evolving quickly, which lowered the price of the set, and programming was improving. Televisions replaced radios as the most dominant broadcast device—and as Radio Clinic's most popular product, the store's name becoming a misnomer. By 1955, nearly 77 percent of households owned at least one television, and Radio Clinic had sold and installed thousands.

My grandfather built a little room in the store to showcase televisions, which grabbed the attention of potential customers as they passed the store. These early televisions were large boxes with small screens. At the time, manufacturers shipped televisions to their merchants in two different boxes, one for the picture tube and one for the chassis, and Grandpa assembled them. By the early 1950s, Radio Clinic's televisions were also the neighborhood televisions. Once baseball started to be televised, Grandpa set up a television in the 98th Street window with the screen facing the street, and people gathered outside to watch. Screen sizes for most home televisions ranged from five to twelve inches, but the one my grandfather angled onto the street had an eighteen-inch screen. After the West Side Rag put a description of my book project in its magazine with my email address in case anyone wanted to contact me, I heard from a lot of people interested in reminiscing. And more people than I imagined had specific memories about watching baseball on Radio Clinic's television. In the fall of 1951, one man told me that he walked home from school and made a detour to stand outside of Radio Clinic for the much-anticipated National League pennant race between the Brooklyn Dodgers and the New York Giants. Before both teams relocated to California in 1957, they had an epic cross-town rivalry, so this was an anxiously watched pennant race. In his email, he described how adults who were able to steal away from their jobs, joined him to watch the final and decisive game of this dramatic series. I could see why he remembered it so vividly: it was a game for the ages. At 3:58 p.m. when Bobby Thomson of the Giants hit "the shot heard round the world," his game-winning homerun brought both cheers and angry shouts from the crowd outside Radio Clinic, as the Giants won the National League Pennant.

As a kid, Dad was a rabid baseball fan. He carefully applied tung oil to his baseball mitt, wrapped it with a rubber band to keep it well cared for, slept with it at night, and played baseball any chance he got. I still feel bad that I lost this mitt in 1979. Dad loaned me his well tended mitt to give me a boost for middle school softball tryouts, which I accidentally left in the gym and never found. It was perfect for Dad that he could watch baseball at his dad's store whenever he wanted. He didn't have to go to the lengths the boys across the street from Radio Clinic did to see baseball played on a television. One older man emailed me to say that sixty years ago his older brother rigged up a homemade telescope, focused it on Radio Clinic's television and then turned on the radio in their living room so they could watch the game through their window.

Dad grew up in Washington Heights, about 90 blocks north of the store, where there wasn't much open space for kids to play. Every public space was contested, and the local schoolyard, with its makeshift baseball diamonds was very much in demand. The entire schoolyard was concrete, and of the three baseball fields, only one was regulation size. The biggest field was the most coveted. The hierarchy was rigid and understood. When Dad was in elementary school, the young kids got to the schoolyard by 7am so they could play on the big diamond. In late morning, the high school kids took over the big field, and the younger kids stayed in the schoolyard playing handball and curb ball. By early afternoon, the college kids showed up and played for money, and all other activities stopped. If Dad had some money in his pocket, he would walk with his friends the 27 blocks south to Yankee Stadium to catch Yogi Berra and Bobby Brown in a late afternoon game. If not, he would take the subway to Radio Clinic, help his dad in the store, and watch the game on television.

My dad holding a baseball bat.

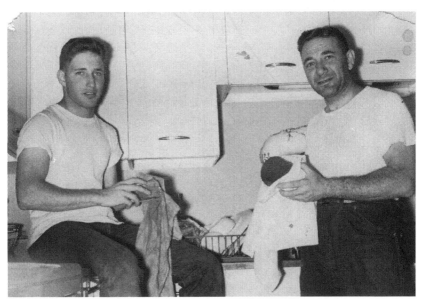

Leon and Alan in their apartment in the Washington Heights neighborhood in Manhattan.

Dad and his sister tried to explain baseball to their dad. He wanted to understand this game that Babe Ruth played. They set up a baseball field in their living room and explained the basics using marbles. Then they all went to a Sunday double header at Yankee stadium, but he fell asleep by the third inning. But having a rudimentary understanding of the game proved useful when the Citibank manager started taking Grandpa to games.

Televisions had the same essential issue as radios. Component parts wear out. Repairs become necessary. Radio Clinic serviced numerous televisions. Philco's electronic warehouse in Long Island City had the best deal for picture tubes, so Dad often made the trek out there to pick one up. It was quicker and cheaper for Grandpa to send my dad by subway than to send a truck. Dad was nervous as he carried the glass picture tube through the city and then sat as still as he could to keep it intact as he traveled up Broadway by subway. As a teenager, he mostly did delivery runs when he worked at the store. He would start his day in the warehouse with Leonzo, lifting and moving the appliances to the trucks that would transport that day's deliveries. Once the delivery trucks were prepared for the day, Dad joined Raymond Harding as he made delivery and installation trips throughout Manhattan.

Raymond, one of Leonzo's friends Grandpa had hired, was in his early 20s when he started at Radio Clinic in 1948. Without a doubt, of all the people that worked at Radio Clinic, Raymond had the biggest impact on Dad. Raymond was initially his mentor and decades later became his employee. The high value Dad placed on their working relationship was the catalyst for a defining decision he made about the business in 1977. As with Grandpa and the other Russian immigrants fleeing Europe and arriving in New York City in 1920, Raymond's story was both incredible and ordinary. He served heroically in the Army and was among the first United States occupation troops that went into Hiroshima after the war was over. Soon after coming home to Florida, he took a risk and left the South, hoping that by migrating north he would find more opportunities in a less segregated city.

Initially at the store Raymond did stock work and deliveries. Grandpa quickly realized his natural ability and sent Raymond to radio technician school. He saw a bit of his younger self in Raymond: physically strong, instinctive repair skill, great with customers and personable. Raymond eventually did repairs, service calls, and, by the time I started hanging around the store in the 1970s, Raymond managed the warehouse. Raymond mentored my dad when he was a teenager and Dad credits Raymond with teaching him much of what he knew about customer service and human nature in general. His childhood memories of running deliveries with Raymond are stories Dad loves to tell. If I were to rank the types of stories my dad told me and my brother about himself, his youthful sporting exploits would top the list and Radio Clinic stories would be second. But as many times as he told me about his second date with Mom, when he thought he impressed her by hitting the winning run in a softball game, but she was chit-chatting with the other girlfriends and hadn't even noticed he was at bat; I heard even more about his house calls with Raymond. It has been more than sixty-five years since he did delivery runs with Raymond and I am still hearing about what he learned from those experiences.

Dad and Raymond went on many service calls for customers who purchased a roof antenna and weren't happy with their poor TV reception. Customers needed an antenna to make their television operational after setting it up in their home. Some customers bought rabbit ears to hook to the top of their television. This was the inexpensive option but it typically resulted in limited reception. The outdoor receiving antenna, with its greater access to television transmitters, was superior, so a lot of customers purchased the more expensive antenna. Before the city was wired for cable TV, the cityscape had many antennae on the roof of nearly every apartment building. Since the city was so densely packed with buildings, TV signals bounced and not every apartment could get great reception. Few people were up for the challenge of mounting an antenna on an apartment roof and connecting it to a television several stories below. Radio Clinic technicians were tasked with installing antennas for the thousands of customers in and around the Upper West Side. No matter how fancy the apartment building, or how much money a customer had to spend on a television, consistently good television reception was hard to come by at the time. The most noticeable difference for my dad was that the less money the customers seemed to have the bigger the tip they would give him and Raymond.

From fine apartment buildings with elevator operators to tenements with steep wooden staircases, each building and each customer came with its own set of challenges. But Raymond was rarely stumped. Back when Channel 5 from the Empire State Building and Channel 13 from Newark were the two popular stations, Raymond knew it wasn't always possible for both stations to come in clearly at the same time from one antenna position. But he also knew that customers wouldn't be satisfied if he told them there was nothing Radio Clinic could do to help the reception. So Raymond often sent Dad to the roof and told him to listen to his instructions but not to touch the antenna. They both wore telephone headsets on each end of a long roll of coaxial cable. Raymond told him to sit down and do nothing regardless of what he said. He spoke into the phone for Dad to move the antenna a little to the right, to the left, back, and so on, until he finally told him to tighten it up and come back down. While Dad did nothing on the roof, Raymond slowly knocked the focus out and then brought it back to where it was originally, at which time the customer typically said it looked terrific and to leave it there. Learning how to install roof antennas came in handy for Dad. Several of his friends' parents hired him to install one for their televisions.

During the 1950s, when Dad was young and spent a great deal of time at the store, Radio Clinic was at its peak. But it's hard to recognize your peak when you are at it. There always seems to be something more you can do to improve and potential can seem infinite. At 30 years old you don't look in the mirror and think I will never look this good again. You imagine that with enough push-ups and a good haircut, you will continue to improve. The Upper West Side was at the end of its tenure as a primarily middle class neighborhood but it didn't know it either. You can't know what you don't know. Economic forces were coming. The ensuing changes to the Upper West Side were a result of a series of cascading policy decisions and, as was often the case in NYC; real estate interests were at the heart of it.

Nothing mattered more to a Manhattan small business than who lived and shopped in its immediate vicinity. Most people in Manhattan did not own a car and relied on public transportation to move around the city. Aficionados might travel 100 blocks to Radio Row, or other more specialized areas of the city to shop, but small merchants relied on the fact that most people preferred to shop where they lived. Radio Clinic depended on this foot traffic and that there were buildings full of people who lived nearby with enough disposable incomes to buy, and later upgrade, their appliances. But that solid customer base was about to shift.

If I wanted to understand why Radio Clinic's storefront window went from a spot where my grandfather picturesquely fixed sick radios to a spot where my dad taped up a 'We Are Staying' sign, I needed to understand how it shifted, and the neighborhood response to this shift. When I first started this book project I didn't anticipate that I would feel the need to dig deeper into the major urban issues of the 20th century; urban renewal, slum clearance, suburbanization, displacement, deinstitutionalization, etc. But Radio Clinic didn't exist in a vacuum. The people who looted Radio Clinic didn't exist in a vacuum. City housing policy didn't exist in a vacuum. Each fall, I teach an 8-week Social Policy class in the Part-Time Program at the University of Wisconsin School of Social Work. It is a required course and some of the students aren't particularly interested in policy. I can get quite animated about context and why it is critical to have a historical perspective about the causes and consequences of poverty if you want to practice social work. My goal is that at the end of the eight weeks each student will agree with me; policy does indeed matter.

Large economic forces, racist housing policies, and a host of overlapping factors impacted Radio Clinic's eco-system. Racism has been baked into the DNA of our housing policies for generations and has shaped our neighborhoods. While these large economic forces impacted all five boroughs of New York City, the two decades after the war brought particularly damaging changes to the Upper West Side. Most essentially, the map of where Americans lived, both inside and outside of the city, changed in the 1950s. The federal government put a huge chunk of tax dollars into an enormous federal interstate system and programs supporting new homeownership, so many people started to leave the city. The opening of the Tappan Zee Bridge in 1955, along with federally supported housing loans, made it possible for millions of people to purchase homes and move to the suburbs. But availability of these loans, and by extension the suburbs, were largely restricted to white people. Many white Upper West Siders took advantage of their opportunity and left the city. Not all the white people left the area, many others stayed and fought tooth and nail in the housing fights to come, trying to keep the neighborhood healthy, integrated and with affordable housing. But the impact of suburbanization was undeniable. Enough white people left the city, taking their middle-class resources with them, and overall the citizenry got poorer. The mostly low-income African American and Puerto Rican people that migrated into the city found a different job situation than earlier white immigrants did.

The same roads that made it easier for people to live in the suburbs made it easier, and cheaper, for factories to operate outside the city. Factory work had historically been the point of entry to joining the New York City economy, which was true for my maternal grandmother when she first got here and started sewing in a factory. But for the large number of southern African Americans and Puerto Ricans that made their way to the Upper West Side in the 1950s, the disappearance of blue-collar factory work often meant they couldn't find a decent paying job and get a secure foothold in the economy.

The changes to the Upper West Side were both emblematic of what was happening in other urban neighborhoods and also quite idiosyncratic. Disparate things were happening at the same time. The Upper West Side was buffeted by many social forces, including white middle class exodus to suburbs, migration of African Americans from the South and Puerto Ricans from Puerto Rico, even as top notch transportation options, proximity to jobs, and cultural institutions helped the neighborhood preserve a core of affluent and highly educated residents.

I wasn't sure how far back to go or how much detail to provide to adequately set the stage for why Radio Clinic's immediate neighborhood changed so dramatically by 1977. Part of the story began at the turn of the twentieth century when the luxury residential hotels were first built to entice the wealthiest people to move to the Upper West Side. Without these enormous apartments, landlords wouldn't have been able to turn a one family residential apartment into a rooming house during the Depression when people could no longer afford to rent their own apartments. This trend then intensified with a post

WWII housing shortage, when the city gave landlord's significant tax breaks to rehabilitate existing apartment buildings. Understanding an opportunity when they saw one, many landlords further divided up these apartments into small, single-room rentals, hastening the transformation of these once-elegant buildings into increasingly run-down rooming houses. So, by the 1960s and 1970s, many of these once grand buildings were now Single Room Occupancy's (SRO), housing the most economically disenfranchised and vulnerable people in the city.

When my grandfather walked between the two stores, from 98th Street to 83rd Street and back again, he saw that city blocks that once housed hundreds of people now housed thousands. This was a seismic change for the neighborhood. It wasn't just one or two blocks that went from having hundreds of people to thousands of people—this statistic was multiplied on many blocks for several of the Avenues in the area. These apartments were cut into so many units, that even though there had been no significant private development in the area since before the Depression, the number of household units on the Upper West Side increased 80 percent between 1934 and 1956.

Neighborhoods like the Upper West Side worried legislators in many cities across the country. They worried the federal government as well. Deteriorating housing stock filled with large numbers of very low-income black and brown people coupled with white middle-class flight is exactly the type of situation that captures a mayor's attention. In the 1950s, then-Mayor Wagner feared these migration patterns would substantially lower city tax revenue and halt private investment. Simply told, he wanted the white middle class people to come back. So, he turned to the powers provided by the 1949 Housing Act to do something about it. As part of an urban renewal plan, the federal government gave cities subsidies and the authority to declare densely populated areas "slums." Through eminent domain, the government purchased property in the slums, cleared out the people who lived there, demolished the buildings, and developed something new. Countless of thousands of poor people were displaced from their homes to make room for something the city considered better. This kick-started a decades-long, intensely fought political battle between city bureaucrats and Upper West Side community activists about what housing should be demolished and what kind of housing should replace it.

Robert Moses, chairman of the New York City Slum Clearance Committee, was in charge of many of New York City's urban renewal projects. His racism and contempt for low-income people was central to how he approached housing development. Based on the median household income he declared neighborhoods slums, and then obliterated the neighborhoods. Displacing people from their homes, without a solid plan for where they would live instead, was an ugly undertaking. Two of the urban renewal projects that had a huge impact on the Upper West Side in the 1950s were Lincoln Center for the Performing Arts and the West Side Urban Renewal Area (WSURA). Before Lincoln Center became Lincoln Center it was the San Juan Hill neighborhood, located near Amsterdam Avenue from 59th to 65th Street, and the most concentrated black neighborhood in Manhattan. Robert Moses decided this neighborhood needed to be destroyed. It didn't matter to Moses that San Juan Hill was home to 7,000 people and 800 businesses; his vision was a, "reborn West Side, marching north from Columbus Circle and eventually spreading over the entire dismal and decayed West Side." And he didn't envision 7,000 low-income African American and Puerto Ricans in this reborn West Side.

Meanwhile, the urban renewal projects on the northern edge of the Upper West Side played out a bit differently. The mayor declared a 20-block radius near Radio Clinic the West Side Urban Renewal Area (WSURA). Robert Moses was not in charge of this project. Neighborhood activists, outraged by the wrecking ball approach the city took in the San Juan Hill neighborhood, pushed the city to help blighted blocks by upgrading, not demolishing, the housing stock. These community leaders were well-informed and dogged. A 1969 New York Magazine article looking back at the Upper West Side of the 1950s described them this way:

> High crime rates, poor schools, indifferent bureaucrats, corruption and graft—all of the classic characteristics of urban disaster—were visiting the Upper West Side in the '50s. The result, however, was surprising. It created the most skeptical, municipally wise, politically organized, reform-conscious community in the city. West Siders became the nightmare of city bureaucrats.

The goal of these community activists was to "revive the neighborhood without destroying its character to maintain its ethnic and economic equilibrium. As a result of their organizing work, the city took less of a wrecking ball approach, demolished only the most rundown buildings, and rehabilitated structurally sound buildings. Neighborhood activists pushed to have a ratio of 30:70 of low-income housing units to middle-income housing units. But even while the WSURA was more accountable to the community than most urban renewal efforts, getting the new housing built was slow going, and many of these buildings stood condemned and continued to deteriorate for years.

The result of these urban renewal projects was that thousands of people doubled and tripled up in the cheap housing scattered throughout the city. SROs near Radio Clinic absorbed large numbers of people and the pockets of poverty in the blocks surrounding Radio Clinic became increasingly substantial. An SRO could have anywhere from 50 to 450 rooms. These was mostly tough places to live, but for people on fixed incomes, it was housing of last resort. Joseph Lyford, a journalist, wrote the *Airtight Cage: Study of New York's West Side* and reported, "Various aid organizations and city officials steered people to live in these buildings: social workers steered people newly released from Rikers Island prison, addicts on methadone treatment, the elderly poor barely getting by with their SSI checks, families surviving on welfare, and recently deinstitutionalized mentally ill patients, to these rooms." Twenty-five percent of the addicts in the country and the largest concentration of deinstitutionalized mentally ill patients lived in the area.

While the neighborhood continued to have a mix of well off, middle class, and poor residents, it seemed like the neighborhood was tipping in the direction of poverty. People without a lot of money continued to be customers of the store. They got their appliances repaired and bought a variety of miscellaneous items, but they only had so much discretionary money to spend. Customers confided to my grandfather that many of their friends were afraid to come to the neighborhood. A woman who had lived in the neighborhood for forty years told a reporter, "A friend of mine got sick the other night and the doctor wouldn't come. He said he was afraid of the neighborhood." It wasn't good news for Radio Clinic and other local merchants that there was a growing feeling that the Upper West Side was a blighted area to be avoided. Whether the residents of the Upper West Side would be enough of an economic force to sustain the area businesses was an open question.

By the mid 1960s, the impact of Lincoln Center started to be felt. Around 65th Street, near the Center, gentrification began and slowly crept uptown. The blocks around 83rd street were an increasingly attractive area for actors and musicians that wanted an affordable place to live near their jobs in the theater district. These performers moved to the Upper West Side in such large numbers they made a big imprint on the overall personality of the area. But the immediate blocks near the 98th Street store were not reinvigorated. These blocks were growing shabbier and more crowded, and the area felt increasingly marginal. The stores on the 98th Street block of Broadway were feeling it.

Phonebook listings show the evolution of the block in the decades after World War II. In 1950 there was no evidence of a decline on the 98th Street block of Broadway. There wasn't an empty storefront on the block. Jean Pathe cleaned your clothes, Jack Stanger cut your hair, Renee made your corset, Max designed your hat, Jack Nelson had your fur coat, and Al Ermann was your butcher. Any number of factors could lead to the end of a small business—a vacant storefront isn't always the harbinger of bad economic news. But by 1965 there were many empty storefronts on the block. That was bad news for Radio Clinic. Ninety-Sixth Street seemed to be an invisible dividing line that many people didn't cross if they could help it. Newspapers cautioned people away from visiting the neighborhood, even for an evening out. With its multitude of theaters and public parks, the Upper West Side had been a destination for people living in other parts of the city to come and spend some time—and some money. But that was no longer true by 1965.

My grandfather could see the changes happening around Radio Clinic. He saw the increasing number of vacant storefronts. But he also knew these were not things he could control. What he could control were changes to his business. Sales slips showed that the 83rd Street store now accounted for two-thirds of Radio Clinic's sales, and while the 98th Street store still turned a profit, it did not do so comfortably. But he knew that the 98th Street store had something valuable that most stores did not. It had an unusually large warehouse for a store its size, in part because of its corner location, but in part because Grandpa had negotiated a lease that extended Radio Clinic's basement space four feet beyond the building line, including some of the residential tenants' space. It also had a 'vault,' so extended beyond the footprint of the building and went under the sidewalk, almost to the curb. Having a place to store large quantities of merchandise allowed Grandpa and Harry to purchase appliances at a significantly better price since they could handle a high volume. Most small retail dealers couldn't do this and had to spend more money per unit. This warehouse opened many new business options for Radio Clinic. Seeing the changes to the deteriorating neighborhood, Grandpa turned his attention to build up a new revenue stream that didn't rely on local customers.

Tapping into his connections with salesmen in several of the large manufacturing companies, my grandfather steered the business into a lucrative wholesale side business. In the 1950s, when the heavy demand for appliances was relatively new, large manufacturers started to use transshipping to move merchandise. Instead of selling directly to small stores, they sold to a middleman, who did the time-consuming legwork of selling to the small operations. The middleman could buy at a large volume and get a better deal on merchandise than a small store would from the manufacturer. The middleman could then turn around and sell the merchandise at a profit to the small store, but for less than it would have cost the small store to buy it on its own.

By being this middleman, Radio Clinic effectively added a lucrative wholesale wing to its operation. This new revenue stream gave Radio Clinic a financial cushion. Grandpa never considered moving Radio Clinic from the Upper West Side, because it never stopped being a vibrant neighborhood to be part of. More than one thing was true at the same time. At the heart of this area, with the deteriorating housing stock and escalating crime, was a lively neighborhood. It had the most eclectic citizenry in the city, and vibrant small businesses.

For 30 years, my grandfather spent 12 hours a day, 6 days a week, on the 98th Street block of Broadway. He had a front row seat to the neighborhood, and what stayed the same and what changed was visible every day. He had time to study his competition and see why some stores closed and others remained viable, and to notice which merchant adapted to changing times and which did not. At the time Radio Clinic's fixed costs were not that hard to deal with. The rent was only 1 percent of his business costs. Radio Clinic had a profitable business on 83rd Street, an outsized warehouse on 98th Street, and a thriving wholesale business. Even as the surrounding blocks deteriorated, Grandpa wasn't too worried. It was the mid 1960s and Radio Clinic was doing fine.

6

The Hornet's Nest

An astonishing collection of artists, writers, middle class professionals,
reform politicians, students, revolutionary political agitators, prostitutes,
welfare families, and a remarkable little group of stark raving lunatics
attracted to our district by its colorful ethos.

—President McGill of Columbia University, Upper West Side Story, early 1970s

So be on the lookout for a new generation. Coming on strong filled with inspiration.

—The Washington Squares

MY DAD JOINED THE family business in 1966. At the age of 31 he was a husband, the father of a three-year-old son and worked as a metallurgical engineer at International Nickel. My uncle Bill, who was married to Gay, had been a plant manager in California, approached his father-in-law about buying out Harry and becoming a partner. Nearing retirement, Harry accepted the offer. Grandpa then offered Dad the opportunity to also come in as a partner, with no cost to join the business. Although Dad had never seriously considered joining the business, his dad had considered it. For the previous year, to earn some extra money, Dad had spent many Saturdays at Radio Clinic helping with paperwork. It was during this year that the idea solidified for Grandpa that it could work out well if his son joined the business. Although Dad liked engineering, he liked the idea of being his own boss and earning a higher salary even

Sandi and Alan Rubin   Uncle Jack, Josh, and me.

more. Reflecting back on this choice, he told me that he knew he would never again have the chance to go into a successful business at no cost. He figured that if in the future he didn't like owning a business, then he could get out and go back to engineering.

My mom also thought it was a good move. She greatly respected her father-in-law. After my brother was born, she and Dad moved into my grandparents' home for six months to save for a down payment on a house. During this time, she got to know him well and thought Dad would learn a lot working in close proximity to his father. Plus, by then she was pregnant with me and the potential for a bigger paycheck was appealing. So, Dad quit his engineering job and began his career as one of three partners at Radio Clinic.

Radio Clinic cleared a major hurdle of longevity by surviving the handover from the founder to the second generation of ownership. (Fewer than one-third of family-owned businesses survive this.) Hundreds of thousands of people have gone into business with a family member. My family was not special in this regard. There are many different types of configurations for who owns these businesses: parent and child, siblings, in-laws connected to the family through marriage. Radio Clinic had a fairly typical set up. One partner was the founder of the business nearing retirement; another was a son who grew up in the business and the third was a son-in-law with management experience. This arrangement started out ok, as most family businesses do. Dad was primarily responsible for the warehouse and deliveries and managed the 98th Street store. Bill worked at the 83rd Street store with his father-in-law and learned purchasing and advertising. From the beginning, Grandpa gave the younger men a fair amount of autonomy and their own areas to manage; but he was the clear senior partner in terms of expertise and clout. This arrangement didn't last long.

In 1968 Grandpa had the very bad luck to be diagnosed with multiple myeloma, a painful cancer of the bones. He continued to work at Radio Clinic after the diagnosis until the pain got to be too much. He tapered down to a couple of days a week until by the end of 1969 it was too difficult for him to travel. Without him at the store as an influential buffer, it became increasingly clear that Dad and Bill didn't particularly see eye-to-eye with regard to the functioning of the business, and it became a growing problem. They did not share a vision for the business, and developed a very strained relationship over time. In this regard my family was not special either. If anything, their uneasy relationship was a bit of a cliché. This co-owning Radio Clinic arrangement was like a hornet's nest, only harmless if neither man poked it.

Although he mostly stayed home, Grandpa kept his hand in the business as long as he could. For several months, the bookkeeper stopped by his house once a week with the accounting, until he assured her that Bill could handle it. Raymond was often at the house, visiting at the end of the workday. Wanting to spend as much time with his dad as possible, once or twice a week Dad stopped by his parents' house after work to visit and talk over business concerns. Grandpa had been thrilled when Dad agreed to join the business, but it was now clear to both men that their short time running it together was over.

With not many months more to live, Grandpa turned his attention to his photography dark room. Photography was a pure pleasure for my grandpa and over the decades he had built an impressive dark room to develop his photos. Dad was going to inherit his darkroom equipment and some of the cameras, and Grandpa put a lot of his remaining energy into helping Dad plan how he would set up the dark room in his garage. He continued to take photos until his last few days and his tinkering skills helped him out when the camera became too heavy for him to hold. While sitting on the back porch, he placed his camera on a tripod and used a cable release to snap pictures.

As the father that was dying, my grandpa was happy for the opportunity to be a mentor to his son for as long as he had the strength to talk. As the son who greatly admired his father, this was Dad's last chance to learn whatever else it was his dad had to teach. These conversations with his dad gave my dad a chance to examine business decisions with an experienced advisor and get an honest assessment about these decisions. As a new business owner, Dad wasn't fully confident in his judgment, but he was fully confident in his dad's business acumen. And Grandpa liked the decisions Dad was making. Slowly, he began to trust his business instincts and felt more prepared to co-own Radio Clinic without his father. In 1971, my grandpa died and Dad and Bill were on their own.

Co-owning the business with just his brother-in-law put Dad in a tough spot. I am guessing it put Bill in a tough spot as well but I have only heard Dad's side of the story. The two men were at an equal level yet they disagreed about fundamental things, making running the business together challenging. Without Leon there as a solid anchor, the two men settled into their roles. Purchasing the merchandise and advertising, Bill spent his days at the 83rd Street store. Managing the warehouse, Dad spent his days at the 98th Street store, where he and Raymond worked together preparing for deliveries. Raymond, a protégé of my grandfather's, taught my dad much of what he knew about running the warehouse, and now needed to transition to a new reality. The boy he had once mentored was now his boss. I don't know how Raymond felt about this at the time. Maybe he was relieved that Radio Clinic would continue to exist and he would remain employed at a good job with a family that respected him and his work. Maybe he wanted to open his own repair shop but knew that wasn't possible for an African American man in the 1960s without his own capital. He certainly would need to show a landlord more than his dream, some chutzpah and the first month's rent. But I do know Raymond and Dad had a conversation about this as they began their new relationship. Raymond had tremendous respect for my grandfather and the opportunity he had offered Raymond as a young man by sending him to technical college. Essentially, Raymond told Dad that he was not his father and their working relationship would be different than the one he had with Leon. But Raymond liked my dad, thought he was a trustworthy guy, and that they would work well together. This conversation was important to Dad. He had high regard for Raymond and it was very important to him that they worked well together.

Meanwhile, there were some variables in play that doomed Dad and Bill's partnership. The primary issue was a differing vision for the future of Radio Clinic. Bill was more ambitious than Dad for the business and wanted Radio Clinic to open more stores and expand to other parts of Manhattan. Dad did not. He instead wanted to invest in and expand the existing stores. He wanted to take over the leases of the stores next to the 83rd and 98th Street stores and create one long window in the front that would catch the attention of more people as they walked by. Without a third partner, there wasn't anyone to break the tie.

Layered underneath the business tensions was a long-simmering family tension that tipped the scales in favor of Bill. Dad's sister wasn't well and hadn't been for several years. She struggled with mental health issues, and my grandmother was very protective of her and understandably didn't want Dad to add any additional stress to his sister's life. My grandmother pressured him not to make waves within the family and to do things the way Bill wanted them done. She often called him to insist that he should just listen to Bill, which strained their relationship. Radio Clinic did open a third store on East 86th Street, although Dad was never happy about it. This 86th Street store was never successful and closed a few years later. But for my Dad this failed experience had a silver lining because it solidified his belief that when he and Bill disagreed about a business decision, he was the one with the better business sense. This did not make for a healthy extended family dynamic.

And so, each man increasingly hunkered into his own domain within Radio Clinic. Whenever Dad would make a suggestion about the warehouse or 98th Street, Bill had a reason why they couldn't do it. Dad stopped consulting with his business partner and just made the changes he thought were necessary. Dad felt Bill ordered significantly larger orders of merchandise than they needed because he wanted Radio Clinic to seem more impressive than it was. Bill stopped consulting with his business partner about the quantities of merchandise he ordered for both stores and didn't include Dad as he developed relationships with new companies. Many of the newer sales representatives didn't even know Bill had a business partner. Handling the day-to-day operations of the business was time-consuming for both men so their strained relationship wasn't always at the forefront. But the tension never really went away.

From Dad's first days as a business owner there were some notable changes to the neighborhood, particularly the blocks near the 83rd Street store. Urban renewal policies were having their desired effect. The young white middle class families, the type that moved to the suburbs after World War II, were moving back into the city, many to the Upper West Side. In 1969 Mayor Lindsay proclaimed, "The Upper West Side is probably enjoying more of a renaissance today than any other single neighborhood of our city." But there was not one simple narrative to the lives being led on the Upper West Side. Nor was there a unifying thread to city policy. City policy provided tax relief for homeowners to renovate neglected brownstone homes, enticing many middle-class families back to the area. City procedure continued to funnel its most disenfranchised residents to the Single-Room Occupancy hotels. Newly renovated brownstones changed the general affluence on some blocks, while squatters moved into abandoned buildings that the city allowed to deteriorate on other blocks.

Six days a week Dad drove down from Rockland County, where we lived, to the Upper West Side, parked his car in a garage on 95th Street near the Hudson River, and walked five minutes to Radio Clinic. He spent a lot of time walking on Broadway throughout each day to either deposit cash in the bank a few blocks away, drop something off at the 83rd Street store, grab some food, or run some other kind of errand. When Dad made his way to work each morning, he walked past a familiar cast of characters that spent their days on the neighborhood benches and walked on streets that were heavily littered. Beer and soda cans, empty whisky bottles, and broken glass filled the islands. The sanitation commission considered upper Broadway to be one of the filthiest areas of the city and planned to assign extra workers to clean the streets. But not the sidewalks. The commissioner felt it was the responsibility of the merchants to keep the sidewalks clean and wanted the city to more rigorously enforce fining those businesses that didn't. While businesses on 92nd Street probably had it the worst with Off Track Betting and Key Foods Supermarket on the block, there was still plenty of trash to clean off 98th Street.

And yet, the benches told the story of the demographic mix of people now living above 96th Street. First installed in 1904 in the median island between the east and west sides of Broadway, these benches remained popular places to sit. Elderly Jewish refugees from Europe reading their Yiddish newspaper, entwined young couples wearing bell bottoms, groups of intellectuals arguing a political point, mentally unstable people resting after pushing their shopping carts filled with possessions around the neighborhood, political activists with their clipboards, and alcoholics nodding off all enjoyed sunning themselves on these benches. Dad also liked these benches and often grabbed deli sandwiches and had a lunch meeting on the bench opposite the 98th Street store. If the weather was particularly nice, he might walk to a bench in Riverside Park and enjoy the view of the Hudson River while discussing business.

But the benches, like the neighborhood as a whole, were an increasingly contested space. A 1973 *New York Times* article, with very dated language, considered what to do about, "the derelicts that vexed residents along upper Broadway." The Broadway Mall Association and the City Parks Department planned to spend a lot of money to landscape the 43 traffic islands between 61st and 114th street, where many of the benches resided. There was a growing concern that some of the people that were fixtures on the neighborhood benches would scare other people away from the area after the landscaping work was done. The people in question, the ones who spent many hours of the day on these benches, sometimes drunk and sometimes not, didn't agree with how they were characterized. One man who sat on a bench at 102nd Street said, "We're really harmless. We just like to sit down on them benches because it's a good place." "These benches give us a front seat in life as it passes by," said an elderly woman who lived in an SRO. But whether you appreciated the democratic nature of whom you might sit next to on these benches or it bothered you, was immaterial. These were public spaces and anyone could sit down on a bench and get comfortable.

As a business on 98th Street, Radio Clinic felt the impact of the thousands of people living in SROs in the blocks around its store. There were nine SRO hotels alone on 94th and 95th Streets. A group of older men alternated between sitting on the 98th Street benches and panhandling outside Radio Clinic. Some of these men lived in SROs and others were homeless, sleeping in subway tunnels at night. When Dad talked to them, usually they were a little drunk and seemed to struggle with mental illness. He wasn't worried about them as a danger, but considered these men a bit of a nuisance since some customers complained about them. Dad understood why they congregated there since the subway ran below Broadway and 98th Street, warming the part of the sidewalk closest to the store. But he also understood that customers might not enter his store if they felt uncomfortable trying to get past these men asking for money.

Dad tends to strike up a conversation with strangers. There is no way to know in advance what person he will start talking to because of some tiny, yet observed, shared interest. This embarrassed me all the time when I was running errands with him as a kid. Although I wish as a young woman I had understood his wingman potential, and taken advantage of his ability to find and talk with attractive young men who shared his interest in soccer and electronics. Each morning, as Dad walked down 98th Street he greeted the men panhandling, asked them how their night was and if they managed okay. He often explained his situation with the customers, and suggested to the panhandlers an alternative: If they stood near the dead spots on the block, they wouldn't block the entrance to any store but could still stay warm and interact with pedestrians who might be willing to part with some money. He did mention to the panhandlers that if they felt like they had the most success directly in front of a store, they would have better luck standing outside Sloan's Supermarket, since it had more foot traffic. His solidarity with other local business owners only went so far.

Mayor Lindsay was excited about the Upper West Side renaissance, but it was primarily occurring below 86th Street. The impact of Lincoln Center was accelerating and heading north and starting to have a ripple effect on the surrounding area. Boutiques, bookstores, theaters, and restaurants began to open up to meet the interests of new residents. In 1969 the owner of the Ginger Man restaurant, on West 64th Street, near Lincoln Center, told a reporter that his business had quadrupled in the last few years. He felt "the whole area has come to life." Businesses closer to Radio Clinic's 83rd Street store were noticing changes as well. Zabar's Gourmet Foods, a fixture on 80th Street, planned to move to 82nd Street and triple its size. Stanley Zabar commented on these changes, saying, "Just five years ago it was considered an adventure, a trek, even dangerous, to come to the West Side and shop in our store. Shopping guides, newspaper stories and magazine article were always knocking the neighborhood when they wrote about the store. That doesn't happen anymore."

Every city neighborhood has its unofficial boundaries. Ninety-sixth Street served as an invisible boundary for the Upper West Side. For many New Yorkers, this was a dividing line they didn't want to cross. The housing stock was noticeably more deteriorated once you crossed 96th Street. An increasingly large swath of humanity walking on these streets seemed dangerous. Mentally ill people often yelled to themselves and sometimes relieved themselves on the grassy median as you walked by, and prostitutes set up shop in the rundown residential hotels that lined upper Broadway. Theaters, such as the Metro, that once showed foreign language films, now showed porn flicks. And pretty much everyone was no more than one degree of separation from a mugging.

While these were not imagined differences between the northern and southern part of the neighborhood, most of the people who lived on these blocks did not consider their neighborhood a place to be feared. The 96th Street block had two low-rise buildings that contained a candy store, coffee shop, counter restaurant, ping pong parlor, a Latin dance hall, and two legendary movie theaters--the Riverside and the Riviera. These theaters had been on the block since the 1910s. They originated as high-end vaudeville showcases when they had been part of the various vaudeville circuits. As a young man my dad took his dates to the Riverside Theater. Although they were now increasingly run-down, they were still immensely popular.

Even a hint of a potential revival in the blocks north of 96th Street piqued the interest of developers. Its proximity to public transportation remained a powerful attribute for the area, since 360,000 people lived on the Upper West Side, but easy access to subways meant the entire West Side population of 800,000 people could shop there. And if developers were potentially interested then the city was ready to do much of whatever it would take to turn that interest into action. The city's Housing and Development Administrator led a group of municipal bond investors through a tour of the West Side Renewal Area. Alexander's, one of the largest retail stores in New York City, had commissioned a two-year survey of the area, and concluded that West 96th Street could be a very successful location for the department store. Alexander's proposed building a six-level block-long store, including a 1,000-seat movie theater. But there was one large stumbling block for this project. Neighborhood activists didn't trust the intentions of the city or the developers and pushed back hard.

Strong community opposition feared the real-estate speculators that would follow Alexander's to the neighborhood. The opposition was led by seasoned New York City activists who knew that the loss of affordable housing meant the loss of a diverse neighborhood. Many of these activists were still battling to have the promised number of low-income housing units built in the WSURA. Their concern, which they expressed at several planning board meetings, was that this type of development would raise property values, and without a commitment by the city to build new or maintain existing low-rent housing, there would be nothing to stop speculators from buying buildings and evicting low and moderate-income tenants. A common sentiment of community activists at these hearings was, "This area has the best population mix in the city and an attempt had to be made to protect this balance." But city planners and developers weren't as fond of this diverse mix and felt confident that big changes were coming to the 96th Street area. "In five years," one city planner boasted, "the only dumpy little shopping bag ladies you'll be able to find on the West Side will be stuffed and behind the glass at the Museum of Natural History."

My dad did not attend these community meetings. He worked very long days and tried to get home in time to have dinner with us each night. But he was rooting for Alexander's. From his perspective, there was no downside to increasing the number of people coming to the neighborhood to shop. He had an untested theory that having a nearby large competitor would help his business. With the department store just two blocks away he was certain he would gain customers. But the neighborhood resistance to this department store chain was so prolonged and vigorous that ultimately Alexander's conceded this skirmish, and withdrew its proposed development.

In the early 1970s, I was in elementary school and heard many Radio Clinic stories during our family dinners. Eating dinner together as a family was something Mom was committed to, so we rarely started eating without Dad. But Dad was rarely home when he said he would be because of one late breaking minor crisis or another. Mom and I become fierce card competitors in the card game "spit" as she tried to distract me, and stop my complaining, about the late dinner. Dad was definitely not the type of person who left his work at work. The affairs of Radio Clinic—the good, the bad, and the funny—were constantly on his mind, as were employee issues and tension with my uncle. And whatever was on his mind was soon in the ears of his children. I zoned out when he described the many frustrations of the day or an argument with Bill, but my ears perked up for the stories about the customers.

As a merchant on 98th Street he talked to a range of people with a range of issues. At times he was incredulous, at times angry, with some customers, but mostly he seemed charmed by them. He talked with parents about their reluctance to buy a calculator since they worried their kids would never learn to do math. He was particularly proud of the help he provided for Alan Lomax, a renowned oral historian and archivist of folk music. As an engineer by training, Dad enjoyed resolving the disparate technical difficulties customers brought to the store. He rigged up a system to keep the temperature cool enough in Lomax's apartment to protect his folk recordings, but without shorting out the antiquated wiring. Customers that kept kosher homes presented interesting challenges when they purchased stoves. The question of what is and what is not work could be an issue when cooking kosher meals, since people who keep kosher are not allowed to work during the Sabbath. One customer wanted to replace her stove with the same model she had used for years but the clock in the new model was digital and not analog. This was a problem for her since she could see the numbers change as the oven warmed and she considered that work. Dad first suggested putting tape over the digital clock so she wouldn't see the numbers change, but she didn't like that idea. He solved the problem by asking a friend who worked in a service company to put in a switch that bypassed the clock and enabled the temperature to be set by an analog control on Saturdays.

The issues Dad helped customers resolve were not always of a technical nature. An elderly man wanted him to fix his radio since he thought the FBI had bugged it to spy on him. Knowing nothing was wrong with the radio, Dad simply kept the radio for a week and when the customer returned, told him it was fixed. No charge. About a month later the customer returned with the same problem; the FBI was back. Dad knew this guy and knew he would never believe there was no bug and would start coming in regularly for de-bugging help. So he suggested that the customer put aluminum foil on his head whenever he listened to the radio to block out the signals. And the customer was relieved to tell Dad, weeks later, that the aluminum foil worked. This isn't to say my dad was part merchant, part social worker. First and foremost, he was a merchant trying to make a sale. But the people at the margins of the neighborhood and the people at the center of it were all customers at the store, and brought their issues with them when they shopped.

Many of Radio Clinic's famous customers I hadn't heard of as an elementary school kid. But Walter Matthau, Tony Randall, Harry Belafonte, Itzhak Perlman, Jerry Stiller, Anne Meara, and countless others were well known to my dad. He was particularly excited the time he helped Robert White. White was a famous tenor, but what excited Dad more was that decades earlier he was "Little Bobby White" from the Horn and Hardart Hour radio show. This had been one of his favorite radio shows as a kid. White came into the store to buy a turntable for a listening party he was hosting to play the advanced copy of his first record. Realizing White didn't have a record collection or an ongoing need for a turntable, Dad wouldn't let him purchase one. Instead he lent it to him for the night of the party. After that, White told his international musician friends that when they were in New York City and needed electronics, they should shop at Radio Clinic. This added to the growing list of musicians that shopped at the store.

Throughout the 1970s the fight for what type of housing should be built and who should live in the Upper West Side continued. The outcome of this fight was consequential for stores like Radio Clinic. Even though the city said that with the West Side Urban Renewal Area it would turn 20 deteriorated blocks of the West Side into an "urban environment truly integrated (economically, culturally, and ethnically) on a stable basis," it was slow going. This ambitious undertaking between 87th and 97th Streets moved in fits and starts, with community activists pushing for more low-income units. When the WSURA originated in the late 1950s, activists wanted the neighborhood to be a place where rich, poor, and everyone in between could comfortably live together. But by the 1970s the political winds had shifted and there was a competing sensibility. The Committee of Neighbors to Insure a Normal Urban Environment (CONTINUE), comprised of hundreds of brownstone owners, wanted to halt any new housing for low-income people. CONTINUE members were very vocal and didn't share the social integration vision of the WSURA.

These competing visions for the area impacted the fate of 96th Street. City officials, merchants, and residents believed the fate of this block was critical for the health of the neighborhood. In one of the several articles the New York Times wrote about this consequential block, in 1972 the block was described as, "...both clean and dirty, going uphill and downhill at the same time." Developers never gave up on the possibility of building on the block. In 1974, Christopher Boomis, a developer, proposed to build a 34-story apartment building. He went as far as sending a wrecking ball through the wall of the Riverside Theater but ran out of money before he could finish the demolition. Eventually the building collapsed, and in 1976 Chemical Bank foreclosed on the property and passed it to Starrett Housing Corporation. Starrett planned to build a 28-story development, with 20 percent of the apartments set aside for low-income residents. But as with the Alexander's Department store plan, there was community opposition to the project—this time from the opposite direction.

Members of CONTINUE and some block associations felt the neighborhood already had the largest chunk of recovering addicts and people deinstitutionalized from state mental hospitals in the city. They feared it wouldn't be possible to attract the middle-to-upper income families they hoped would move in to these apartments if they shared the building with low-income families. Starrett's project stalled out, and community gardeners took over the vacant block.

As a kid I walked past the 96th Street corner several times a day when I worked at Radio Clinic. One of my main responsibilities as an older elementary school aged kid was to run errands. I didn't have any technical skills, or interest in acquiring any, so the job of walking around the neighborhood was perfect for me. At least once a day Dad would send me down to 83rd Street to either pick something up from the other store or drop something off. It was impossible not to notice that the sidewalks near the store were some of the dirtiest in the city. Although an existing law made it a $100 violation for merchants that allowed litter on their sidewalk, it was only enforced on rare occasions and the penalty was only $1. The pooper scooper law wasn't passed until 1978 and sidestepping dog poop was a key part of the walk. Gutters were filled with garbage, the ground beneath the benches in the islands in the middle of Broadway was covered with cans and empty liquor bottles, and I also had to side-step broken glass.

It might sound unpleasant, but I loved this fifteen-block walk. And I particularly enjoyed walking it alone. I noticed the partially demolished buildings on 96th Street and later the community garden, but didn't think much about it. I just knew, as a young suburban kid, that the Upper West Side was an exciting place to spend time. It could not have looked more different than the homogenous suburbs where I lived. With the sheer numbers of people walking on the street, I never knew who I might see: beautiful people and ugly ones; well-dressed people and disheveled ones; men with bras and women without; young muscled men with oversized Boomboxes hoisted on their shoulders, forcing the rest of us to listen to their personal soundtrack. The mass of humanity came in all sizes and colors. I loved being surrounded by people, yet anonymous.

My love of small businesses took root during the Saturdays and summers I worked at Radio Clinic. I shot the price gun's neon stickers onto film and packs of batteries, dusted televisions while watching Loony Tunes cartoons and picked up food for the salesmen. They worked on commission and preferred to stay in the store and not miss a sale. I was happy to do it since there was so much tasty food on Broadway. Maybe someone would want a morning cruller from the Italian bakery. Or they might want me to run across the street to pick up Chinese dumplings for a late morning snack. My preference was to be sent for deli sandwiches from the Korean delicatessen, since my favorite guy behind the meat counter always gave me a free half-sour pickle. But mostly I was sent over to a coffee shop around 100th Street to pick up fried egg sandwiches and coffee. I usually got something for Raymond to eat, and back in the store I took the steep staircase down to the warehouse where he worked. The warehouse was cavernous, and I liked to push the dollies loaded with merchandise over to the freight elevator and sit on top of the major appliances as Raymond and I rode the elevator up to the sidewalk.

My work at the store could best be categorized as "special projects." On a good day, I played Atari video games in the storefront window. Or I helped my grandmother cook bacon in microwave ovens to draw attention to these appliances that were rapidly becoming a standard fixture in homes. She positioned the bacon operation near the front door so people would smell the irresistible bacon as they passed by. The days leading up to Christmas were a family affair since these were the busiest days of the year. At the time, Radio Clinic sold many small appliances such as hair dryers, Boomboxes, food processors and stereo components. During this busy week I was given my own domain: the complimentary holiday gift-wrapping station. I liked having a job that was my own. My brother made sales and kept track of inventory. Surely I could do something more useful than use the price sticker gun and use paper towels to soak up bacon grease.

My wrapping station was a folding table with large reams of wrapping paper, a pair of scissors, and plenty of tape. The system seemed simple enough.

A customer wanting an appliance gift-wrapped would bring the merchandise and receipt over to the table, where I would wrap it. Give me a regularly sized book with appropriately sized wrapping paper, and I could make quick work of the project. But a hair dryer in an 8-inch box and a paper dispenser 36 inches wide? The proportions were all wrong. Do I wrap the paper around the hair dryer box four times? I couldn't get the paper to lie flat when I did that. Do I instead cut the paper, leaving a jagged edge and an often not quite long enough piece of paper, forcing me to either start over or tape additional scraps of paper to the box? As complicated as I found the small boxes, the large ones were worse. Televisions, humidifiers, and stereo components were often wider than the wrapping paper. I never knew how to approach these boxes and more often than not approached it wrong. One wrapped television could have six different strips of paper cobbled together with more than 50 pieces of tape.

It took just one painstaking wrapping job for the line to build. There could be as many as eight New Yorkers waiting in line for free holiday wrapping, and a ten-year-old girl to butcher the job. With a line of impatient New Yorkers waiting with boxes in hand, I didn't take one minute to measure the box and determine how much paper I needed. No time for that. Instead I just pulled and ripped what looked right and spent the next five minutes taping small amounts of paper to cover the exposed cardboard. Some customers waited patiently. Others shouted out wrapping instructions for me. And then there were the customers who just couldn't take another minute of watching my slow progress and simply made room for themselves at the table, grabbed some paper, and wrapped the boxes themselves. Other customers asked me to rip them a large piece of wrapping paper for them to take home. I really only relaxed when a customer approached the table carrying a Boombox or small fan. Like baby bear's porridge, the sizes of these packages were just right for my style of gift-wrapping.

My mom joined us at the store for Christmas Eve. Last-minute shoppers made this a huge sales day, and she often had the task of watching the store to make sure things weren't stolen. Plus it was my parents' wedding anniversary. It wasn't a romantic evening, but it was the only way for Mom and Dad to spend time together. Mom had been a kindergarten teacher, and it was common for Jewish teachers to marry on Christmas Eve since they had the school break for a honeymoon. They met on a blind date that was put into motion by Dad's mother. She had noticed my mom's sister in a fabric store and liked the look of her. Mom's sister was married to Seymour, who owned the store, and my grandmother asked him, in her signature blunt style, if there was another one like her at home. There was, and thus the blind date set-up. After the store closed on Christmas Eve, my parents, brother, and I would go out to dinner at Marvin Gardens, a restaurant on 83rd Street. While I doubt it was Mom's first choice to spend her anniversary with the kids, in practical work clothes, it was always a fun dinner. Dad was in a good mood after such a great day of sales, my brother and I were in good spirits after being paid well; and being useful all day.

As the years ticked by, they did not soften, but instead exacerbated, the disagreements between Dad and Bill. There was no end to them. Both big picture and small. They had some important decisions to make about the overall health and direction of the business. Radio Clinic's wholesale business was on the decline in the mid 1970s, which was potentially troubling news for the business. Radio Clinic had developed a successful wholesale business with the smaller dealers who could only buy in small quantities. Manufacturers realized they were losing out on significant profits by using other businesses to do the trans-shipping work, so they started phasing out Radio Clinic and other wholesalers. Losing this portion of the business was having an impact on Radio Clinic, and my dad and uncle needed to reevaluate the business. But these were not easy conversations to have since it brought to the surface how little common ground they had for their vision of Radio Clinic. In 1977, a difference of opinion on how much to pay Raymond pushed their business partnership to its breaking point.

In an effort to keep costs down, Dad and Raymond ran the warehouse alone. They still employed delivery crews, but the two of them did the work of getting the merchandise ready for the next day's deliveries. Physically this was not easy work. They had to pull and route the merchandise for the next day's deliveries. They spent their days lifting, carrying, and moving air conditioners and other large appliances. If they couldn't get everything ready for the next day, then they took turns either staying late or coming in early to get it done. What Dad gained in autonomy by owning his own store, he lost in hours of his day spent at the store.

In the early summer of 1977, Raymond told Dad that he felt he deserved more money. He was doing the work of two people, was tired, and wanted a raise. Dad agreed with him but first needed to discuss it with Bill. Bill did not agree. Bill's position was that he was also working hard and he would also like a raise but there wasn't enough money to do that. Radio Clinic wasn't as lucrative a business as it was when the two men became owners a decade earlier and they hadn't taken a raise in a long time. Dad felt that you couldn't compare a worker to an owner. The owner gets innumerable gains to owning a business; a salary isn't the only benefit. Dad's feeling was that along with those benefits, the owner also gets all the headaches and is paid last if money is tight. Maybe at this point the animosity between the two men was such that Bill disagreed with Dad just on principle. Or maybe the two men did have a philosophical disagreement on the difference between employees and owners. I am not sure Dad would have been willing to push this issue to the breaking point for any other employee, but this was Raymond - the man whose time at Radio Clinic predated the two owners by decades, was a good friend of his father and trusted my dad to do right by him. He wasn't willing to back down on giving Raymond a raise.

This argument spilled unpleasantly into other arguments. It was clear to both men that they couldn't continue to run the business together. The next morning Bill offered Dad three options: Each buy the other out of the business or sell the business. Dad decided to buy Bill out of the business. While the paperwork wouldn't make it official for a few months, as of the first week of July, my dad was unofficially the sole owner of Radio Clinic. And for all intents and purposes, on the night of the blackout, the responsibility for the business was his alone.

7

The Looting

We've seen our citizens subjected to violence, vandalism, theft, and discomfort.
The Blackout has threatened our safety and has seriously impacted our economy.
We've been needlessly subjected to a night of terror in many communities that have
been wantonly looted and burned. The costs when finally tallied will be enormous.

—Mayor Beame, the night of the Blackout, 1977

...before the blackout, you had about maybe five legitimate crews
of DJs. After the blackout, you had a DJ on every block...that blackout
made a big spark in the Hip-Hop revolution.

—DJ Disco Wiz

THE BLACKOUT OF 1977 was not New York City's first blackout. New York City suffered many electric power blackouts since it started to depend on utility-supplied electricity. The Brush arc lighting system failed as early as 1881, burned cables caused a two-hour blackout contained on the east side of Manhattan in 1948 and a more significant blackout lasting over eight hours in upper Manhattan in 1959. It wasn't even its first widespread extended blackout. That was in 1965, when New York experienced a utility system failure so massive that over 30 million people in seven states and Ontario were left without electricity for up to 12 hours. This night became legendary in New York for recording less crime than on any other night since New York started keeping track of crime records. Providing the yin to 1965's yang, the 1977 blackout also became a legendary blackout, but this time for its unprecedented civil disorder.

How electricity traveled from hydroelectric plants to my light switch had never been something I gave much thought to. Utility system functioning is one of the many things in modern life whose mechanics I don't fully understand but expect and rely on to keep happening. My dad blamed Con Ed more than any other entity for his damaged business, so I was curious what Con Ed could have done to avoid such an epic failure in 1977. Providing electric power for all of New York City was not a small task. The Edison Electric Illuminating Company, the original name for Consolidated Edison (Con Ed), had been a dominant player in 1880, supplying power to just 59 customers. But by 1977 it served 2.7 million customers in all five boroughs of Manhattan and parts of Westchester County. Given its population density and location, New York City had outsized demand for electrical power and unique constraints. Con Ed didn't pull its power from within the city but instead relied on plants in upstate New York and a variety of neighboring states. To harness this power from outside the city and deliver it to the city, Con Ed used 77,000 miles of underground cables. I found it remarkable to imagine all those miles of cables underneath such a relatively small amount of land in the Tri State Area. 77,000 miles is a lot of miles; you could drive back and forth from the Atlantic Ocean to the Pacific Ocean 25 times and still have miles of cables to spare.

Digging through newspaper archives, I came across, "Nobody Loves Consolidated Edison," the title of a 1966 Fortune magazine issue in response to public anger over the 1965 blackout and frustration with its policies. The cover showed a manhole cover and a caption that read, "Con Edison: The Company You Love to Hate." To me, these newspaper and magazine articles read like a case study of why industries need to be regulated; and why they can't be trusted to regulate themselves. Con Ed resisted efforts to improve utility reliability after the 1965 blackout. When Congress explored interchange "reliability" legislation in the mid 1960s, Con Ed opposed it, arguing that federal intervention would hinder the company. Government oversight bodies tend to take a laissez faire approach when a corporation prioritizes maximum profits over the provision of reliable basic services. It would have been in the public interest for the Federal and State Power Commissions to require Con Ed to prove that their utility interchange system was improved and adequate after the 1965 blackout. But they didn't.

I could see why Dad was angry with Con Ed. And why he was not impressed with the Con Ed official who declared the blackout "...an act of God" to distance the company from any culpability. While a small appliance store has little in common with a utility company earning billions of dollars, on some level every business decides what its operating philosophy is and runs the business accord-

Radio Clinic in the early moments of the 1977 Blackout

ingly. As a small businessman, Dad understood the challenges and stresses involved in running a company. He knew that not a day goes by when a business has the opportunity to maximize profit by cheating a supplier, misleading a customer, or providing shoddy service. Small business owners do a daily cost-benefit analysis—their very survival relies on it - on how much they should invest in infrastructure, merchandise, salaries, staff training, and innovations. He knew that the people he employed were human, and therefore costly errors were always a possibility. Dad understood very well about cutting corners to keep a business viable, but he expected total preparation for a power failure to be part of Con Ed's business calculation. Con Ed's negligence, enabled by government regulatory agencies, meant that in the wake of the blackout, small businesses like Radio Clinic were now in danger of going out of business.

A direct line could be drawn from the lesson not learned and the steps not taken from 1965 to 1977. So, on July 13th, an improbable sequence of events began with the first of several lightning bolts hitting power lines at 8:37 pm and ended with a massive power failure at 9:36. For the 59 minutes in between, an enormous demand for electricity coupled with lapses in preventable maintenance, improperly operating protective devices, inadequate communication and training and human error led to the total collapse of Con Ed's power grid.

Sitting in a meeting on the east side of Manhattan at 9:36, Dad was immediately pragmatic. After waiting five minutes to see if the lights would kick back on, he hustled to his car and drove to Radio Clinic to check on the warehouse elevator. He believed the blackout would be temporary and wanted to be at the store when the power returned to fix whatever damage was done to the two marine pumps that ran 24 hours a day to protect Radio Clinic's elevator warehouse motor. He wanted to be on top of the situation.

But the only people that were on top of the situation that night were the people doing the looting. Stores on Broadway had iron gates ripped off by hand, with clubs, or by chains attached to cars. Twisted iron gates now pierced empty window displays. Fuller Drug Store on 103rd street had empty racks where appliances and perfume had been the night before. Lorette Sportswear, a business on 105th street since 1944, was left with just dismembered store mannequins. At Irene's Jewelry on 104th street all that remained was her sign, "On Vacation, Back September 1st." Watching families carry furniture into the housing projects near his 92nd street store, the owner of Capri Furniture was amazed at how quickly his store was emptied. What would have taken him several trucks and a week of delivery runs was gone within 3 hours.

I read anecdote after anecdote of that night, and most people were slow to figure out what happened when the power first went out. Some thought they personally caused the blackout by plugging in a fan, tripping over a power cord or turning an air conditioner on high. DJ Disco Wiz and Grandmaster Caz, early innovators of Hip-Hop, were in the middle of a DJ battle at a park on 183rd Street in the Bronx and thought they caused the blackout by draining power from the street lamppost they tapped to power their equipment. Mayor Beame was talking to a room of elderly residents at Co-Op City in the Bronx and initially thought the lights going out was a temporary situation. But other people only needed a few minutes to consider the possibilities and get to work. Neighborhood residents were more aggressive than the police in protecting their neighborhood stores. Some banded together with a very hands-on approach. The owner of Marsh Liquors, seven blocks north of Radio Clinic, reported that tenants from 924 West End patrolled the block with baseball bats to make people think twice before ransacking neighborhood stores. On other blocks, tenants deterred would-be looters by dumping water on their heads. Others drove their cars to Broadway and shined car headlights on the storefronts to scare away potential looters. Some stores were protected and some were not.

A few years ago, the West Side Rag published an excerpt from an essay I wrote about Radio Clinic and the blackout. After reading this excerpt a documentary producer, making a film about the blackout for PBS's American Experience, contacted me. He wanted to interview Dad for the documentary. Turns out he knew my dad and the store. Over the course of writing this book, a surprising number of people I contacted had at some point in their younger lives, delivered and installed air conditioners for Radio Clinic. Along with Elzora Williamson, former owner of the store, Trophies by Syl, he was featured in the small business owners portion of the film. Elzora described seeing her merchandise in the street, driving her car up on the sidewalk and parking near the doorway to try to keep more people from entering the store. While she had a car at her disposal, her night didn't sound much different than Dad's standing on the grassy median, watching the destruction of his store. Elzora perfectly described the experience of local shopkeepers that night. "There was no police to stop them...who would stop them from taking whatever else was there."

As soon as the lights went out, the officers at the 24th Precinct got in their patrol cars to see what was happening in the neighborhood. Sargent Freud, the patrol supervisor, drove south down Broadway and Radio Clinic was the first store he saw being looted. It only took 9 minutes from when the power went out until he came across dozens of men working together to pry off Radio Clinic's gate. After reading through an extensive 240-page Ford Foundation report about the blackout, it didn't surprise me that the first looting the patrol officer encountered was Radio Clinic. The report authors culled through municipal and arrest records, interviewed merchants, police officers, people who looted, and neighborhood leaders to provide an analysis of what exactly happened. What happened in the first stage of the looting was that young men, between the ages of 20 to 30, many of whom lived in SROs near Broadway, were the first to hit the stores.

Radio Clinic was in the sweet spot for this first stage. It resided in the part of the Upper West Side where a high concentration of men experienced with breaking into locked and gated stores lived. They broke into the store, quickly took what they knew they could easily fence and left. And what could be easier to fence than electronic equipment and other appliances. Once this first group of looters opened the stores and took what they were going to take, open season began. Next, taking advantage of the chaos, came the teenagers. They cleaned out the remaining Boomboxes, stereos, and electronic components. By midnight, when it was clear that the brakes of civilization were off and the police were barely making arrests, some people who had jobs but low incomes, could see no reason not to take advantage of the opportunity the darkness created and took whatever was left.

The blackout occurred in the aftermath of New York City's narrowly averted bankruptcy. Because of a newly imposed austerity budget, the police department, like their city, was stretched pretty thin in 1977. Austerity budgets might sound like a good remedy on paper but it doesn't feel so good when the austerity is targeted at you. At the time of the blackout the police weren't feeling too charitable toward the city since 5,000 officers were laid off in 1975 and Mayor Beame had recently threatened to have only one officer in each patrol car, expecting the police to absorb even more budget cuts. When the lights first went out there were 2,500 police on the beat, which was nowhere near enough manpower to deal with the thousands of people that started looting. In response, Police Commissioner Codd invoked the civil emergency plan, requiring every able-bodied officer to report for duty but somehow only 8,000 of a possible 25,000 managed to report for duty. To make matters worse, in one of the biggest miscalculations of the night, Codd ordered all officers to report for immediate duty at their closest precinct. Once upon a time, the Lyons Law required New York cops to live in the city they served, but that law had been repealed in 1962. Nearly half of the off-duty police had to come in from the suburbs or the far reaches of Queens or Staten Island. The looting could gain momentum in the hardest hit neighborhoods in part because there was a very minimal police presence in the early part of the night. One officer said, "by the time we got enough men to do anything that night, it was already too late."

Between the pitch-black night, limited police presence, and free for all energy of the night, the blackout was a golden opportunity. People in every corner of the city saw what was happening on the commercial blocks in their neighborhoods and considered what they would do. Not a single neighborhood that had a concentration of low-income people escaped damage. This was true in the Bronx, Manhattan, Brooklyn, Queens and Long Island. Whether looting occurred in a neighborhood or not was a good indicator about how deep the pockets of poverty were in a given neighborhood. For many people struggling to pay their bills, the pull of stealing coveted merchandise with no consequence was irresistible.

Decades later, during our interviews, Dad was still angry with the city and his belief that neighborhood police were deployed to protect midtown department stores and left businesses like Radio Clinic on their own. He told me that, "if just one policeman had stayed none of this damage would have happened." When Dad walked me up and down Broadway to talk to other neighborhood merchants, I asked them what they remembered about the 1977 Blackout and several also thought the police were absent because they were protecting department stores. I can see why long standing small business owners thought this, prioritizing very large businesses at the expense of small businesses was typical operating procedure for New York City. But the fact was that when the lights went out people looted where they lived and took advantage of whatever opportunity they could make. No one took the time to run 50 to 100 blocks south to midtown. It wasn't practical to run miles, and possibly even across a bridge, in the dark, to rob a midtown department store with its more expensive merchandise. People looted where they lived and they lived on the Upper West Side.

The question on everyone's mind in the days after the blackout was who to blame for the extensive damage. Like my dad, many people pointed their finger at Con Ed. But they pointed their fingers in other directions too. There was plenty of blame to go around. Con Ed was guilty of negligence. The state power commission was guilty of not enforcing regulations. The city was guilty of significantly cutting the number of officers in its police force two years earlier. The police themselves were guilty because when the police commissioner invoked the civil emergency plan calling on every able-bodied officer to report for duty, not enough showed up. The looters were responsible since they took advantage of the power outage. The depression-level unemployment in the ghettos was responsible for the disenfranchisement people felt. A credible case could be made to point blame in each direction.

The looting provided a Rorschach test on how New Yorkers viewed the health of their city. For the neighborhoods that were affected, thousands of people erupted in violence. Maybe you were one of the people doing the looting or maybe you were scared of the people doing the looting. Regardless, it was clear to everyone that the police officers were almost comically ineffective in trying to quell the eruption of violence on the city streets. One merchant reported, "seeing a policeman try to corral a looter while brandishing a toilet bowl brush." Thousands of people were arrested, beaten, and kept in substandard and dangerously hot makeshift prison cells. The looting was personal. And whichever your vantage point, the looting probably confirmed whatever truth you already knew about the city. But the truth can be a slippery thing, since we all tend to pick and choose the facts that align with what we already feel.

The looting was also a Rorschach test on how New Yorkers thought about race. There was no ignoring the fact that the people who did the looting were overwhelmingly African American and Latino. Many middle class New Yorkers, most of them white, were scared and angry about what just happened and the city's ineffectual response. Many poor New Yorkers, many of them African American and Latino, had been scared and angry for a long time about their displacement, lack of economic opportunity and the city's overall neglect of their communities. Like those Rorschach inkblots, the various New York City newspapers were exhibit A for what New Yorkers were thinking. A firestorm of debate about who was to blame played out in newspaper articles, editorials, and letters to the editor in the weeks after the blackout.

Each newspaper had a different story it wanted to tell and a different agenda to pursue. I grew up reading the *New York Times* and as a teenager added the then-very-lefty *Village Voice* to my repertoire. *The New York Times* led with the factual, its banner headline reading: "Power failure blacks out New York; thousands trapped in the subways; looters and vandals hit some areas." Anyone who walked past the newspaper stands that populated the city was already familiar with the screaming headlines of the *New York Post*, and the paper certainly didn't disappoint. Newly owned by Rupert Murdoch, doing its part to scare readers into thinking a race war was imminent, the *Post* headline screamed: "24 Hours of Terror." *The Village Voice* did extensive investigation into the culpability of Con Ed and the treatment of the arrested looters. *El Diario*, the largest and oldest Spanish-language daily newspaper, was succinct and perhaps said it best with the headline, "¿Porque?" *Amsterdam News*, the oldest black owned newspaper located in Harlem, had the most thorough analysis of the looting. The front page led with the results of extensive interviews and let its readers know that "widespread, violent looting that ravaged more than 2,000 businesses in the black communities in Brooklyn, Harlem, Queens and the Bronx during last week's blackout has bitterly divided black leaders and ordinary black citizens throughout the city."

New Yorkers weighed in with opinions about the looting and what it said about the people who did it. "Animals," said one store owner. An angry neighborhood resident said, "I thought we were through with this...but we got mothers and fathers looting out here. Now what do they expect for their kids, for their future?" A person who looted commented that people looted, "not because they're thieves, not because they mind working ... but because self-preservation is the law of nature. Opportunity arrived." A police sergeant said, "The lights went out. A bunch of greedy people took advantage. Plain and simple. Don't go with all that sociological bullshit." Another person said, "Man, times are hard and it was the chance of a lifetime to get over. There is no work for anyone. Black folks don't have much and we are kicked and stepped on every time we turn around. I feel sorry for those who got caught." A resident of Harlem said, "Looting is never justified. I've been poor and raised two children and never stole anything from anyone. I worked hard and long. Too many people feel that the world owes them a living. No one owes anyone anything." My dad added his two cents about the looting. "...But most people in this neighborhood are nice. It's these SROs. (The people who live here) have nothing to do. Soon they'll be in the store buying batteries for their new appliances."

Reading this newspaper quote from my dad, amidst all the other quotes, it occurred to me that growing up, I never heard Dad talk about the people who did the looting of Radio Clinic. I heard him talk plenty about Con Ed and the city's indifference toward small business owners during and immediately after the blackout. But I had no memory of Dad talking about the people that did the actual destroying of his business. I grew up in what I consider a fairly typical white Jewish liberal New York household. As such, we didn't consciously think one racial group was better or worse than others, but we had the same inability to grapple with the structural and systemic realities of racism as the next white person. I was curious and asked Dad how the looting impacted his feelings about race. He said, "My attitudes did not change as I did not consider the looting of Radio Clinic to be racial. It was more about opportunity as many of the looters lived in a SRO down the street." I get what he was saying, that people looted because of their economic circumstance, not their race. But after decades of racist housing policies and limited employment opportunities, the circumstances and race of New Yorkers were entwined.

While a great deal of ink was used to comment on whether people stole because of need or greed, this debate didn't interest Dad. Each of the impacted neighborhood merchants spent the days after the blackout assessing the damage to their stores, drawing their own conclusions about what just happened, and making plans for what to do next. Dad was already consumed with the work of saving his business and wasn't following the arguments in the news. But even a quick look at what types of stores were looted shows that people stole for both need and greed. More than a third of the stores that were looted sold the basic necessities of clothing and food. If a store had sneakers in their inventory they were completely stripped of their stock. All over the city blackout black-markets sprung up where you could buy needed day-to-day items such as pampers and toilet paper for a steep discount. After food and clothing, stores that sold household appliances and home furnishings were the third major category of looted stores.

I imagine that not a single electronic component was left in any appliance store in the areas of the city where looting occurred. While I was trying to satisfy my curiosity about the general fate of stereo components on the night of the blackout I came across a very fun book to read, Yes Yes Y'all: The Experience Music Project Oral History of Hip-Hop's First Decade. It turns out that stores like Radio Clinic had an impact on the early growth of Hip-Hop. Granmaster Caz and DJ Disco Wiz, early innovators of the Hip-Hop movement who were part of the multitudes that stole electronic equipment, talk about the impact the looting had on the proliferation of Hip-Hop. Caz says that after that night "… everybody was a DJ. Everybody stole turntables and stuff. Every electronic store imaginable got hit for stuff. Every record store. Everything. That sprung a whole new set of DJs." Radio Clinic's merchandise wasn't critical to anyone's survival, but to an ambitious teenager with no money, electronic components can factor high in their personal hierarchy of needs. There was no getting this equipment back. The damage had been done almost forty years ago. I liked thinking about it all these years later, that the stolen electronic equipment was put to good use and found its way into the hands of one of these new crews of DJs.

Mayor Beame shared my dad's view about Con Ed. Outraged, the mayor demanded explanations from the utility and appointed a special board to investigate. "We cannot tolerate, in this age of modern technology, a power system that can shut down the nation's largest city. I believe the people of this city must be assured that this will never happen again. Con Edison at best has shown gross negligence, and at worst something far more serious." But even with all his tough talk, the blackout ultimately doomed Beame's political career. The blackout occurred during a mayoral campaign, and Ed Koch, also campaigning, capitalized on this fear by positioning himself as the law in order candidate. Ed Koch challenged Mayor Beame's decision to not call in the National Guard during the blackout. Beame felt similarly to how my dad felt when offered a gun by the owner of Riverside Pizza, that the National Guard might cause more violence than it stopped. Dad saw Koch for the first time when he walked the streets with a bullhorn asking the people on the sidewalks, "All those who thought we should have called in the National Guard during the blackout, raise your hand."

However you parcel out the blame or consider the solutions, the thousands of storeowners that saw their businesses severely damaged or completely ruined by the looting hoped the city wouldn't forget them. From the list of stores that were looted, it's clear that the people doing the looting didn't discriminate: those owned by children of immigrants whose stores had anchored the neighborhood for decades, first-generation black-owned businesses, and unpopular merchants all suffered. Feeling a sense of urgency and ever pragmatic, Dad wasn't too concerned about the motivation of the people who looted. Whether a television was stolen because someone wanted a bigger one, or a stolen air conditioner helped make life more bearable for a family living in a sweltering tenement, or some teenagers now had the equipment for a legitimate Hip-Hop crew, or some toasters were sold for cash to help someone ward off eviction, was really beside the point for him. For my dad, there was only one issue that consumed his thinking. He was staring at the wreckage of Radio Clinic and knew he had a steep uphill battle.

Worried that the city might not prioritize the damaged small businesses, he talked to any reporter that came knocking to push the city in his preferred direction. He knew that politicians and city officials often lose interest in a problem once the television cameras go away. For all of Mayor Beame's tough talk about how things would be different with Con Ed going forward, he didn't talk about how the city would help the looted businesses. For all his yelling into the megaphone about the National Guard, Koch didn't mention what he would do as mayor to help the merchants whose businesses were destroyed and the people employed by these stores. The writing on the wall wasn't looking good for the small businesses and Dad hoped to shift some thinking by talking to reporters. A very quotable man, he gave a comment to the press that perfectly encapsulated the situation as seen through a small business owner's eye. The quote was picked up by local and national papers and even *Time* magazine. This was the moment when Dad went from being one of many neighborhood merchants to taking a leadership role in fighting for New York City small businesses. "I'm responsible for twenty-five families—the families of people that work for me," he said. "What's going to happen to them if I pull out? As bad as I got hit, there are other guys that got wiped out. What's going to happen if they can't reopen? What can the city and government do to keep people like us from leaving these neighborhoods?" It was a reasonable question with an unsatisfying answer.

8

Better Than
A Kick in The Head

It's not the size of the dog in the fight, it's the size of the fight in the dog.
—Mark Twain

At the end of every hard earned day people find some reason to believe.
—Bruce Springsteen

'**F**OR THE PAST SEMESTER I have taught you how to start and operate a small business. Today we are going to do something a little different. I want you to listen to this man. He will tell you what to do when everything goes wrong." This was a Columbia Business School professor, introducing my Dad as a guest lecturer in his class four months after the looting. One of Radio Clinic's customers was a professor there and he asked my dad to come and talk with his class. The night before his presentation, Dad wrote down *Rubin's Rules for Survival* on seven index cards. His survival rules are as follows: I. Attitude, II. Ego, III. Common Sense, IV. Instinct, V. Patience and Planning, VI. Negatives lead to Positives, VII. Flexibility, VIII. Understand the others' problem and, IX. Relax. Not all of these rules proved easy for him to follow.

In the initial days after the blackout, residents of the Upper West Side were trying to make sense of what had just happened in their neighborhood. Murray Kempton, a well-known West-Sider and a Pulitzer-Prize winning journalist, captured what many people were feeling in his *New York Post* column,

"The Pride of the 44th." He wrote about a police precinct in the Bronx and how it responded to the blackout and 25 hours of looting. And in the column, Kempton mentioned Radio Clinic, writing: "Radio Clinic is run by pleasant men whom I think incapable of cheating anyone on Earth." Kempton quoted Police Captain John P. Henry saying, "All we were doing all night was trying to hold civilization together. Where are we if we can't protect the dignity of an enclosed store?" Kempton initially questioned whether a store could have dignity, but after walking in his Upper West Side neighborhood and seeing Radio Clinic, he changed his mind. He wrote, "We are used to holding the dignity of the person higher than the dignity of a store. And yet yesterday morning I looked at the shell of the Radio Clinic round the corner from where I live, and all of a sudden it became horridly clear that a store does have its dignity and that it can be violated."

The day after the looting, the fact that Radio Clinic was violated was already old news for Dad. He saw it happen. In the bright sunlight of the next day, he stood on the sidewalk contemplating the ruins of what, just hours earlier, had been Radio Clinic. It was 7:00 in the morning and his attitude was clear. The store was a disaster; his employees who made it through the city were dazed by all the damage, but Dad was not. Sweeping up the ruins of his store, he felt the same way that he did when he first heard the glass vestibule shatter. He would reopen Radio Clinic as soon as was humanly possible, which he decided would be in two days' time. The light and electricity were still out, and there was no way to know whether it would be hours or days until the power outage was resolved, but he was sure the worst was over. So, he got to work.

With the brutally high temperatures, people were going to want to buy air conditioners at the 83rd Street store, which was not damaged and opened for business. Luck can be a fickle thing. The heatwave almost destroyed Radio Clinic, but then ironically, the heatwave helped save it. Every summer day, when Dad drove across the George Washington Bridge into the city, he would look toward midtown. If there was enough haze that he couldn't see the Empire State Building, he knew it would be a good day at work. In the days after the blackout, it was all hazy views.

But the air conditioners were trapped in the 98th Street basement with no functioning elevator to get them out. A work around would need to be figured out since people were desperate for air conditioners. Temperatures hovered at around 100 degrees before topping off at 104 degrees on July 21st. Intense heat in a dense urban area burns more than in the suburbs or countryside. The combination of exhaust fumes, asphalt, concrete, and massive buildings ratchets up the heat. With fewer trees and grassy areas to absorb the sun, Manhattan became an oven. Dad's work-around plan was to spend the next two days filling the store with only air conditioners and fans and on Saturday re-open the store with an incredible day of sales. He figured he had nothing to lose. If he was immobilized by the damage or took a day or two to plan, then Radio Clinic would lose hundreds of air conditioner sales and most likely go under. But if he worked around the clock for the next 48 hours, the business might have a fighting chance.

Keeping the store open wasn't the only option available to him. He could have liquidated the merchandise, closed the store, and collected the insurance money. But he never seriously considered that option. On his index cards he wrote, "Follow your gut feeling. Long deliberation leads to rationalization and vacillation." Looking back at this moment, even from the distance of forty years, it still seems to me like this was exactly the kind of situation that required deliberation. My mom, by far the more pragmatic one of the duo, certainly would have liked him to do a cost/benefit analysis to consider the potential financial implications for the family in keeping the business open or closing it, then deciding on the better option. But Dad was sure this was the right thing to do, and just started doing it. Believing his chances are good of overcoming any number of obstacles had always been an elemental part of Dad's personality. When in doubt, he went with his overarching life philosophy: follow your instinct.

Follow your instinct. This was Roman numeral four for *Rubin's Rules of Survival*. I heard variations of this story many times growing up. My dad is a guy who likes to share a story, and his favorite stories operate on an endless loop to circle back around when he feels they are needed. I was a kid who didn't have a natural affinity for school or standardized tests and lived with a sibling who never met a test he couldn't ace. Dad often sat me down to talk about the value of common sense versus school intelligence, and he thought I would do well in life because, like him, I would be able to trust my instincts. I was never sure if I was being complimented or insulted during these talks, but his lessons stuck with me. Every time he went against his gut in business, he had been wrong.

Dad was right to think there would be a rush on air conditioners the Saturday after the blackout. Radio Clinic only had air conditioners in the store and Dad hired an extra delivery crew to get them delivered that day. Customers came in ready to buy, from the moment the store opened on Saturday morning until it closed later that evening. This cash infusion resolved the immediate question of whether Radio Clinic could make payroll and afford to stay open. Yes it could. But it didn't resolve the looming problems: paying back his creditors, paying his employees in the months going forward, paying for critical infrastructure repairs, and purchasing new merchandise. Radio Clinic bought itself some time, but whether it could remain open in-the-not too distant future remained to be seen.

For Radio Clinic, everything on the selling floor was gone. Televisions, hi-fis, speakers, calculators, Sony Walkmans—basically any minor appliance you can think of from the 1970s was gone. The store suffered a loss of more than $200,000 (which in today's dollars would be close to $800,000), and a significant chunk of its merchandise was stolen. Most small businesses use retail floor planning to purchase high-cost inventory like air conditioners. With floor planning merchants do not pay up front for merchandise and instead are invoiced later. This arrangement only works when the supplier trusts the merchants; if payments are not made on time, very steep fees are added. Radio Clinic had not yet paid for the merchandise that was stolen. Simply put, my dad had to pay back suppliers with money he didn't have for merchandise that no longer existed. It was an ugly circle.

On Friday, Dad and his employees moved every air conditioner and fan out of the basement and onto the selling floor. As they slowly but surely moved these large appliances, neighbors kept coming into the store both to offer their condolences and to find out if Radio Clinic would remain in the neighborhood. While he appreciated their concern and well wishes Dad didn't have the time to talk to everyone; he had way too much work to do. So, he rummaged through the back office until he found a large piece of paper and a thick marker and wrote the answer to the question people were asking. With some duct tape, he put the sign, 'We Are Staying' on the unbroken window facing 98th street and then got back to work.

After he hung the "We Are Staying" sign in the window, reporters sought my dad out. They wanted to know why, the day after the looting when there was still smoke in the air, he was so definitive about staying. Close to 1,600 New York City merchants had a damaged business to contend with and more than 1,000 stores were set on fire. In the days after the looting, only 68 percent of the looted Manhattan stores reopened, 47 percent in the Bronx, and 36 percent in Brooklyn. New Yorkers were still trying to understand what had just happened in their city. Why did Dad have no hesitation? Outside the store, the street was garbage-strewn and littered with broken glass from storefront windows. Inside the store, the flooring was ripped and instead of being surrounded by merchandise, he was surrounded by empty shelves. Standing on 98th Street, reporters looked at the damaged storefront and asked my dad what he planned to do. But Dad was ready for them. Already on a mission to rally the city to the small business owner's side, he said: "We are not going to move out. We've got to get some aid from the city, state, or federal government, or a lot of people are just going to move out. And New York can't afford that."

At some point during that Saturday, an entourage of local politicians came into the store. Assembly member Jerry Nadler, Ruth Messinger, who was running for city council, and Gail Brewer, her chief of staff, were among the group.

It was hectic in the store, and Dad wasn't happy to take the time to talk to them, but he knew they were in a position to help. The politicians told him that they were going to assist the looted businesses get loans. Dad told them that he needed support, but he didn't want a loan since he would not be able to pay it back. He believed he was in this mess because the city couldn't protect his business, and what he really needed was grant money, or a moratorium of July's taxes; or some other creative solution. Nadler and Messinger said that he wasn't the first merchant to tell them this and made plans to come back and talk more with Dad when he wasn't so busy.

My dad knew he needed city support to rebuild the business. The small business owners couldn't do it alone. He believed the city would help its small businesses keep their doors open. This wasn't excessive optimism on his part. Just two years earlier, the city was on the verge of bankruptcy, and it wasn't too big a leap to think the city would put some muscle into keeping the looted businesses from boarding up their windows or moving out of the city and taking their taxes with them.

Nothing about Radio Clinic's recovery from the looting was straightforward or went the way my dad thought it would. Right from the start, President Carter set the tone for a disappointing governmental response. He quickly refused to declare New York City a disaster zone, which meant small businesses would not get badly needed federal funds. Dad had hoped Carter would come through with tangible support since just one year earlier, when campaigning in the city for much needed New York votes, he declared his support for the city and juxtaposed himself against then-President Ford who refused to aid New York City as it headed toward bankruptcy. But the 1976 Presidential election was long over, and President Carter didn't need New York anymore.

The City's Office of Economic Development set up an emergency phone number and received reports from businesses about their losses. From the Friday after the blackout until the next Wednesday calls came in from storeowners, wholesalers and manufactures. Collectively they reported about $35 million in losses from theft and close to $3 million in non-theft costs. The office planned to set up 14 neighborhood business assistance teams with volunteer lawyers, accountants, bank representatives, and specialists in filing insurance claims to help the merchants of looted stores seek moratoriums on existing loans.

An emergency relief fund was established for the looted businesses. The mayor worked with business leaders, labor leaders, and philanthropists to make small grants available to the businesses. Radio Clinic was one of the 373 Manhattan small business owners that applied for and received a $1,800 grant. Dad quickly spent the $1,800 repairing the storefront. A *New York Times* article published a couple of weeks after the looting reported that most of the looted businesses got a small grant from this fund. Radio Clinic was featured as a typical recipient, and the author said that the "workmen all but fell over one another in a rush to install another storefront at Radio Clinic."

Dad doesn't remember who he hired to fix the storefront but he does remember that he didn't have enough money to pay him in full. He gave the carpenter the entire $1,800 and as much of his working capital as he could spare. The man was generous to do the work and wait until later for the remainder of the payment, when Dad had more money. He couldn't believe that this grant money, which he characterized as "better than a kick in the head," was all the city had to offer. Since these grants were such a small fraction of what stores needed to survive, they wouldn't impact whether a store remained open or closed. As far as Dad was concerned, the city abandoned its small businesses during the blackout. Now it was doing the same thing in its aftermath.

It wasn't until writing this book that I fully understood how my dad's approach to owning Radio Clinic affected the work my brother and I have chosen to do. Neither of us took a significant leadership role in the store or had interest in owning it. But both of us have spent work and volunteer time engaged in progressive policy change on the local and state level. Diving into the details of Dad's work life after the blackout, the direct line between what I absorbed watching him continually try to wrangle a response from bureaucracies and powerful institutions, and the work I have done for much of my career is clear. Over and over I absorbed his lesson that government as an institution will not care about what you need, but there are good people working within the government who will. You just need to find them. And to find them you need to be tenacious. Maybe you need to make dozens of phone calls. Or write dozens of letters. Or talk to someone who knows someone who can get the ear of the right person. If the right person wants to help you but isn't sure how, then figure it out yourself and then tell them exactly what they need to do to help you.

While he was scrambling to figure out how to bring more cash into the business, Dad called Radio Clinic's suppliers to let them know what happened. Mainly he wanted them to give him extra time before paying for the stolen merchandise. Also, he needed the suppliers to ship new merchandise so Radio Clinic would have something to sell. He was surprised to learn that not only would most of the suppliers not grant Radio Clinic additional time, they refused to ship new merchandise. This was not the best time—or the best way—for Dad to learn that Radio Clinic had an ongoing payment problem with some of its suppliers. It had never been a healthy thing for the business that my dad and uncle kept to their separate spheres and didn't really communicate with each other. And now the fallout from this problem came home to roost.

At the time of the blackout, Dad was in the process of taking sole ownership of Radio Clinic. But he hadn't yet started ordering the merchandise and

handling the billing. With each phone call Dad made to a credit manager; he
learned something he hadn't known. Radio Clinic was months behind with payments to multiple suppliers. The upshot for Dad was that Radio Clinic newly
had a credibility problem with its suppliers at the exact time when the only
thing the store had going for it was its integrity. Radio Clinic couldn't be without merchandise, money, and credibility, and still survive.

Dad spent hours on the phone calling every credit manager for every supplier that Radio Clinic used for merchandise. He was amazed to learn that several of the suppliers, and even more credit managers, didn't know that he was
a partner in the business. One by one he told each credit manager that he now
solely owned the business and the business had been looted. He did not hide
from Radio Clinic's payment problem and told them that from this day forward
he would be the only person authorized to make financial commitments for
Radio Clinic. Things would be different. 'Ego' is listed under Roman numeral
two in Rubin's rules. "Admit mistakes and failures...look for help wherever
you can find it and don't care what others think." Temperamentally Dad was
well suited for rallying suppliers behind the Radio Clinic cause. He can be very
dogged in his determination.

There are not many things my dad likes to do more than tell a story. His
stories can be pitch- perfect, non sequiturs, boring or repetitive; but regardless
he cannot be deterred in the telling. I imagine that the credit managers heard
a story about where Radio Clinic had been and where it was going, tipping the
scale in favor of them giving Dad extra time. Dad explained that he would be
getting money from the insurance company in a few months and asked if they
could figure out a way to work together on new merchandise and pay the old
debt later. Every single credit manager said yes to extending credit. It didn't
hurt that, recent credit problems notwithstanding, no one wanted to see the
business go under and lose what had once been a great customer. Being Leon
Rubin's son didn't hurt, either. Grandpa had enjoyed a great reputation within
the industry, and people still respected him.

Without any significant government support, Dad turned his attention to
insurance. He knew two things about his insurance company; they would give
him some money and it wouldn't be anywhere near enough to cover the damages. He started contacting everyone he knew, looking for any angle or any idea
he could hook onto to save the business. In yet another newspaper article he
was quoted saying, "I began making the wearying rounds of city and state agencies, such as the Office of Economic Development of the City of New York. At
each, I was listened to courteously and was given expressions of sympathy and
apology. But I received no financial aid." He estimated that he made more than
100 phone calls to officials to arrange an interest-free loan, a grant, anything
that would help him get on his feet again. He was full of ideas on how the city

could best be of help, such as putting a moratorium on July taxes for looted businesses. In Radio Clinic's case, the $30,000 saved from skipping July taxes would have made an enormous difference at the exact moment he needed it most. If the store closed, the city would receive no future taxes from Radio Clinic, so getting a pass for one month seemed like a reasonable request to my dad. But reason didn't win the day.

In the wake of a surprisingly limited governmental response to the looted small businesses, Dad felt cornered. Without assistance, he knew he couldn't get Radio Clinic in the black. So he came out fighting. He pushed and pulled at every seam to try to unravel the indifference he encountered. On a fundamental level, Dad believed in our political and economic systems and that there are good people within its institutions. And that good people can make a difference. His approach was that he just needed to find these good people and talk to them. When confronted with a bureaucratic system that was getting in the way of Radio Clinic's survival, he called his Senator to help sort it out. When a loan officer wouldn't seriously consider Dad's request, he contacted the bank president. He had faith that calling his legislator, or a credit manager, or the public advocate, or writing a bank president would be effective. That each would take his call, read his letter, see the clarity of his position, and consider his request. In some instances he was right and in others he wasn't.

Radio Clinic's insurance claim was fairly straightforward. This was a good thing since Dad was relying on this money to pay off his waiting creditors. Dad, my brother, and Raymond went carefully through the store to do an inventory of what was destroyed and what was stolen. The insurance adjusters came the week after the looting and determined that because of the magnitude of the damage more than one insurance company would pay the claim. Two insurance companies would each write Radio Clinic a check for $31,500, which Dad would receive in February. Sixty-three thousand dollars would certainly help in the store's recovery, but most of it was already promised to his creditors. He called his four major suppliers and told them a check was on the way but not to cash the checks until February. The checks were made out for the amount owed but dated for Feb. 28, 1978. Each supplier agreed and started shipping Radio Clinic new merchandise. While getting this assurance from his suppliers was a relief, it didn't change the fact that with the insurance money effectively spent, Dad needed to find additional sources of money.

For the next six months, Dad steered Radio Clinic through a very convoluted road to recovery. If there was a unifying theme to this tortuous path, it was that at each stop along the way the responses he got from bureaucrats, bankers, and government officials, made no sense. Business students weren't the only students that could benefit from Radio Clinic's experience. Dad as a case study would also fit well in a philosophy class. There was something almost universal in the question Radio Clinic's fight for survival raised. How does a rational person fight to accomplish something when there is irrationality at every turn?

I am going to boil his efforts down to its essential elements, since there are too many twists and turns for me to maintain the thread of the story. The banks were a complete disappointment. The New York City Economic Development Department organized local banks to talk to the affected small business owners to give them a chance for a loan. Since Radio Clinic had made its loan payments to Citibank on time since the 1950s, Dad thought he had a good chance for a new loan with them. But when he asked for a $30,000 loan, he was told he needed $30,000 in collateral to be eligible. Dad pointed out the longevity of the business, its history with the bank, and that if he had that kind of collateral he probably wouldn't need the loan. But it was a nonstarter.

Next came the Small Business Administration (SBA) and a very convoluted process. It was a victory of sorts that Dad even got to meet with an SBA loan officer. The conversations he and other merchants had with Jerry Nadler and Ruth Messinger the days after the blackout paid off. They and other local politicians put pressure on Washington to allow SBA disaster loans. These loans were useful to merchants because they came with a relatively low interest rate of 3 percent instead of the typical 8 percent. It wasn't as good as a grant, but there would be no more grants. The interest rate was low enough that my dad thought he could pay it back.

Sitting down with the SBA loan officer was a high stakes meeting for Dad. He had exhausted all his options and without an infusion of cash the store wouldn't make it. The fate of Radio Clinic hinged on its outcome. Initially it seemed to be over before it really started. The loan officer took a quick look at Radio Clinic's profit and loss sheet, handed Dad back the sheet and said the SBA couldn't justify the loan. In other words: no. A no was impossible to my dad. Without this loan his business was dead. He hadn't even had a chance to state his case. He had to do something. So he again followed his instinct.

Another all cap entry on the *Rubin Rules for Survival* declared, "You as a person are most important here." Like any good salesman, Dad understood that customers are more likely to believe you if they feel like they know you. Maybe you let them in on a confidence, show vulnerability, or make some other kind of human connection. Ignoring the no, Dad made his case. He told the loan officer that Radio Clinic had been his father's business, and that both his father and his father's business partner were dead now. He wasn't in the business when they made their decisions and he didn't want to be penalized for their actions. Additionally, he was newly the sole owner of the business. He figured he had nothing left to lose so he told him the truth. The profit and loss statement looked worse than it was because his dad saved on taxes by lowering the statement. In the moment of silence that followed, Dad could have kicked himself. Maybe he went too far in telling the loan officer that his dad doctored the books and it would be too costly now to bring the payments truly current. But the SBA guy didn't flinch. If anything, it won him over to Radio Clinic's side. He smiled and said not to worry, that he knew there are things that small businesses need to do to survive. He then advised Dad on how to best navigate the federal loan process.

Next Dad learned the counter intuitive way the Small Business Administration worked. The now-friendly SBA guy gave my dad two pieces of advice. First, he should apply for the physical damages and economic damages separately, because if he applied for both at the same time he would probably be denied everything. Once he received a check for physical damages, then he could apply for harder-to-substantiate economic damages. That was straightforward enough. The second piece of advice, however, was problematic. If Dad wanted to be granted an SBA loan he needed to check *yes* on the form, agreeing that he would give his insurance reimbursement to the SBA in exchange for the loan.

This made no sense. The only way he could get a chunk of money from the SBA, money which came with 3 percent interest, was to essentially sign away his rights to a different chunk of money: money that was interest free. But even though it was not a great deal, since ultimately Radio Clinic would get less money, it was still worth it. The SBA loan would come in many months sooner than the insurance money and Radio Clinic needed the money now. He did, however, hedge his bets and only told the SBA about one of the $31,500 insurance settlements, leaving the other one to pay off his creditors. It took me a few minutes in this interview for what my dad told me to fully register: he lied to the SBA.

Initially this news surprised me. As a merchant Dad was careful to not take advantage of situations that might benefit him, but would harm someone else. For example, he wouldn't process stolen credit cards even when he was given approval by the card processor. But the more I thought about it the more sense it made. The rules of the business game were not written to help small stores like Radio Clinic, and it would not survive if Dad played completely by the rules. Fundamentally, Dad felt that anyone who understood the economic realities of running a small business should be able to see this rule did not make sense. Created in 1953 with the mission to "aid, counsel, assist and protect the interests of small business concerns"—it didn't seem too much to ask that the Small Business Administration understood these realities. He knew the SBA loan would fall far short of $200,000, the full amount of damages that occurred. The government response was underwhelming. Citibank wouldn't help. Dad was not opposed to doing the right thing or doing the best thing, but doing what makes sense always wins for him. And hedging his bets made sense.

To submit a claim for physical damages, Dad needed to include an inventory of what was stolen and what was damaged. An SBA adjuster spent time in the store taking notes on the electrical wiring and flooring that were destroyed. The SBA guy's advice turned out to be helpful since the SBA gave out 535 loans to looted businesses, and Radio Clinic got one of them. A check for $74,600 arrived in October, and it took my dad the next 20 years to repay it.

After he got the money to compensate for the physical damages he learned that Radio Clinic was also eligible for $50,000 from the SBA in economic damages. But before he could apply for that he needed to turn over the insurance money. This was the same insurance money he needed because his major suppliers were sitting on checks waiting to cash them. So if he didn't make those checks good for his suppliers, they would stop shipping him merchandise. But if he didn't send the SBA $35,000 now they wouldn't send him $50,000 later. The absurdity of the situation irritated him. So, he went back to the phone.

Figuring that politicians are supposed to be responsive to the needs of their constituents, and he was a constituent, Dad contacted Senator Moynihan. He was hopeful there was a way out of this bureaucratic labyrinth. Moynihan's chief of state was sympathetic, but unsure he could do anything to help. Unwilling to let this sympathy amount to nothing the way it did with his earlier phone calls to the city, Dad pitched him a plan. This plan had the benefit of costing the government nothing and helping Radio Clinic. But it might have had too much nuance for the SBA bureaucracy that deals in absolutes. Radio Clinic would keep the $35,000 of insurance money now and waive his right to $50,000 in economic damages, saving the government $15,000.

The first thing the chief of staff said to Dad was that it was a good idea but could not be done. Before Dad had a chance to marshal his arguments, the chief of staff then gave him the name of his SBA contact and said to call this man. He will tell you how to get it done. I have heard this story many times as exhibit A as to why you never give up. Find the right person to talk to and then make it easy for the person in charge to say yes. Financially Radio Clinic was existing on fumes and could have used the extra $15,000. But in the months immediately following the blackout, Dad had to choose the bird in the hand. The insurance money was enough for him to pay off most of his creditors.

And Radio Clinic lived to see another day. Both stores remained open. No employees were laid off. This was an enormous relief for Dad, since several of the men he employed in 1977 he had known his whole life. Dad did not disappoint when he talked with the Columbia business students a few months after the Blackout. As advertised by the professor, everything really did go wrong for Radio Clinic. The fight to save the store was a case study in resolving one thorny problem only to have another one pop up. At the bottom of the first index card of *Rubin's Rules for Survival*, I saw a phrase that perfectly encapsulated his efforts to bring Radio Clinic back from the brink. It caught my attention since Dad wrote it in all caps, had arrows pointing toward it, and pushed down hard on the pen so the letters almost looked like they were written in bold. It read, "Define problem—make decision—all else are obstacles to be overcome." My dad had made his decisions. And for now, Radio Clinic had overcome.

9

An Occasion Worth Remembering

I've learned that people will forget what you said, people will forget what you did, but people will never forget how you made them feel.

—Maya Angelou

I'm back, back in the New York Groove.

—KISS

IN THE YEAR AFTER the blackout, Blocks for a Better Broadway, a community group already dedicated to improving the avenue from 86th to 96th Streets, decided to create a community cultural center in the neighborhood. Ethel Sheffer, one of the group's founders, suggested to her husband Isaiah Sheffer, a playwright and stage director, that they do something with the old movie theater on 95th Street called the Symphony. They teamed up with Allen Miller, a conductor and filmmaker, and together they planned a 12-hour community event and renamed the theater Symphony Space.

As with almost every old building on Broadway, the building that now houses Symphony Space had an eventful past. Before 2537 Broadway became Symphony Space, it was a market opened by the very wealthy Vincent Astor. Within a few years, it turned into the Crystal Palace skating rink with a restaurant below. Two hundred people could watch the skaters from balcony seating. But nothing stays the same for very long in New York City, and the space became the Symphony and Thalia movie theaters. By the summer of the blackout, the building had fallen on gritty times, and instead of showing films the building rented out for boxing and wrestling matches. As they prepared the space for their inaugural event in their newly envisioned space, Ethel Sheffer and Miller needed to dry-clean all the gum off the floor.

The first event was called "Wall To Wall Bach," where for 12 hours an orchestra and local musicians came to the theater to play music by Bach. They rented the space for one day, January 7, 1978. Ethel Sheffer went door to door to get financial support from local businesses and my dad chipped in. Along with thousands of other people, Dad was curious about the 12-hour event and attended some portion of it. He walked back and forth between his store and the theater throughout the day to listen to the music and check out the turn-out. Chairs were on the stage and you could sit up with orchestra and come and go as you pleased. The event, and Symphony Space, were a big hit in the neighborhood.

Excited about how this theater could rally the neighborhood, Dad wanted to contribute. In the year after the blackout, his thinking about the store's role in the neighborhood had shifted. Being told by customers and local politicians that keeping Radio Clinic in the neighborhood was important to them had an impact on him. It wasn't that he didn't understand before that Radio Clinic had a significant stake in the health of the neighborhood, but he simply wasn't oriented toward effecting change. He was running a business, not actively trying to improve the neighborhood. After the looting, that changed.

Dad got an opportunity at one of the next Symphony Space shows, "Wall to Wall John Cage and Friends." Isaiah Sheffer came into Radio Clinic looking to rent Boomboxes since John Cage planned to use them on stage. He didn't know how many would be needed in the show, so Dad lent him several and told him to save the boxes and repack them when done using them. He didn't want any payment, but asked if Sheffer could let the audience know where the machines came from. When Sheffer dropped off the Boomboxes, he told Dad that when he announced Radio Clinic's support, the audience cheered.

Before writing this book, I hadn't known about Dad's early involvement in Symphony Space, or at least hadn't remembered it. It came up during an interview with my brother, who was proud of Dad's early involvement, and he encouraged me to include it in the book. It turned out to be a great way for my dad to do his part to add value to the neighborhood and to be visible as a business while doing it. For weeks after "Wall-to-Wall John Cage," new customers came into the store happy to support a business that supported Symphony Space, reinforcing for Dad the importance of being an engaged community member. In addition to donating equipment, Dad had other ways he supported Symphony Space in its early days. At the time, Radio Clinic ran a monthly ad in the *New York Times* stereo section. Dad kept these ads clean, with a lot of space and little copy. Any event Sheffer wanted publicized, Dad included in the ad. He also violated his rule to never hang posters in his window in support of local causes, since it was too controversial to play favorites with events. But Symphony Space was special.

Ed Koch was then Mayor. In his 1978 inaugural address, Koch encouraged "urban pioneers" to move to the city. He urged people to play a role in the city's revival saying, "A better city requires the one ingredient that money cannot buy, people who are willing to give of themselves." The Upper West Side had been filled with activists willing to give of themselves for decades, but Koch was thinking of different people. He definitely stepped into the neighborhood's active political battle about how much housing should be built for low-income people versus middle class and wealthy people. Considering brownstones to be a stabilizing economic force for the city, he used tax policies to encourage people with money to move into the city. By using incentives and tax abatements to help people rehabilitate deteriorated housing stock, he planned to reinvigorate neighborhoods. More and more middle class people who had the energy to rehab these row houses and brownstones moved to the Upper West Side, used this public money, and got to work.

In the year that followed it sure seemed to Dad that the West Side revival that had been heralded in 1969 had landed in his section of the neighborhood. These new brownstone owners were promising customers since they needed many appliances to set up their new homes. Also, more and more people traveled to the neighborhood for performances at Symphony Space. He noticed that Radio Clinic had a growing number of younger customers, many of whom were interested in stereos. Seeing an opportunity, my brother encouraged Dad to add a sound room to the store. Josh was 15 and Dad trusted him to do many of the jobs in the store. He alternated between making sales and working with Raymond in the warehouse. An avid music listener, Josh was the kind of guy that would eventually run his college's radio station and he thought a sound room could help Radio Clinic showcase its audio equipment. It meant a lot to my brother that my dad had the confidence in him to green-light the project and just let him have at it.

Space was at a premium in the store, so there was a limit on how many stereos, speakers and other components could be displayed in the sound room. The idea was that a separate sound room would provide space for customers to linger and listen to music to compare and contrast each stereo and speaker. The interior of the store was L-shaped and my brother envisioned a three-walled space in the back of the store, somewhat removed from the noise of the store. Creating the sound room was a lot of fun for Josh since it involved conceptualizing, trial and error, and a great deal of wiring. Teaching himself how to do the wiring was probably his favorite part and he spent many hours putting together this complex multi -audio room.

Once he was done, using an AB switch, customers could mix and match stereo and speakers to see which combination they liked the best. Several loyal customers were professional musicians and they helped Dad sort through the options to select which audio equipment to carry. With their highly trained ears they directed Dad to the stereos that had the best sound fidelity but were relatively low priced. Looking back on it, Josh isn't sure the sound room was the best business decision for Dad since Radio Clinic couldn't meaningfully compete with the audio shops. Dad probably wouldn't have created a sound room if my brother wasn't so excited about it, but it was much appreciated by the store's existing customers. I know I loved the room and spent hours in the sound room doing some mundane task while I listened to music. Grabbing whichever headphone had the softest ear cushion, I plugged into each stereo until I found the one I liked best and sat on the floor using the pricing gun to label boxes of film and cassettes.

Dad noticed something curious about the female customers shopping for stereos in the sound room. Women were shopping for stereos but not buying. They would invariably say, "I will wait for my husband before I buy a stereo," or "I don't know enough about stereos to buy one." Yet Dad knew from talking to them that these customers usually had a pretty good idea of what they wanted in terms of size and sound for a stereo. Typically, when a woman returned with her husband or boyfriend, she let him talk her into something different than what she wanted. The same customer who knew she didn't need a stereo with a high degree of sound sensitivity for the receiver, who believed my dad when he told her that you needed a super ear to tell the difference in sound quality with the more expensive systems, would wind up leaving the store with a more expensive stereo than she needed.

Roland Surena, a salesman at Radio Clinic who also taught an audio class at Westchester Community College, noticed the same problem. Both men believed that female customers felt intimidated when buying stereos and that this was a problem that could be solved. Their solution was to take the mystery out of buying stereos and teach an audio class for women one evening a week for eight weeks on how to buy and maintain a stereo. They advertised in local newspapers and posted flyers in the two Radio Clinic stores. Ten women showed up for the first class in 1979, which quickly grew to 70 women per class.

Local reporters liked these audio workshops. The *Daily News* featured the classes with a photo of Dad with his time capsule sideburns, surrounded by women listening intently, and framed by a backdrop of shelves filled with televisions and Boomboxes. "We served coffee, cake, and knowledge" was how Dad described the class. Hans Fantel, who wrote a popular "sound" column for the

New York Times promoted these audio workshops in a surprising number of columns. Here's one excerpt:

> Music, after all, is not sex specific. There are as many women interested in music as men; and in an era when most music is heard through electronic means, women as well as men rely on good audio as a source of esthetic pleasure. As more and more women, at least in urban centers, live singly and are economically independent, the proportion of women as buyers of audio equipment also rises. One prominent New York audio dealer - RCI[1], on Manhattan's upper west side - reports that women constitute as much as one third of his clientele. We asked him if women, on average, were competent buyers... I wouldn't say that men are more knowledgeable about audio than women, says Roland Surena of RCI. To me it seems they're both equally confused and bewildered—most of them, that is. The difference is that women admit their ignorance.

These classes even caught the attention of Gloria Steinem, a leading feminist and one of the founders of Ms. Magazine. She thought it was an innovative workshop and wanted Dad to do a presentation about it at a consumer appliance tradeshow. I was 12 years old at the time and never did take this workshop. But I should have. I don't have any memory of it, but if my dad tried to practice at home what he preached at these workshops, it certainly didn't work with me. Our house had a never-ending stream of new appliances. Dad brought these appliances home to see how well they worked before investing in inventory. It seemed to me he brought a new VCR or stereo component home on a monthly basis. Between my brother and me, Dad could gauge a wide spectrum of human response to any given appliance to determine if user-friendly. Josh was very technically inclined and liked to figure out how things worked. I preferred for someone to show me how something worked and then for it to simply work. Many of the stereo components and VCRs that Dad tested out on us were complicated. Each stereo system tended to have several switches that needed to be up and down in a very specific pattern to get music to play. Just when I got the hang of one, Dad would replace it with a new one. I attribute the fact that I am very loyal to my aging appliances to how much I hated continually learning how to use a new one.

The nights of these workshops and other community oriented events and meetings, Dad got home after dinner. Since Dad worked such long hours at Radio Clinic he missed many of the activities my brother and I were involved with in the years after the blackout. Plus, we still lived in Suffern, the town my

---

1 In 1979 the name of the store changed from Radio Clinic to RCI (Radio Clinic Incorporated). I refer to it as Radio Clinic throughout the rest of the book.

parents moved to when Dad worked as an engineer at International Nickel, in the suburbs. They had often considered moving back into Manhattan but hadn't yet, so my dad had a commute in and out of the city. Josh was a soccer goalie, the position Dad played in high school, college, and a club team. Both he and Dad were both disappointed that Dad could rarely make his soccer games. I would have liked Dad to be home more but I also liked that he had a double life. At least that is how I thought of it at the time. Mild mannered suburban dad by night and owner of a store on BROADWAY in MANHATTAN by day. I very much wanted to live a double life. Sure, I was a socially awkward and not very popular suburban girl, but maybe I could be something else too. Most of my peers in Suffern didn't spend much time in New York City. And if they did it was either on a school trip or a family outing. They did not spend time on upper Broadway unchaperoned. There wasn't much about me that impressed my peers in middle school. I spent my lunch hours scared and alone in a stairway reading a book and hoping to get through the day without being bullied, but my getting to roam Broadway alone did impress.

During the years before I started high school, spending Saturdays working at Radio Clinic with Dad was a nice refuge from my life in Suffern. My neighborhood friends, inexplicably all Catholic, went to Catholic school and had an entire life outside of me. My Hebrew school friends, also inexplicably, looked like gorgeous women when they hit puberty, started dating high school boys, and no longer had time for me. Since Mom was the one who was home, the thankless tasks of parenting fell to her. She was the one who had to deal with an unhappy and uncommunicative kid whose grades were quickly heading south. She was the one who witnessed my slightly pathetic afternoons, eating crackers, pepperoni slices and watching soap operas alone because I didn't have anyone to hang out with after school. Her concern for me was palpable, and I resented it. No one likes to be pitied, even the pitiful, and I preferred my Saturdays at Radio Clinic to home.

A Saturday at Radio Clinic started out with a 40-minute car drive. I loved this drive, particularly if my brother wasn't in the car and I got to ride in the front seat. Dad let me choose the music, would regale me with his New York City childhood stories and we strategized about what flavor of donuts to buy after we parked the car and walked to the store. This was certainly more fun than staying home and doing homework, my eye exercises to correct a lazy eye, back exercises to ward off further scoliosis, and any number of other things I didn't want to do. When I look back on these middle school years, I am amazed at how little use I was at Radio Clinic yet how willing my dad was to have me join him at the store. When he was my age, Dad learned how to repair radios, traveled to Radio Row and Hell's Kitchen to buy parts and was part of installation runs. Josh was often down in the warehouse learning how to chart deliveries. There was no way Dad, or any of the employees, found me helpful in any meaningful way. Yet on Friday nights he would ask me if I had plans the next day and whenever I didn't, he would say, "Good, I could use you at the store tomorrow." In a couple of years, I would start high school, find things I was good at, make friends, and get too busy to spend many Saturdays at the store. But for my unhappy middle school years, when each day felt like a month, the days I spent at Radio Clinic were an oasis.

Two years to the date of the Blackout, Radio Clinic had an "Apple Power" sale. Dad modeled the slogan after the city's "I heart NY" logo, which was launched in 1977 to persuade tourists that New York was a safe place to visit. He wanted to commemorate the store's recovery, thank his customers for supporting the business through a tough time, and send a vote of confidence to the other merchants on the block. Jean Pathe Cleaners and Dyers, Nedick's, Riverside Cleaners, and a stationary store had helped Radio Clinic anchor the block since 1940. New businesses such as Broadway Army and Navy, Ialdo Japanese Fencing Center, Mejia Grocery and Hunan Balcony opening on the block fueled my Dad's optimism. For the sale, he printed bright red T-shirts and tote bags with an image of a large apple and the words "apple power" in black blocky lettering. My mom, brother and I were all at the store for the sale, wearing our apple power t-shirts, and with each purchase, handing a shirt or bag to customers.

At the time of the sale, Dad was very upbeat. Radio Clinic had survived the initial crisis and was chipping away at its debt. The business still had its struggles, but he was talking to his bank to resolve some credit issues, and, other than one major supplier, he was in decent standing with his pre-looting suppliers. While he was certainly still bogged down by the past, he was looking toward the future. My dad changed the store's name to RCI (Radio Clinic Incorporated) in recognition of the fact that it was no longer primarily a radio service shop.

To help publicize the Apple Power sale, the West Side Shopper, a local newspaper, featured him in what I can only describe as a gushing "profiles in courage" article. The reporter compared Radio Clinic's customer and community service to that of a small-town merchant, and detailed several anecdotes of Dad creatively helping a customer. Between the stereo workshop articles and this one declaring that "responsibility, integrity and the knack of listening to customers" was the root of its success, Radio Clinic's reputation as a good place to shop was broadcast loud and clear to the new neighborhood residents. Dad didn't know it yet, but he was going to need all the help he could get with this type of publicity. In the not too distant future, mega-stores and chain stores would see the growing financial opportunity and move into the neighborhood. Radio Clinic's reputation for personal service would be the main way the store held its own against them. But this was not yet on my dad's mind and he was ready to celebrate. For three days, Dad offered reduced prices, free gifts and a raffle. The West Side Shopper summed up his mood well. "It was two years ago this month that the blackout and subsequent looting almost jeopardized the store's survival. Alan Rubin feels this is an occasion worth remembering."

10

Aftershocks

New York City is a great monument to the power
of money and greed... a race for rent.

—Frank Lloyd Wright

THE SUN WAS SHINING on a bright spring day as Dad walked from Citibank
to Radio Clinic. He shared the sidewalk with musicians heading over to Symphony Space, people making their way to a bodega to get lunch or maybe some cigarettes, elderly women pushing their belongings in shopping carts, people enjoying the cookies they bought at Lichtman's, and young couples entwined on a park bench. For every elderly person walking over to the benches on Broadway's median strip, my dad saw a young woman pushing a baby stroller. New apartment high-rises would not be built for a few more years, but the Wall Streeters and lawyers who would soon be its tenants were already here. Landlords and merchants both noticed the changing fortunes of the neighborhood. During his walk that day, Dad ran into Radio Clinic's landlord, Leon Weinreb, who said, "Alan, the neighborhood is looking up, I want more money." My dad said, "Okay, but I want more time." So they set up a meeting to renegotiate the lease.

When Grandpa signed Radio Clinic's first lease in 1934, the landlord at the time didn't hesitate to rent him commercial space. As a general rule in the 1930s, landlords weren't making or losing a fortune on their property because there wasn't a fortune to be had. The brick and mortar goldmine that would soon erupt all over the Upper West Side was dormant.

With the growing affluence of the area, Leon Weinreb knew the commercial space he owned was now worth more than the $700 Radio Clinic was paying each month in 1980. Or would be soon. Dad had seven years left on his lease and didn't need to agree to pay the additional $800 a month that his landlord wanted. But Dad was thinking ahead as well and was willing to trade money for security. He wanted the stability of a longer lease. Radio Clinic had now been on the block for 46 years, and he didn't want to relocate the store when his lease expired. He worked too hard to save the business; he certainly didn't intend to move out of the neighborhood.

The two men reached an agreement. The new rent would be $1,500 a month, with an escalator clause increasing the rent over time. In exchange, the new lease would last 20 years, until the year 2000. Leon Weinreb also required merchants to pay a percentage of the real estate tax of the building. The building tax can be an unpredictable expense, and landlords typically pass as much of that expense on to their commercial tenants as possible. The jump in rent from $700 to $1,500 a month was significant, but it only went from one percent to two percent of Radio Clinic's costs. It was a small enough percentage that Dad felt it would be manageable. Paying a small percentage of the real estate taxes was a wildcard, since it went up in tandem with the property's assessment. But in 1980, that too seemed manageable. (The real estate tax would ultimately become less and less manageable over the 20 years of the lease as the taxes on property soared.) He was pleased with the new lease, optimistic about the future both for Radio Clinic and for the block. My dad was always confident about the future: that with hard work something better was around the corner. But even someone with a pessimistic nature could see that the neighborhood was changing, and Radio Clinic, with its brand new 20-year lease, was well-situated.

At the time that Dad signed his new lease, the area was in the midst of its "brownstone renaissance." Brownstones told the story of the neighborhood, where it had been and where it was going. They were coming full circle to when they were built for middle and upper middle class families in the 19th century. A rundown brownstone that could barely sell for $30,000 in the late 1960s was renovated and sold for $300,000 by 1980. The housing development momentum was undeniably heading toward building expensive housing. Mayor Koch provided tax abatements and exemptions to developers to facilitate the conversion of SRO's into high-end housing and the development of new high rise luxury buildings. Large numbers of people between the ages of 25 and 44 moved into the area, shifting the demographics.

As the number of young customers in the store increased, Dad and Roland built on the success of the stereo classes and offered an air conditioner workshop. These classes accomplished two things that made my dad happy. It

Alan leading a 1980 air conditioner maintenance class.

brought new customers into the store and gave him an opportunity to do one of his favorite things: proselytize about the importance of appliance maintenance. They began each class with the basic principle of how air conditioners work since Dad considered that the basic building block. From there he believed it was clear why basic maintenance would prolong the life of each air conditioner. I imagine Dad's enthusiasm for sharing this information was one reason these classes were so popular. It didn't make sense to him that anyone was intimidated by an appliance and he was happy to do his part to demystify. He liked the idea that by sharing what he knew, he was giving women some tools to stand up for themselves. This newspaper quote from a woman who took the class made him happy, "I also don't feel like a victim to the repairman, as I used to. I feel secure now that I know how it works and I really don't think I can be conned."

Growing up, time and time again I saw Dad puzzle out why an appliance wasn't working and then fix it. Family legend says that when I was little and something broke, I would say "daddy fix it" and put it aside until he got home from work. With a tape measure or pencil and paper he would approach a problem through trial and error and eventually get to the root of the problem. On a regular basis, I saw him do basic maintenance work to prevent a problem from starting in the first place. Whether cleaning out the air conditioner filters or washing the refrigerator coils so the compressor wouldn't overheat, he believed he could keep our household appliances working. Every summer I watched him install window air-conditioners by himself, making it look easy to fit an air

Jen in high school.

Jen's first attempt to install a window air conditioner.

conditioner into the right spot and then use the window extensions and mounting brackets to get an air-tight fit.

I got the message loud and clear. Humans are smarter than appliances, and if I took the time to figure it out, then I could find the solution to whatever problem the appliance posed. But although his enthusiasm for this subject matter was infectious for customers, it didn't work so well with me. As many times as I was given a tutorial on how to install an air conditioner, I made the most basic mistake the first time I tried to install one on my own. It was a hot and sticky day and I decided to try the air conditioner that I found in the basement of the home my husband and I bought in Madison. I didn't take the time to secure the unit while installing it and dropped it out the window a couple of times. Slightly the worse for wear, and with no window extension or brackets, I couldn't get an air-tight fit. Instead I made due with old encyclopedias and rags to fill the open space between the air conditioner and the window frame, and just got used to having some bugs in the house. Throughout my adult life I have never proactively cleaned an appliance or tried to find the source of the problem for a broken one, instead I rely heavily on duct tape to help the appliance get through one more month or one last season. I can't really explain why this is true about me, because I know better.

By the time I was in high school in the early 1980s, Radio Clinic carried many appliances that were perfect for a teenager. With the increase of young adult customers, Dad now stocked the store with a wider range of electronics. The shelves of Boomboxes interested me more than the stereos in the sound room. In addition to being much cheaper, I preferred Boomboxes because they were much easier to use and were portable. When in the store I would bring in a favorite cassette tape to try out each new model and see which one I liked best. The acoustics couldn't compare to the stereos, but I am always happy to trade sound quality for ease of use. But no appliance could compare to the Sony Walkman, the first portable tape recorder on the market. I was not alone in that assessment, Sony sold over 385 million units worldwide. This device brought countless customers into the store, but it would be hard for anyone to match my devotion to the Walkman.

At the time, it was incredible that you could make a mixed tape of favorite songs, insert the cassette in the Sony Walkman, put on the headphones, and listen to them as you traveled throughout your day. Having a portable device to listen to songs of my choosing and not just whatever songs were playing on a portable transistor radio was thrilling. Radio Clinic sold thousands of the sporty version, with the hard-yellow plastic casing and the large clip on the back that could be attached to a pant pocket or a belt loop. In high school, I was a serious runner. After middle school Mom insisted I turn off the tv and join a school club, so I joined the track team. It turned out I loved to run. I also loved to listen to music. The Walkman let me do both at the same time and made me very happy. For my first run with the Walkman I headed out with a carefully curated mixtape playing in my ears. I had a very pleasant first five minutes and then noticed my right arm was aching. I moved the Walkman to my left hand but that arm didn't last any longer. I didn't account for my lack of arm strength and how heavy a couple of pounds of plastic would feel to me after ten minutes of running. Clearly, I needed better arm muscles and started doing push-ups, but this was a long-term project. Clipping the Walkman to my running shorts pulled them down. Clipping the Walkman to a belt left bruises since it bounced. I was sure Dad could help me rig up a way to run with the Walkman but that would require a long discussion about the mechanics of what I was trying to accomplish. With my aversion to spending too long on problem solving, I decided adhering the Walkman to my body with duct tape might be the solution. It did pull skin off my stomach, but it worked well enough until my arms got stronger.

Many of my Saturdays were taken up by cross-country and track meets. My mom's decree, that I join something and suggested track, turned out to be the best advice that anyone has ever given me. As a big fan of sports and his daughter, Dad was excited that I joined my high school cross country and track teams. He treasured his memories of running track, playing softball and soccer when he was younger, but it was hard for Dad to spend too much time away from the store. Occasionally my team raced at Van Cortland Park in the Bronx or the armory in Midtown, and Dad would watch and then hustle back to the store. Being out of the store for more than a few hours at a time worried him. He never did the requested presentation at the women's trade show because he was afraid to be gone from the store for two days. Since the looting, he maintained a constant juggling act watching his cash flow, managing his debt, and fending off creditors, and he didn't trust anyone else to keep the balls in the air. Even though many aspects of the business were healthy and the volume of sales was increasing, it didn't alter the fact that its working capital had been an issue since the blackout. Working capital is the cash available for the day-to-day operations of a business, and back in 1977 Dad used about $60,000 of it to rebuild his store. Radio Clinic had slowly increased its sales volume, meaning the quantity of goods sold went up, but he still struggled to fully pay off all his creditors. The business's current assets were not greater than its current liabilities, and cash flow was so tight that some months it was difficult to operate.

In 1980 my dad tried to get another bank loan to provide a release valve to the financial pressure he was under. First, he again made the wearisome rounds to find some financial aid from the city, the office of economic development, and other state and federal programs designed to help businesses expand. But none of those programs lent money for working capital. Thinking his bank would be impressed that Radio Clinic had reduced its debt in the last three years and substantially increased its volume, he approached Citibank to restructure Radio Clinic's debt. Basically, he wanted to switch who he owned money to. A bank loan would allow him to pay off all his creditors and only owe money to one place—the bank. The bank's interest rate, and therefore his monthly payments, would be lower.

On his loan application, Dad was very positive about what this loan would do for the store. Once his money wasn't tied up in old debt, he could spend money to save money. Suppliers like it when customers pay their bills early and offer trade discounts as encouragement. Radio Clinic never had the cash flow to do this and invariably paid an extra $30,000 each year to suppliers. If he could take advantage of these trade discounts, he could use that money productively and put it toward growth. With the demographic changes to the neighborhood, Dad wanted to expand into the video and home entertainment market. He just needed the capital to do it. In the loan application, he stated his case: "Radio Clinic is in two neighborhoods of New York that have been considered marginal. We have been a stabilizing influence in these areas for many years. These communities are now experiencing a renaissance. We want to be able to respond to the growing and changing needs of our community." In other words, some merchant was going to make money from the young urban professionals moving into the neighborhood spending money on their home entertainment, and it might as well be him.

Radio Clinic didn't get the loan. He was told that the bank doesn't take risks. This risk comment particularly frustrated Dad and touched a nerve. Or maybe it was more of a scab on a barely healed wound than a nerve. Government officials and banks had said the same thing to him after the blackout each time he was denied the assistance he wanted. Scribbled in the corner of his

Rubin's Rules for Survival cards was, "Banks are negative and conservative." This risk comment just reinforced Dad's central premise about life as a small business owner: governments and banks assume risks all the time for business interests—just not for the small ones.

He penned an op-ed piece to the *New York Times* three years, to the week, after the blackout. "The Blackout's Legacy" described at length what Radio Clinic had contributed to New York City's economy by staying open. Nineteen jobs were saved, which meant nineteen fewer people were on unemployment. At the time, Radio Clinic's annual wages and sales tax was $200,000. If you multiplied this by the 10 similar Upper West Side businesses that stayed, that was $2 million the city would have and the neighborhood would have lost out on, my dad explained. Again, he was cheerleading for the value of small businesses. And again it did no good.

> I can't help but think the Chrysler Corporation is being rescued from its own bad judgment by the same United States Government that will not come to the aid of tax-paying small-businessmen when they are the victims of criminal acts. It is this policy that has cost New York City as many jobs and taxpayers over the years as would be lost if the Chrysler Corporation went bankrupt. The small businessman is always being praised for being the backbone of the economy and for providing stability for the community. And yet the small businessman is in the same position as the victim of a crime who never regains all that he has lost. So, too, with New York City.

In 1981 Dad circled back to Citibank and asked for another loan, this time for $50,000. He had recently been featured in a New York Times article about small businesses that were squeezed, but not necessarily ignored, by banks they have used for years. He described how each year since the looting, he had to pass on opportunities to buy a large number of air conditioners at unusually low prices, because he didn't have the cash flow to buy them. Each time the bank declined to lend the money without collateral, but he hoped this article would have an impact and change the thinking of his bank. He was also worried about Texas Instruments, a significant electronics supplier. The company had lost interest in giving Radio Clinic time to pay off its debt. He had worked out a deal with this supplier after the looting, but they later reneged on it and wanted to be paid in full. Radio Clinic couldn't pay them in full and still pay employees and keep the lights on. The article ended on an up note, which was Dad's signature move. "By next year," he said, "Citibank will understand me."

But any increased understanding of Radio Clinic was not immediately apparent. At least not by Citibank's Community Business Team, which approved or turned down loans. Citibank did approve the loan application, but at a very high interest rate. Not only that, if Dad took the loan, the bank would also apply the higher interest rate to an existing loan Radio Clinic had with the bank, which predated the blackout. Once the loans were added together, the new loan would add, not detract, from Radio Clinic's monthly financial obligations. So Dad refused the offer and returned to a tactic that worked well for him in the months after the blackout. Instead of taking no for an answer, he wrote a letter to Walter Wriston, the head of Citibank. Relying on his reasonable people theory, he explained his situation:

> Although we may be considered a 'small business' when compared with Citibank's corporate and international clients, we are a major business within our community. We have been a stabilizing influence on the West Side during many difficult years and we are a part of the drive that has led to its renaissance. We have supported many community activities, both financially and personally. I am on the board of directors of the West Side Chamber of Commerce and Symphony Space; I have represented the business community in many capacities including Councilwoman Ruth Messinger's task force on small business financing.

He also shared his frustration with Citibank:

> In all my discussions with various representatives of the Community Business Team (CBT), there has been no understanding of how small businesses function, no willingness to consider areas of compromise, and a constant message of----Citibank does not take risks.

He closed his letter with classic Alan Rubin optimism:

> Mr. Wriston, I have written to you because I have read so much about your reputation as an innovator in the banking industry and one who is not afraid to take risks. I do not feel that the CBT shares your spirit and philosophy...

As a kid, I didn't know the details of Radio Clinic's troubles and all the steps Dad needed to take to keep the business going. Over the past few years, each time I interviewed Dad I learned about another frustrating interaction with the bank or with the city. There were so many of them that I needed to create a timeline to understand where each bank loan denial was in relation to the blackout, or in relation to having a business partner, or in relation to closing a store, etc. I knew I couldn't write about each discrete event unless I wanted this book to turn into a how-to primer, or perhaps a cautionary tale, for new small business owners. In this instance Citibank was eventually willing to lower the interest to an amount Dad could work with. Dad's guess was that Wriston picked up the phone and called the loan officer and told him to change the terms. It was a satisfying victory for Dad, and reinforced his belief that making the phone call or writing the letter can make a difference. But it came too late to be a useful victory. Unable to get out from under the Texas Instruments debt, Radio Clinic had filed for Chapter 11 bankruptcy one month earlier.

Recovery from the looting was not a very linear process. Radio Clinic survived the initial seismic shake, but the lingering debt continued to destabilize the store. Aftershocks might be small compared to the actual earthquake, but sometimes it's the aftershock that gets you. Chapter 11 was designed for a business in debt to reorganize its affairs for the purpose of remaining in business. Which is an official way of saying that the business in Chapter 11 no longer had to pay the full amount of debt it owed. The Texas Instruments debt was an albatross around Radio Clinic's neck, and Dad needed to get rid of it to breathe. Chapter 11 did for the business what Dad had hoped the Citbank loan would do: consolidate his debt. At the bankruptcy hearing, Texas Instruments didn't show up to contest it, so they lost by default. In the end, Radio Clinic was too small for them to bother with, and Dad was no longer responsible for that debt or any debt accrued before November 1981. While he was relieved to have that slate wiped clean, he was anxious about its ripple effect.

Filing for Chapter 11 was a risk for Dad. He knew it would hurt Radio Clinic's reputation with his suppliers and worried it would impact other suppliers' willingness to work with Radio Clinic. The creditor's committee that forms after each Chapter 11 determined that Dad needed to pay 15 cents on each dollar owed. Worried that his four major suppliers would no longer work with him, Dad quietly violated the terms of Chapter 11 and told those four credit managers that he would pay them back 100 percent on the dollar. But he needed more than those four suppliers to run the business. In the year after filing for Chapter 11, Dad struggled with getting good pricing from other suppliers. He lost access to credit with floor planning, and not having this type of credit to finance inventory would have dire consequences for the business. Since the late 1940s, a part of Radio Clinic's success was that it had good access to merchandise at favorable terms. This allowed the store to sell merchandise at lower prices than other comparably sized stores and still made a decent profit. Radio Clinic relied heavily on a good word of mouth throughout the neighborhood on both its prices and customer services. This was starting to feel like it was in jeopardy.

As a result of filing for Chapter 11, Dad decided he needed a business partner. He hoped that the right partner would bring both working capital and strong connections in the appliance industry. Mike I.[2] fit the bill on both counts. One of Radio Clinic's salesmen was friendly with Mike, which is how Dad got to

2 I only used the first letter of his last name since I couldn't locate him to get
   permission to include his name in the book.

know him. Mike bought into the business for $60,000. And as a well-regarded sales representative at Topps appliances and Newmark and Lewis appliances, he would be valuable in helping Radio Clinic get good deals on merchandise. Mike kept his regular job and worked in the store on Saturdays. In many ways, this arrangement suited Dad, since the fact that he was at the store every day meant he called the day-to-day shots. The working capital and connections combination were so critical to my dad at this point that even though he worked six days a week to Mike's one day, he brought Mike in as a 50:50 partner.

This access to appliances was quickly useful for both Radio Clinic stores. The 83rd Street store had newly acquired a tough competitor for household appliances. Zabar's. Over the decades Zabar's steadily grew into a deli power-house. And now it wanted to be a retail powerhouse. Murray Klein, a longtime Zabar employee, ran the retail operations in the late 1970s and 1980s and started selling the same type of appliances that Radio Clinic sold. Zabar's was a well-known institution on the Upper West Side and thousands of people shopped there for food each day. Located two blocks from Zabar's, the 83rd Street store was increasingly in competition with it for household appliances.

Charlie Mackoff, Radio Clinic's 83rd Street store manager, and Murray had a friendly relationship. Charlie had managed the 83rd Street store since my dad bought Bill out of the store in 1977 and had been employed even longer. He knew the neighborhood well and paid close attention to the nearby competitors. At some point, Charlie noticed that Zabar's was underselling Radio Clinic by ten dollars a unit on humidifiers. While not an enormous problem, humidifiers were a phenomenally successful appliance for Radio Clinic. Dad relied on the 83rd Street store to bring in two thirds of the business and both men were concerned about Zabar's encroaching on Radio Clinic's turf. Even though Radio Clinic was the first store in the neighborhood to sell humidifiers, Zabar's, the larger store with deeper pockets, could buy 1,000 humidifiers at a discounted rate. Charlie asked Murray why he was selling a humidifier at such a low cost. Zabar's made a lot of money on food, its primary merchandise, so why sell humidifiers for so cheap? Murray said to Charlie, "I have to be the best on every product. I am not going to change the pricing. You're playing with the big boys. Are you a big boy?"

Being undersold was concerning, but there was nothing to do about it. "Don't fight battles you can't win" was an important enough point to Dad that he flagged it with an asterisk in his rules of survival. But now, with his new partner Mike, Dad had access to discounted merchandise. Mike got a fantastic deal on a Toshiba humidifier, considered the best on the market at the time. Dad thought it was an ugly unit, but it was easy to use, and Topps Appliances had a ton of them. Radio Clinic could sell it cheaper than other stores and still make a good profit. One day a man was standing in line at Zabar's holding the

Toshiba humidifier when someone behind him in line told him he should buy it at Radio Clinic since they sold that same humidifier for $10 less. The man put the humidifier back on the shelf and went across the street and two blocks north to purchase it at Radio Clinic instead.

Murray heard about this and sent his Toshiba representative over to Radio Clinic to figure out why there was such a price difference. The sales rep went to Radio Clinic one afternoon, and he never came right out and asked Dad how much he paid for the merchandise; instead, he danced around the question. He asked Dad why he was willing to lose money on the humidifier. Dad knew that Radio Clinic was underselling Zabar's by $10 and still making a 40 percent profit, but he learned from his dad to never answer an unasked question. He answered, "Who said I am losing money?" The sales guy then asked, "Why are you selling it so low?" My dad parried, "I can sell it even lower." The rep again asked, "Why lose money?" and Dad responded, "I can sell it lower and still make money." Back and forth and around in circles they went. Finally, Dad leaned into the sales rep, smiled and said, "Why don't you go back to Murray and tell him that we are big boys."

11

Follow the Lease

They're young and rich, single or starting families, and they're making over an old, mixed neighborhood in their own upwardly mobile image.

—Patricia Morrisroe, *New York Magazine*, 1985

He's not idiotic. He's the Wiz. And nobody beats him. Nobody.

—Elaine Benis from Seinfeld talking about the Nobody Beats the Wiz pitchman she dated.

TWO YOUNG PEOPLE CARRYING clipboards stopped by the store in 1985 with a survey they wanted Dad to fill out. They wanted to know how long local stores planned to stay in business. He told them to follow the lease. The number of years left on a lease was the answer to the question of how long a business was going to last on the Upper West Side. "Add those years to today's date," he told them, "and that is the day they will go out of business. All this other stuff you're asking doesn't mean anything."

It wasn't as easy to get a lease as it had been in the past. As the demographics in the neighborhood shifted, so did how much money a landlord could get in rent. By 1985, Mayor Koch's housing tax policies had an enormous ripple effect on the Upper West Side, particularly around 96th Street. Sparing developers the full cost of property taxes was a powerful economic incentive, and many took advantage of this opportunity. From 1981 until the tax exemption program

119

ended four years later, developers built high-end housing for young urban professionals. By 1983, only 35 of the Upper West Side SRO's remained. More than 7,500 people between the ages of 25 and 44 moved into the area. Young people with money had arrived and settled in.

William Zeckendorf, a developer, put to rest the question of what should happen on 96th Street. He bought the 40,000 square-foot lot and succeeded where Alexanders and other developers had not. The Columbia, a 32-story and 320-unit building, was unapologetically high-end housing. It included over 30,000 square feet of commercial space, a 200-car garage, a 7,000 square-foot garden, a health club, and a pool. Unhappy community groups greeted the bulldozers with protests and chants when the Columbia first broke ground, but there was no stopping it. The Columbia's impact was quick and evident. A reporter for the New York Times described it as, "crossing the old 96th Street frontier that once divided the trendy Upper West Side from the troubled Upper West Side." Half of the buildings 302 units were sold in two months.

Longtime neighborhood residents used the construction of the Columbia as a marker in time. Comments like, "That was before the Columbia" or, "After the Columbia there was scaffolding everywhere," drove home the point that this building was a big deal. Once the Columbia broke the ice, other development quickly followed. Dad couldn't walk more than a few blocks past Radio Clinic without seeing scaffolding, construction cranes, and wrecking balls during this time. Ten buildings with more than 2,000 apartments were constructed in a very few years. The other ones closest to Radio Clinic were the Princeton House on 95th Street, New West on 90th Street, and the Savannah on 89th. Depending on your point of view, the Columbia was either the beginning or the beginning of the end. For landlords and realtors, it was good news. As one broker described it, "The I won't look above 96th Street market is getting soft." The same one-bedroom apartment that rented for about $250 in 1980 now cost more than $1,500 in one of these luxury buildings. Through newspaper advertisements, brokers declared the Upper West Side "yuppie country" to entice the young and upwardly mobile to buy apartments in the neighborhood.

My parents also moved to the Upper West Side. After getting her Master's Degree while I was in middle school and working for a state senator while I was in high school, Mom then worked for the Jerusalem Foundation in Manhattan. Since both of my parents now had a commute to and from work, they decided it made more sense to live in the city. More specifically, they moved into the Endicott Condominium on 81st Street and Columbus Avenue, two avenues east of Broadway. The Endicott was one of the many fancy apartment hotels built around 1900 and at the time was described as, "in all respects, the finest and best appointed in this part of the city" and often served as a meeting place for the city's Republican party. As with many other grand buildings on the Upper West Side the Depression didn't treat it well and it quickly spiraled downward. By the 1970s it was considered such a dangerous building, known for violent crime and homicides, that Dad would not send any delivery crews to the Endicott. But gentrification revived the building and by 1986, my parents moved into a remodeled studio apartment.

A 1985 New York magazine did a feature called "The Yupper West Side" to describe this rapidly gentrifying neighborhood. The tagline read, "The Upper West Side is the hottest neighborhood in New York right now. Young professionals are colonizing the area, squeezing out many poorer people who've lived there for years." The same brownstone that could be bought for $300,000 in 1980 sold for $1 million five years later. Wall Street financiers used their bonuses to make down payments on a brownstone or co-op.

Many longtime residents hadn't quite wrapped their heads around these rapid changes. An older man interviewed for the New York magazine article while buying Rice Krispies at the Red Apple supermarket didn't understand why anyone would pay that kind of money to live on Broadway. "Didn't anyone tell these people it's a commercial street? If I had the money for a condo, I'd move to Florida," he said. Others did understand, but weren't happy about it. A middle-aged woman at a corner newsstand buying the next day's newspaper watched twenty-somethings drunkenly leaving the Caramba!, a newly opened bar. As she purchased her New York Times, she shouted, "Yuppies. Go home."

But these young people were home. And most local merchants did not feel doom and gloom about it initially. What's not to like about an influx of people living near your store that have a great deal of disposable income? It was good news to have so many people who could afford to eat in local restaurants and to spend their money in local shops. There was no end of what appliances these new customers might buy. Televisions, stereos, speakers, air conditioners, toasters, hair dryers—all were within their budget. But they were bad news in the long term because they pushed the rent prices way up. Real estate prices don't lie. First the rising rents came for the long-term residents. And if the higher rents were coming for the people who lived in the neighborhood, they were coming for the merchants too.

With the changing neighborhood demographics, the city started paying more attention to how the area looked. Dad noticed an immediate difference. After the Columbia was built, the emphasis on garbage collection increased, which was a huge pain for him. Not that he liked when the block was strewn with litter. But he liked being fined even less. City regulations had long required small businesses to pick up the trash outside their store, but it wasn't until the 1980s that Upper West Side businesses were regularly fined for not doing it. My dad had always tried to keep his part of the sidewalk clean. But now the city was enforcing the ordinance that he was responsible for 18-inches into the street from the store being kept litter free. He found this maddening because it was an impossible task. No small business had the manpower to have an employee go outside every hour to sweep and make sure no one dropped garbage on their 18 inches. But that didn't stop the city from issuing fines. Eventually the city agreed to only check between 11:00 a.m. and noon and then again between 4:00 and 5:00 pm., but it was still imperfect. If an ill-timed wind blew some garbage into the street in front of Radio Clinic at the wrong hour, the store might be fined.

As the neighborhood grew cleaner and safer, people with money continued to move in, driving up property values and rents. This process kept reinforcing itself until the rents became untenable. For commercial tenants, the content of their lease determined their fate. Landlords were now in a power position with their commercial tenants. They no longer wanted to enter into a 10-year lease with a commercial tenant, let alone a 20-year one. No one knew how much higher the rents would rise, and landlords did not want to lock themselves out of potentially frequent rent hikes. Merchants, even the ones that had paid their rent on a timely basis in the same location for decades, were powerless. One developer bought the Powelton building on 97th Street to convert the building to co-ops and wouldn't renew the lease for any commercial tenant. Even though the owner of the Army Navy Store was willing to pay a higher rent, the developer thought the store "...didn't give the building a good image."

A lease with many years remaining on it provided some protection, but surprisingly it was still no guarantee for business owners. Merchants were vulnerable if their lease had a demolition clause, allowing a landlord to sell a building to a developer, regardless of lease terms. Merchant after merchant had the same story to tell. Confronted with a sharp rent increase, they gambled and renewed their lease, figuring the new residents of luxury apartments would bring in enough revenue to cover the extra costs. These were merchants who had been in the neighborhood for the years when business was slow, and now they were optimistic enough about the future to invest money into their stores. To attract the wealthier people who lived in the Columbia and the Savannah they installed new floors, repainted their stores, and bought new awnings. But often, within a few months, their landlord sold the building to a developer who demolished it. For many other merchants, if there was not a demolition clause, the landlords just waited out the lease and then demolished the building. Small businesses were taking up increasingly valuable land, which could be converted into something far more lucrative. Many small businesses died in the gold mine that the Upper West Side had become.

But Radio Clinic was in a different position. Its landlord didn't sell the building. And with the store only five years into a 20-year lease, Dad wasn't going to need to renegotiate until 2000. While the escalating lease clause and the percentage of the property tax that he needed to pay were going up and causing concern, it was still manageable. The long lease gave my dad a buffer, and he went about the business of running his business. But he had a new type of competitor to contend with. Chain stores had moved into the neighborhood to take advantage of the growing number of young professionals. Two popular chain electronic stores, with reputations of being affordable, muscled their way into Radio Clinic's domain. Crazy Eddy was first to make its claim on the Upper West Side. With its non-stop advertising, the business aggressively proclaimed that its prices were so insane no other store could beat them. Jerry Carroll, a radio personality, played Crazy Eddy in the commercials to great effect. With his maniacal stare, he boomed, "We are not undersold. We cannot be undersold. And we mean it." People believed him.

A few years after Crazy Eddy paved the way on the Upper West Side, Nobody Beats the Wiz opened a store on 96th Street and Broadway. It was one of the commercial tenants that lined the ground floor of the Columbia apartments. Thanks in part to its ever-present commercials with an insidiously catchy jingle, everyone soon knew that when it came to low prices, nobody beat the Wiz. As a major sponsor of New York sports teams, with a commercial narrated by Joe Namath and a voiceover by Tiny Tim, this business had incredible name recognition.

Radio Clinic didn't have a popular shtick or catchy jingle. It's hard for a small business to contend with the power that a chain store brings to a competition. Today, both of these chain stores are long gone, one founder indicted for tax evasion and the other indicted for lender fraud and both bankrupt. But before their fall from grace, Crazy Eddy and Nobody Beats the Wiz sold a hell of a lot of appliances, made millions of dollars in profits, and were formidable competition for Radio Clinic. Nobody Beats the Wiz, just two blocks south, should have given Dad the most concern. But after watching his sales go up once Crazy Eddy opened, he wasn't concerned.

Dad was worried when Crazy Eddy first moved into the neighborhood. He knew Radio Clinic had a good reputation locally, but everyone wants a good deal. The one thing everyone knew about Crazy Eddy was that "his prices are insaaane." It didn't matter that it was false advertising. Radio Clinic couldn't counteract the blitz of Crazy Eddy advertising, and Dad saw Crazy Eddy's one store on 77th Street sell more air conditioners than the two Radio Clinic stores did combined. But Dad noticed something interesting; Radio Clinic's air conditioner sales went up as well. Later, when The Wiz opened on 96th Street, the same thing happened. The Wiz also sold more air conditioners than both Radio Clinic's stores combined, and still Radio Clinic air conditioner sales went up. Dad realized that for Radio Clinic, the addition of these stores was good for

Alan in Radio Clinic in the early 1980s

Jen and a highschool friend painting
Radio Clinic's gate in the early 1980s.

business since the Upper West Side had become a destination for air conditioner shopping. He knew Radio Clinic would not get the customers that believed the hype of Crazy Eddy and The Wiz. But anyone who took the time to price shop up and down the neighborhood would soon be Radio Clinic's customers.

Dad developed a winning sales strategy one day when a customer asked him if Radio Clinic would match The Wiz's price. He essentially said, no, let a dramatic pause build, and then said he would not raise his prices just to match The Wiz. The customer, believing the jingle, asked him what he meant. My dad told him that Radio Clinic's prices are lower, and he didn't plan to raise them. When the customer didn't believe him, Dad suggested that the customer walk the two blocks and compare the prices himself. He figured the customer was going to leave the store anyhow, so he might as well acknowledge it and try to use it for his advantage. The customer came back ten minutes later and agreed that The Wiz was $30 higher and bought the air conditioner from Radio Clinic.

This became the Radio Clinic's technique: use Nobody Beats the Wiz as a showroom. Salesmen would tell a potential customer just that, visit their showroom on 96th Street, find what they liked, and then come back to Radio Clinic to buy it for less money with the bonus of better customer service. Radio Clinic was never the very successful business that The Wiz was at the time, with profits over a billion dollars and more than 94 stores. But that doesn't change the fact that on any given day in the mid 1980s, when hot and sweaty New Yorkers were looking to buy air conditioners on the Upper West Side, Radio clinic did, in fact, on occasion, beat The Wiz.

Dad may have found a way to coexist in the same neighborhood as these two chains, but there was no denying that time was not on the side of the small merchant. With their deep pockets, chain stores could contend with rising rents. Whether a business was robust or fragile, innovative or stodgy, its success still depended largely on its lease. High rents were bearing down on merchants and outside their control. New York City small businesses were starting to be uncomfortably squeezed. A merchant can prepare for a dip in the economy, slow months, chain store competition or fickle consumer trends. But a cushion can only do so much to soften a blow. A cushion cannot absorb a 100 percent and climbing increase in rent. It can't protect a business when its building is being demolished. Even with his relative security, Dad recognized this as a losing business model. He might have been successful with his creative approach to the neighborhood chain electronic stores, but what would that matter when he was no longer able to cover his monthly expenses? It was becoming increasingly evident that at some point each small business would hit a rent threshold it couldn't cross. For some it was immediate. For others, it took years. Either way, the leases were ticking time bombs.

My dad knew it was just a matter of time until he was in the same position as the owner of Golden's Stationery located on 96th Street. This store had two years left on its lease, and the owner knew he wouldn't be able to afford a new lease because he couldn't substantially raise his prices on stationery store goods. "There is only so much anyone will pay for an envelope," the owner told a reporter. "I can't start charging $2.99 for scotch tape when everyone else sells it for $2.49. I planned that this would be a nice retirement for me. It's a family business. I've put in 30 years. I'm 59 years old. It's all worth zero now, zero." When the fixed costs of rents are higher than even a reasonably profitable business can handle, that business is ultimately doomed. A merchant can't triple his prices and expect to retain customers. But there wasn't anything to do about it. New York City landlords weren't doing anything illegal. You could follow the lease all you want; it wouldn't get you anywhere illegal.

New York magazine interviewed Dad for another story on the Upper West Side. He once again beat the drum that it was ultimately bad for the city to lose its longtime small businesses.

> Because all the leases now are short ones, the merchant can no longer plan for growth in his business. It isn't just the marginal businesses that are going under, either. Good strong businesses are folding. These places can absorb a certain amount of rent increase, but they can't go from $2,000 to $10,000. And if an RCI that's been around 50 years disappears from your

neighborhood, some chain comes in. If it's at all uneconomical, they'll pull out. Whereas a business that only has one, two stores, they'll stay during the tough times. In the '77 blackout, our 98th Street store was looted and damaged. I could have collected my insurance, got out, and done quite well. But I stayed.

It was around this time that my dad joined then-Councilwoman Ruth Messinger's Small Business Rent Stabilization committee. In the 1980s Messinger was contacted regularly by area small businesses and their customers worried about the shops that were being forced out by rent increases. Real estate developers were buying up land on the Upper West Side to build luxury apartment towers. Messinger and her chief of staff, Gail Brewer, knew that "real estate pressure had put the neighborhood under siege" and were concerned that neighborhood businesses would continue to close unless there was some regulation put on commercial rents. They were concerned for the merchants, who often invested all they had in the business, and for the residents, who would be deprived of needed goods and services. It was getting harder and harder to find repair shops and stores that sold practical things.

They drafted the Small Business Preservation Act (SBPA) to set guidelines on rents for stores 10,000 square feet or less. The act basically built in a legislative recourse for when a longstanding store's rent was going to increase by more than 25 percent. An impartial third party, the arbitrator, would look at the landlord's costs and balance that with a fair rent for the merchant and the needs of the neighborhood. In my grandfather's day, a landlord and tenant would meet when a lease was about to expire, and bargain in good faith to arrive at lease terms that allowed both parties an acceptable profit. The committee envisioned that an arbitrator would recognize the need for an increase on the part of the landlord but wouldn't allow for rent gouging.

Dad was an early supporter of this bill; he thought it offered a mechanism that added fairness to the process. To him, the bill placed the landlord and the merchant on somewhat equal footing. My dad, who never met a baseball analogy he didn't like, explained it to me this way:

> We wanted to approach landlords with something that is palatable to them but also gives us a chance to survive. At that time arbitration was big in baseball. Each side makes their best offer and the arbitrator chooses which offer they want. Both sides have an incentive to compromise because you would get nothing if the arbitrator didn't choose your offer. The idea of SBPA was to put pressure on each side to compromise. The hope was that merchants would be realistic and say to the landlord 'look, I can go this far. I can pay this high a rent'. Then the landlord would say 'I can live with this.'

I only vaguely knew about Dad's involvement in the push for commercial rent stabilization, while it was happening I was in college and not paying close attention to my parents' lives or Radio Clinic. At college, I was busy running cross country and track, trying to figure out how to flirt, and taking as many sociology courses as my liberal arts college would let me. The more sociology courses I took in college, the more suspicious I became about whether there truly was equality of opportunity for everyone in the United States. And I wasn't so sure capitalism was such a great thing, with its demand for winners and losers. By the sheer fact that it existed and was a business, I would have placed Radio Clinic in the winners' category. Not being a fan of nuance at the time, I didn't differentiate between types of businesses nor pay attention to policy favoring big business at the expense of small business. If I had been a fan of nuance I would have understand that it was no accident that small businesses were beginning to close throughout New York City. That through tax advantages, selective enforcement of regulations and other mechanisms, federal and city policy intentionally made it possible for large businesses to dominate their markets and crush the mom and pops. Had I taken more than a cursory interest in my dad's life, I would have been proud that he was standing up to the Chamber of Commerce, one of the most powerful corporate special interest groups in the country.

Today, I have no problem being involved with lost causes that go against the grain of our free market economy. I believe in the bumper sticker that I placed on my first car, that "housing should be a right and not a privilege." When I was single, Dad once asked me if I would refuse to date someone just because he had a lot of money. He was happy to hear that I would not. My dad was and is more mainstream in his politics than I am. When describing the committee to me in further detail he said there were:

> typical liberals on the committee. I mean I am a liberal, but not a typical one, because I look at both sides. They wanted to screw the landlord and all this kind of crap. I said that is ridiculous. The landlord has a right to earn on his investment. He can do whatever he wants with his property. Our problem is that landlords are putting us out without any real recourse to be able to afford it and jeopardizing long standing businesses.

I wasn't exactly sure where Dad thought the common ground was here. Either a landlord could do whatever he wants with his property, or he couldn't. Either the city put regulations on what a landlord could charge, or it didn't. These were two inherently different worldviews. Yet Dad held them both. If he were forced to define himself ideologically, I am sure Dad would choose pragmatist. In many of the conversations we had since I attended college, he has emphasized that he is more interested in practice than theory. He makes decisions based on what is useful. In theory, he understood that a landlord has a right to charge whatever rent he or she wanted. But in practice, landlords were killing small businesses and that was not an ok outcome. Surely that was obvious to everyone involved. As a businessman and the son of an immigrant who started the business, he didn't have a problem with our economic system. But it was Bonfire of the Vanities in New York City, and he did have a problem with greed becoming a business virtue. He was just trying to make capitalism reasonable.

I interviewed both Ruth Messinger and Gail Brewer, more than twenty-five years after their fight for commercial rent stabilization. Messinger had represented the West Side on the city council, became Manhattan Borough President, and was then the CEO of American Jewish World Service. Brewer had been Messinger's chief of staff and had later become Manhattan Borough President. Messinger shared many details about the organizing around the Small Business Preservation Act. She told me that she knew that SBPA, which first went before city council in 1984, would be defeated. Once a bill was defeated you can't have a hearing, and she wanted a hearing to give people a chance to testify. So, she never called for the vote. She wanted people from the West Side and other neighborhoods who were experiencing the same pressures to come and speak.

> I became known for having this legislative platform which made me less popular with people with money. I love the small business people. I loved your Dad. But I knew reasonably early on that the legislation is not going to pass. The question is, can we keep highlighting the problem in ways that will allow magazine writers to do stories, and more thoughtful urban planners and sociologists to join the fight?

While this publicity might have had an impact on the people who lived in the city, it did not have an impact on the mayor. Mayor Koch consistently opposed any effort to enact commercial rent control. Messinger set up public hearings to push the city to grapple with this issue in 1984 and 1985. There were many public hearings where people came to vocalize their support or opposition to the bill. Passions ran high at these hearings, with some referring to the bill as the "anti-landlord greed act" and others declaring the act a "poisonous disincentive to investment in the city."

At the time of the rent stabilization hearings, Dad was a member of the West Side Chamber of Commerce. He had joined the Chamber a few months after the blackout in his efforts to be more involved in the community and thought an association of business owners was a good fit for him. When the president of the chamber learned Dad was on the Rent Stabilization Preservation Committee, he was initially upset with my dad for working with Messinger, but he quickly tried to enlist his support. He wanted Dad to spy on "Red Ruthie" and report back to the chamber what she had planned for the bill. Realizing that the local chamber was more aligned with real estate and bigger business interests, Dad became disillusioned with it. By actively opposing the bill, the chamber showed it wasn't concerned with the needs of the mom and pop type businesses, so Dad ended his membership with them.

Members of the West Side Chamber of Commerce turned out for hearings, in opposition to commercial rent stabilization. Philip Rudd, a member of a property-owners' organization and the chairman of the West Side Chamber, was a vocal critic of the bill. An exchange between him and the owner of Community Bookstore, a Brooklyn Heights shop, encapsulated the larger debate. The bookstore owner described that his rent was $1,300 and he had offered to pay his landlord $2,600 when the lease expired. The landlord refused to renew the lease since an ice cream entrepreneur had agreed to pay more. Rudd said, "It's not my job to give you a subsidy in the form of rent so you can stay in business. Maybe your neighborhood needs an ice cream chain more than it needs a bookstore. If people don't want an ice cream store, then they won't buy ice cream, and then the store will become vacant." The bookstore owner asked: "Then what will happen to me?" "That's your problem," Rudd replied. He went on to say, "The first thing a retailer learns in a business course is how to negotiate a lease. Rent, as a retailer, is the least important thing you have to deal with if you are doing a good business. If you're not doing good business, it's the most important thing - and it's impossible." The storeowners at the hearing took exception with Mr. Rudd's statement. "It doesn't mean a thing to know how to negotiate a lease," one man said, "if nobody is going to negotiate."

Mr. Rudd, one of the biggest property owners on Amsterdam Avenue (the avenue directly parallel to Broadway), typified why my dad became disillusioned with the West Side Chamber. Rudd believed that to be successful merchants only needed "...to meet the community need." Yet on Amsterdam Avenue, as with Broadway, merchants with needed services (the locksmith, exterminator, and shoe repair) stores were being replaced by a revolving door of boutiques. In 1980, comprising more than 20 percent of the Upper West Side, more than 41,000 Latino residents lived between 59th to 100th Street. The tenements on Amsterdam Avenue were the most heavily populated with Puerto Ricans. Yet the Latino-owned bodegas, beauty parlors and carnicerias were vanishing and being replaced by trendy boutiques, that mostly went under after a year or two.

Dad attended and spoke at many of the hearings in 1984 and 1985. Being involved in this effort was a perfect fit for him. He wanted to see the bill passed and was hopeful in 1985 that election-year politics might help that happen. Mayor Koch was running for another term with one challenger from the left,

Carol Bellamy, and one from the right, Diane McGrath. If Bellamy won, city hall might get a whole lot friendlier to the idea of rent stabilization, which was a topic during the mayoral campaign. Koch created the Small Businesses Retail Commission to officially study the issue. His opponents believed he only created this commission to neutralize concern about rising commercial rents.

All sorts of groups weighed in during the campaign. The Coalition for Small Business Preservation had thousands of members involved with merchant associations, community groups, trade unions, churches, and block associations. They knocked on doors and attended hearings. More than 15,000 petitions, postcards, and letters were sent to city officials from merchants and community members wanting protection for the small businesses. But they squared off against the Real Estate associations that spend millions of dollars to lobby for their interests. While part of the West Side Chamber, Dad sat in many meetings with real estate developers, including Donald Trump, who had purchased 76 acres of land on the Upper West Side and intended to develop luxury apartments. When he asked these developers if they planned to set the rent levels for their commercial space, at a rate local small businesses could afford, they made vague assurances. But together the real estate developers poured a lot of money into their campaign to stop commercial rent stabilization.

The Greater New York Real Estate Board wanted Koch to be reelected and weighed in. The board shared Dad's assessment that escalating rents were hurting small merchants. Where they differed was that the board didn't think anything should be done about the problem. Dad was standing in the back at one of the hearings, talking to two guys from the Real Estate Board. He wanted to hear what they thought about the bill and let them know why he thought the bill was fair. In his mind, they were having a productive conversation. They told him that, while they were not in favor of the plan, it might be workable. Just then, as if they were in a movie, a man walked over to the two men and whispered in their ears. They turned to my dad and told him that the polling suggested Koch was going to win a third term so they didn't need to stay and "listen to this crap." Dad watched them walk out of the hearing. "It's a shame," he told me, "The idea was workable. It was fair. But that was the end of it."

After Koch's reelection, the commission issued its findings. Similarly to the Real Estate Board, the majority of the commission acknowledged that rents were a problem but felt confident in the free market and opposed any rent controls. The dissenters on the commission, though ineffectual, argued that there was too big "a distortion in bargaining between landlord and tenants," a "public emergency exists," and the city needed to get involved.

In a 1987 editorial, the *New York Times* agreed with Mayor Koch and described why restrictions on the free market would be worse than any benefit. "On what basis," the editorialist wanted to know, "would arbitrators decide whether it is better to keep an existing shoe store, say, in business, rather than allowing a bakery to take over the space? The market is surely the most effective mechanism for determining whether a neighborhood's residents want a Chinese laundry or a French wine store." This was a common argument, that government regulation strips individuals of free choice. In fact neighborhood residents did want a Chinese laundry and a French wine store and a bakery and a repair shop. But ultimately none of these could afford to stay in the neighborhood.

The businesses continued to close—stores that had been on Broadway for more than half a century and stores that opened just five years earlier. Repair shops, restaurants, clothing stores, and bookstores. Popular stores that were successful businesses, and stores that never gained traction in the neighborhood. Gone. There was story after story of good businesses going out of business in the 1980s. It wasn't a question of poor sales or changing markets or unprepared merchants. It was a question of sky-high rents and building demolitions. And the city wasn't willing to do anything about it.

Many people are uncomfortable with the notion that our government might tell landlords what they can and cannot charge for commercial rent. This seems like a handout to a small business at the expense of the landlord, who is also running a business. The thinking is that either a small business can compete in the market it occupies or it can't, but city hall doesn't need to get involved. Critics who are philosophically opposed to government regulation are impatient with stories about the demise of a beloved store or restaurant. Surely economic decisions should not be dictated by nostalgia. The fact that neighbors have affection for a business, or that it's an integral part of the community isn't relevant to these critics. No business has an inalienable right to exist. You can't freeze time.

These critics will say a shuttered store must not have been a good fit for a changing neighborhood. That neighborhood values and preferences are expressed through the businesses that thrive. Or a strong business doesn't need government support to prop it up. But in the 1980s, the Upper West Side was littered with successful small business that weren't successful enough to handle the rent increases. These were businesses like Radio Clinic that met the needs of their neighborhood and were satisfied with their one or two stores. They were businesses that provided a valued service, sold sought-after merchandise, paid their small staff a decent salary, and turned a modest profit. They didn't need to grow into a multi-chain store or be bought out by a multinational corporation to be a success. But increasingly that was needed to survive the rents on the Upper West Side.

What happened with Upper West Side small businesses was a bellwether of what was to come across the country. The demise of the small business reflects a crisis of our time that has reverberated through cities and small towns alike.

People having no meaningful say in the fate of their communities. Neighborhood residents could knock on doors, attend rallies, organize hearings and rabble-rouse all they wanted; the rents weren't coming down.

"Of course we didn't win," said Gail Brewer when I talked to her about the fight for commercial rent stabilization. "But we had rallies, hundreds of them. We fought like crazy on the issue of our small businesses. We spent almost 10 years fighting for this issue but we knew it wouldn't pass. It couldn't pass. We couldn't get enough votes because the real estate industry had a fit. The real estate industry of New York is the answer. It is always the answer."

12

Air Conditioners

Hot town, summer in the city. Back of my neck getting dirty and gritty. Been down, isn't it a pity. Doesn't seem to be a shadow in the city.

—Lovin' Spoonful

THE ELDERLY WOMEN WHO stopped by my office couldn't decide if my being too skinny was the problem or that I didn't make enough of an effort with my face was the problem. Each had a theory about why I was single and how to help me. I had just graduated college and got a job working at Victim Services Agency (VSA), a large agency with small community offices scattered throughout the boroughs. My office was on 72nd Street between Columbus Avenue and Broadway, with our service area extending from West 72nd Street to West 110th Street. Both Radio Clinic stores were in this service area. Any victim of crime in our area could, and it sure seemed like they did, stop by VSA for assistance.

Each office had a director, senior counselor, junior counselor and administrative assistant. I was the junior counselor. Within two weeks of my first day the director left for a different job. By six weeks, the paperwork for the transfer to a Brooklyn office that the senior counselor requested months ago was completed and she too was gone. The administrative assistant, recognizing both my naiveté and an opportunity, taught me incorrectly how to log in the petty cash so she could funnel some of it to support her cocaine habit and took increasingly longer lunch breaks. It was just a bonus that it later looked like I stole the money. I was young, inexperienced, alone in the office for half of each day and out of my depth.

My office was on the fourth floor of a fairly nondescript building near Tip Top Shoes and Éclair bakery. The interior was run down and the hallways were dark. There was no pleasant way to get to my office on the fourth floor. Either I could take the stairwell, where it was not uncommon to find someone sleeping in the urine-stained stairwell. Or I could take the elevator. Generally, I like to take elevators, I hadn't fully lost the thrill I felt as a kid pushing those buttons, but this one made me nervous. Mounted on the wall of each elevator was a list of when it was last serviced and who serviced it. As I listened to the elevator cables loudly grind their way up and down, I kept glancing at the notification telling me that this elevator hadn't been serviced for over a year.

My days mostly alone in the office were intimidating because a steady stream of desperate people knocked on the door each day, hoping to convince me to part with some petty cash. The same petty cash that the administrative assistant siphoned out of the petty cash drawer to support her lunch-time drug habit. The crack epidemic had hit the Upper West Side hard by 1988 and there were a lot of people in urgent need of money to buy three-dollar vials of crack. I told one of the managers from the downtown office about my situation and once a week another director stopped by to theoretically keep an eye on things. It wasn't much of an improvement for me since he spent most of his limited time in the office trying to press up against my body. Not sure how to handle this situation, I considered asking my parents for advice, but I was worried they would pressure me to quit this low-paying job. Without a job, I might take the path of least resistance and work at Radio Clinic. I already was living with my parents in the two-bedroom apartment they moved to on 92nd Street, since they only charged me $100 for rent, allowing me to save money to eventually move out. Both living and working with my parents did not bode well for the new independent young adult life I hoped to live, so I said nothing and stayed at VSA.

Many of these elderly Jewish women were customers of Radio Clinic and knew my dad and/or my grandpa. For elderly women, purse snatching was commonplace on the Upper West Side in the 1980s and VSA was the place to go to fill out a crime victimization reimbursement form. Those that thought I was too skinny would return with rugelach and other baked goods. Those that thought I needed to make more of an effort with my appearance would bring me their half-used perfume and lipstick tubes. I shared their collective concern that I was single, since I never did master the art of flirting, but mainly wanted to encourage their visits so I wouldn't be alone in the office. So, after the paperwork was completed I would do my best to keep them talking and settle in for a visit.

Each day I walked the 20 blocks from my parent's apartment to VSA and then back through this neighborhood of contrasts. The impact of gentrification and displacement was on full display. On Columbus Avenue, I tracked the progress of Poiret, a new French bistro, as artists put up a mosaic on its outside wall, and the vacant storefronts were replaced by a revolving door of boutiques. On Amsterdam Avenue, I walked by Popover Restaurant with its strawberry butter and also by bodegas with young men smoking outside the doorway while people left the store with their lottery numbers. On Broadway, I saw professional women heading to work wearing their color-coordinated dress suits and running sneakers, giving wide berth to the people who were homeless sleeping on park benches.

Dad and I would sometimes meet for lunch on 72nd Street, get a hotdog from Gray's Papaya, and sit on a nearby bench. As we ate, we swapped crime stories. Radio Clinic had been contending with petty theft, probably since the day it first opened. Warding off theft was a daily challenge for small businesses; my one-year of VSA stories were no match for his. Radio Clinic's delivery guys couldn't leave merchandise unattended for even a second when unloading a truck. Someone would try to steal any small appliance that wasn't tied down. Teenagers stole six dollar packs of batteries and sold them on the street for 50 cents. Dad's favorite was a woman dressed entirely in black, who slithered silently across the floor with a wire cutter, hoping to stay out of anyone's line of vision as she tried to free a radio and slide back out unnoticed.

While I was working at VSA, Josh started working for Franz Leichter, a New York State Senator. Each summer during college he had worked at Radio Clinic six days a week and occasionally, while he was looking for a job, after college. From these summers at the store, it was clear to my brother that he didn't want to have a career in the business. He saw how hard our dad worked, how nonstop the stress was, plus he found the work limiting. This was never a problem for Dad, he wanted his kids to find the work they liked to do. Maybe it would eventually lead us back to Radio Clinic, but he knew most likely it wouldn't. Josh enjoyed working for Leichter, a senator consistently willing to take on New York City's banking and real estate industries. This was good news for Dad, since he was happy to have a direct line to someone who worked for a state senator. Dad brings his small business mentality with him wherever he goes. He was always looking to find the person who might be able to help him with X headache or help him resolve Y situation, and now my brother knew some of the useful people. Once he was fully settled in Leichter's office, Dad started calling Josh for advice, a practice that continued for the next two decades.

Radio Clinic was eight years into its 20-year lease. For a healthy business, according to Dad, rent should be no more than five percent of your gross margin. Not five percent of total money a business takes in, but the percentage of the money that is left over once the cost of goods is deducted. In other words, if Radio Clinic purchased air conditioners from a supplier at $70 a unit and sold them for $100 the gross margin for each air conditioner was $30. When Dad joined the business in 1966, the rent was one percent of the gross margin. After the 1980 lease renewal, it went up to two percent. But by 1988, even though the long lease provided Radio Clinic a buffer from the steepest rent increases, the escalator clause and paying a percentage of the property tax was starting to make an impact. Radio Clinic was feeling the pinch.

When costs go up, a merchant needs to look at the store's expenses and adjust. Dad reconsidered the store's hours of operation, merchandise, and staffing. Radio Clinic was then opened seven days a week. And he started to phase out small appliances. In the past, Dad had relied on a good Christmas season of small appliances sales to provide a winter cash infusion to get the store through to the following air conditioning season. But small appliances were becoming less profitable. Selling the Sony Walkman did not pay the bills. For the 83rd Street store, this was in part because Zabar's was too strong a competitor. Zabar's had much greater buying power, so other than the occasional blip, Radio Clinic couldn't sell its toasters and food processors at as low a price as Zabar's. At the 98th Street store, the chains caused problems. In general, customers preferred Radio Clinic to the chains for appliances that required good customer service and expertise, such as stereo systems and refrigerators, but not for the smaller items. Chain stores could afford to have a large selection for everything they sold. They might have 20 different types of Boomboxes to choose from while Radio Clinic might only have four. By not having as deep a selection, Radio Clinic didn't look as attractive for these small appliances.

Not only was the store being outperformed with its small appliances, selling them was increasingly not a good use of time. Selling a small appliance could take just as long as selling a large one. And Radio Clinic just didn't make that much money on these items. A salesman might spend fifteen minutes selling someone a 15 dollar Walkman, earning the store maybe six dollars on the sale. In the same amount of time a salesman could earn triple the money on a larger appliance. Dad also phased out stereos since too many stores now specialized in them and he couldn't buy merchandise at a large enough volume to sell competitively. He even started phasing out color televisions, although it was hard to convince the salesmen it was a good idea. Televisions were about five percent of the total volume, and the store made roughly 15 percent profit on each sale. But once he factored in the staff time needed to make a sale, the unpaid support time, delivery, and installation time, Dad realized the cost of doing business for televisions was too high.

Merchandise changes in a longstanding business were not unique to Radio Clinic. The many drugstores that lined upper Broadway in 1934 and the block-long Duane Reade's of today all sell pharmaceuticals, but that is where the similarity ends. The soda fountain where Grandpa made malts has been replaced with the self-service carbonated fountain soda and Slurpee machines. With rare exception, either a store kept up with the rapidly shifting consumer interests and updated its merchandise, or the store closed. Any product that starts out popular can wind up in the dustbin of history. Nothing is immune. Think 78 rpm records. Think Sony Walkman. Nedicks, a very popular corner stand restaurant chain where generations of New York City kids bought a hotdog and orange drink for 10 cents, couldn't compete with McDonald's and Blimpies and they closed the 98th Street branch in 1981. Robert Payne Furs, whose owner was a longtime customer of Radio Clinic, was the last neighborhood furrier to relocate to the fur district on 30th Street in 1990.

As Radio Clinic phased out its small appliances, the larger ones became more important. And none were as important as the air conditioner. Air conditioners had been a valuable product for decades, but now they were the linchpin to the health of the business, accounting for one third of the appliances sold. Radio Clinic's good warehouse space had become even better during the 1980s, allowing my dad to store an even greater number of air conditioners. Then, thanks in part to a long story involving litigious residential tenants in the building, Dad was able to absorb even more of the basement until by 1990 Radio Clinic had half a block of warehouse space.

With this additional space, Radio Clinic stored as many as 800 air conditioner units during the winter. It was a great way to monetize air conditioners even if it wasn't a hot summer. Dad charged customers $170 to pick up the unit from their home, clean it, store it, and deliver it back and reinstall it before the start of summer. Factoring out the cost of doing that work, the business made $100 a unit and netted as much as $80,000 a year. Customers could also hire Radio Clinic to do a "steam clean" of their air conditioners, which didn't cost the business too much in terms of labor. Essentially they just sprayed hot water out of a hose to clean the dust off the cooling coils in the air conditioners.

Air conditioners. The neighborhood had an endless number of people who needed to buy one. But it was not for the faint of heart to rely heavily on an appliance that needed hot weather conditions to be in demand. A really great air conditioning season between May and August could earn Radio Clinic as much $1.3 million. But a cool summer, or even a summer that didn't get hot until August, was going to be a disappointing summer. Sales could be less than $700,000 those summers.

Dad did what he could to mitigate the outsized influence weather conditions had on his business. He and Mike worked their considerable connections to get a better deal than other merchants on air conditioners. These connections were invaluable. While researching this book, I spent one day in the microfiche room of the New York City public library, reading the phone book listings from 1934 until 1993. Tracking the stores between 80th Street and 100th Street on

Broadway, I could see when long-standing businesses closed. The closer I got to 1993, Radio Clinic was among only a handful of long standing businesses that remained. Part of its staying power was the 20-year lease agreement. But another factor in its staying power was Dad's ability to build connections with people and his skill in working those connections.

These connections didn't provide a direct line to the sun to force a heat-wave on the city, but they did give Radio Clinic a leg up with their competition. Dad was friendly with a guy who was a distributor for Fedders, a large air conditioner manufacturer. This guy had a lot of "scratch and dent" units, air conditioners that were sent back because they had scratches, needed repair work, or were damaged in some way. Scratch and dents were popular because the functioning of the air conditioner wasn't damaged; it just didn't look good. Or new. So they had to be sold at a discount. Fedders didn't want to deal with selling these damaged units so it turned the merchandise over to an independent distributor to deal with it. During the 1990s, Radio Clinic would buy thousands of slightly damaged air conditioners each year for a fraction of their cost and sell them for a sizable profit.

One summer Radio Clinic had an unusually good opportunity to buy a large number of scratch and dents right before the air conditioning season started. It was shaping up to be a hot summer and Dad knew Radio Clinic would sell out the units in 6-8 weeks. The trouble was he needed to finance the $10,000 worth of air conditioners up front, and Radio Clinic didn't have that money. The business had no reserve to pull from. So, Dad and Mike went to Citibank to try to get a loan. Citibank turned them down, saying they were not in the business of financing risk capital. Dad suggested to the loan officer that if he thought this was a risk he didn't understand small businesses, but he knew further discussion would be fruitless. But Mike knew a guy who knew a guy who made short-term loans. The condition was they needed to pay back the loan in one month or incur steep interest payments. Taking this loan was only a good idea if the weather for the next four weeks was as hot as projected. If the air conditioners didn't sell as expected, they would owe a lot of money and start the winter months in a deep hole. It was a risk, but Dad took it. The weather cooperated and the risk payed off. This time. But Dad knew that always owing other people money was no way to live. He couldn't get the loan he wanted from a bank. Loans from outside the bank came with too much risk. But there was one person he knew who was willing to provide an interest-free loan: himself. This was the third part of Radio Clinic's staying power, Dad's willingness to invest personal savings into the business

Air conditioners helped me earn some extra money the year I lived with my parents. I was saving up money to eventually move out and wanted to supplement my salary. So, Dad paid me whatever the minimum wage was at time to track down a sales slip for every energy efficient air conditioner Radio Clinic sold in the last few years. It was an easy yet painstaking job. Radio Clinic sold thousands of air conditioners each summer. Some of them were energy efficient models. I had a list of each model number that was energy efficient, and I needed to cross-check the thousands of sales slips against this list. He showed me how to do the paperwork and then left me to it. It was air conditioner season, and he was busy. Deciphering the sloppy handwriting on each sales slip was the hardest part of the job. I filled out the requisite paper work, and Dad sent the paperwork to the State of New York.

I did some of this paperwork at our kitchen table, but mostly on Saturdays I sat at Dad's desk in the back office of the store. Usually I avoided the back office other than to take the sailor staircase down to the warehouse or to use the store's sole bathroom. The office was filled with three or four large metal desks, file cabinets, risqué jokes thumbtacked to the walls, piles of paperwork, and overflowing garbage cans; clearly, it wasn't in anyone's job description to clean the office. With no windows or decorative touches, it was not a very attractive place to spend time. But it was lively in the back room. Salesmen hustling to look up an invoice in a file cabinet to answer a question for a waiting customer. Delivery guys emerging from the warehouse or returning to the warehouse after a delivery run. Suppliers trying to convince Dad to try out a new product. The soundtrack was the constant clicking of nails against hard plastic as the book-keeper, with her very long and artfully done nails, ran numbers on the accounting machine.

The receipts I was tracking were to use in a New York State incentive program with the aim of lowering energy consumption. Con Edison was running out of capacity and wanted to avoid building a new power plant. Since this would cost taxpayers a great deal of money, the state wanted to avoid this too. Taking a different approach, the state put money into an incentive program to encourage consumers to use less energy. Every energy efficient air conditioner Radio Clinic sold equaled a certain number of points. These points had a great deal of practical value since they could be used to buy merchandise from a catalogue or for travel. During a hot summer the points could pile up pretty quickly.

The fact that these points came indirectly as a result of the blackout was satisfying to Dad. It still annoyed him that the New York State Public Service Commission hadn't pushed Con Edison to invest in its infrastructure or put safeguards in place that might have prevented the cascading system collapse in 1977. Government agencies had no end of regulations it required of its small businesses. Yet unlike large corporations, Dad and other small merchants couldn't convince their regulators to let them fix problems on their own—without government interference. The city continually sent inspectors to Radio Clinic to check if municipal regulations were being upheld and didn't hesitate to issue a fine if the business was in violation. These energy-efficiency points felt a little bit like karma.

While I was happy to do this project on the side, I didn't want to work full time at Radio Clinic. I still worked at Victim Services Agency and after about six months the situation in the office improved when more counselors were assigned to the 72nd Street community office. I could now start doing community outreach, which I liked better. While plenty of people came into the office wanting to submit a claim to the state victim compensation board to get reimbursed for new eye glasses or new apartment keys, I knew plenty others didn't know this compensation board existed. This seemed like a problem that could be fixed if I just went outside and talked to people in the neighborhood. Knowing how useful local merchants can be, I went to all the neighborhood stores that sold eyeglasses, hardware stores and locksmith that made new keys, and asked them to share information about the compensation board with their customers. The merchants were happy to post a flyer by their cash register or give one to each person replacing a stolen item.

After more than a year working at VSA, I moved to the Midwest. I wanted to find my adult footing outside the watchful gaze of family and decided to go to graduate school. Because I enjoyed community outreach work I applied to the University of Michigan's School of Social Work which had a community organization emphasis. Several of Michigan's faculty began their careers active in the civil rights movement and I was excited to learn from them. I figured I would be back in New York City in a few years.

My parents rented a minivan for the move and we needed to figure out how to fit several large pieces of furniture and most of my possessions into a not very big space. Early on the morning we left, Dad lined everything up on the 92nd Street sidewalk next to the van and considered his best approach for the task. People walking by stopped to offer him advice on how to get everything in the car. The consensus seemed to be that he would never make it all fit. I was ready to leave a chair or bookcase behind. But Dad did not agree. Bystanders offered their advice: leave behind the chair or the bedside table or the air conditioner. Using his tape measure, bungee cords and rope, Dad methodically fit things in the car. Sketches on paper were involved. By the time he was done every last inch of the van had been used and everything that had been on the sidewalk was now in the car. The crowd of people that gathered to watch his progress broke into applause. We left New York City on a high note.

I enjoy a good road trip. I like being in the car removed from the demands of daily life. I like stopping at gas stations and loading up on soda, pretzels and chocolate. And I like the level of intimacy being in such close proximity to another person can bring for the endless hours of travel. Dad had to remove all the back seats from the van to get everything to fit, so there wasn't room for my mom in the car. We had ten hours of driving between here and there with nothing to do other than talk, listen to good music and nap. Cellphones hadn't been invented yet so he couldn't check in to see how things were going back at the store. It was a fun trip and it would be more than 15 years before I saw him this relaxed again.

13

The Time Bomb

Thus it goes in this great town—sections changing so rapidly that the New York of one generation remains little more than a memory to the next.

—Real Estate record and Builder's Guide, 1924

AFTER **GRADUATING FROM THE** University of Michigan School of Social Work, I visited my folks in New York City during a five-day heatwave. Customers were so desperate for air conditions they lined up and down the block of Radio Clinic. Initially people weren't so orderly and tried to push their way into the crowded store. Trying to control the flow of people to prevent hostility, my dad locked the door. He allowed older people and pregnant women into the air-conditioned store, asked the others to form a line and then let people enter in little bunches. My job was to do runs between the closest bodega and Radio Clinic to bring cold sodas and juices to the sweaty people in line waiting for their turn to enter the store. An uncomfortably hot June was Radio Clinic's sweet spot and Dad was in a great mood. A couple of hot June days with lines down the block and my dad could almost forget Radio Clinic's troubles.

I couldn't decide if I should move back to the city or stay in Ann Arbor for a few more years. I interned at the Housing Law Reform Project while in graduate school and made some connections that I thought might help me get a job. But at the moment I didn't have one. An obvious choice would have been to come back and join the family business, but I never seriously considered

People lined up to buy air conditioners during a 1993 heat wave.

it. People asked my brother all the time if he planned to do what our dad did all those decades ago, and join the family business. But he wasn't interested. I liked the idea of being part of a neighborhood fixture, but I had no interest in being responsible for anyone's salary, having to deal with cash flow and budgets. Owning the store no longer looked like a pleasant way to spend your days, I could see how tied to the store Dad was and how tired he looked each night. Plus, I could see all the "lost our lease" signs taped onto storefront windows in businesses on every block of the neighborhood. I stayed in Ann Arbor.

As the rents continued to rise, the small stores continued to close. Ed Koch was no longer mayor, but the city's guiding principle for small businesses remained that the free market would determine what businesses remained open. It was increasingly clear that one thing the market couldn't bear was small businesses. Dad remained optimistic about Radio Clinic and its potential, but that didn't change the fact that in slow months he had trouble paying the bills. His optimism for himself and people that he loves has always been a curiosity to me. Warranted or not, it was ever present. He never doubted I would figure out algebra and pass my various math classes or that I would have a boyfriend one day, even when there was ample evidence to the contrary. He never doubted that my young teenage son would evolve out of a difficult phase and want to reconnect once he did. But the evidence to the contrary was growing for Radio Clinic. When money was tight he didn't take a paycheck. The following year, a particularly chilly early summer, set the store back considerably since air conditioner sales were low. Without a surplus of cash from air conditioner sales, he couldn't pay all his winter bills. So he went to his new source for loans and issued himself one. He borrowed money from his and Mom's personal savings. Just to get the store over the hump. But the hump kept moving. As the 1990s ticked by, it became more common for Dad to have insufficient cash flow in the months before the summer. Each time he was sure that just one more infusion of money from his personal savings would do the trick and carry the store into the next summer. He hoped that this summer would be a hot one and make up for the deficit.

Mom did not share this confidence. And this put her in tough spot. It was hard for her to have a productive conversation about the wisdom of investing in Radio Clinic since Dad couldn't really separate himself from the store. Not letting him invest their savings in the business meant the business wouldn't be able to pay its bills. And yet. She didn't see how they would get this money back and didn't want their all their savings sunk into the business. Both of their children were done with college, and it was time to turn their attention to retirement savings. As a small business owner, Dad didn't have a pension. Mom had a good job and earned a good salary, but she had only been working at the Jerusalem Foundation a few years and hadn't yet built up a healthy pension. Her balancing the need to be supportive of her husband and the business that had provided for the family for years with the likelihood that this money was never coming back, became an ongoing part of their relationship. And there was nothing particularly pleasant about this dynamic for either of them. So occasionally, when he had a sudden cash crisis, Dad avoided an argument by investing their money in the business without telling my mom.

Until writing this book I hadn't put all the pieces together before as to why Radio Clinic was one of the few small businesses on the Upper West Side that didn't tape a 'lost our lease' sign to its window. The main reason Radio Clinic remained open when businesses were closing around it was that Dad cumulatively invested large amounts of personal money in the business. The 20-year lease certainly helped, but at some point it stopped being enough. Between the escalator clause and the rapidly rising property tax, by the mid 1990s the rents were higher than a small appliance store could handle. And this made life very stressful for him and explained why I rarely saw him relaxed. He needed these cash infusions to work. If the business went under, it would be a financial disaster for my parents. In addition to the economic damage of owning a failed business, he would lose much of their personal savings.

While business pressures continued to mount, I was in Ann Arbor, 622 miles away from New York City. I was occupied with my fledgling life there. I made great friends, became very active in the fight to build permanently affordable low-income housing, and exchanged my unrequited relationships for requited ones. I started working at a Community Development Corporation, which operated a micro-loan pool. The idea of the loan pool was that a low-income entrepreneur could apply for a loan of up to $3,000 to kick-start a business that was typically run out of a home. Mostly the loan pool recipients were single moms receiving Aid for Families and Dependent Children (AFDC) who were trying to build up a micro business that they could run out of their homes while taking care of their children and once their children were in school they hoped to build on these businesses. My grandfather started his business with less than $3,000 and over time grew it to provide a middle-class life for his family and descendants. While I had no interest in running a business, it appealed to me to be part of an organization supporting a new generation of scrappy entrepreneurs.

The same banks that were unwilling to support longstanding established small businesses like Radio Clinic were even less willing to support low-income entrepreneurs wanting to get a toehold in the economy. If anything, they erected additional barriers to keep them out. Many of the women who wanted to start businesses couldn't even open a checking account at a local bank. At the time in Ann Arbor you needed to maintain a $1,000 minimum to open an account, which was simply too high. Many women "banked" at Kroger, since the local grocery store would cash their checks for five dollars. While I had absorbed enough stories from Dad to be suspicious of banks, surely local banks weren't allowed to make it impossible for people that live in its community to open a checking account. My colleague Lendell M.[3] wondered the same thing. For her, this was even more personal. She had a long-term goal of getting her kids out of public housing, owning her own home, and creating a track record with a bank so she could build her business.

We did some research and learned about the Community Reinvestment Act (CRA). The idea behind the law was that any financial institution that accepted public deposits from the community needed to meet the credit needs of the entire community, which includes low-income people. The women I worked with at the Community Development Corporation weren't trying to upend banks or challenge our economic system. They just wanted in. Each bank was required to have a public file with the most recent CRA performance evaluation and a list of credit-related services provided by the bank. Lendell and I went bank to bank because we wanted to see what was in their files.

We made quite an impression. The bank tellers didn't know where to direct us and sent us to the loan officers. The loan officers sent us to the public rela-

---

3 I only used the first letter of her last name since I couldn't locate her to get permission to include her name in the book.

tions manager. The public relations manager found us an empty conference room and brought us two glasses of water. The bank president poked his head in to see if we were comfortable. No one really wanted to help us, but they were pretty sure they didn't have a choice. I was a 25-year-old white woman who dressed as if I was colorblind and symmetry was a crime. Lendell was a 35-year-old African American woman who would iron the crease out of leggings if need be and was always impeccably dressed. We did not look as though we belonged together and we made people nervous when we visited the main office of every bank in Ann Arbor together and asked to see their public files. I knew from Radio Clinic's experience how disinterested banks were in the credit needs of the small potatoes accounts. It was satisfying to spend some of my workdays trying to unrig the game.

During my regular phone conversations with my mom and brother, the health of Radio Clinic, and, by extension, Dad, was a common conversation topic. They both provided troubling descriptions of how Radio Clinic was doing. At times, it was tricky talking to Mom since she was tense about Dad and what was happening with the business. Between Dad spending most of his waking hours at Radio Clinic and the money invested, I commiserated with her, but it was awkward to talk about it with her. Josh, who had become a sounding board for Dad, was also frustrated with him. Since my brother had spent many summers working in the warehouse, he had a good understanding of the business and its operations. Plus, he had a very detailed and lawyerly mind and liked to dig into something to have a complete understanding of an issue. A couple of times a week Dad called Josh at work to explain a situation or problem to him, looking for advice.

Like me, my brother had very positive memories of working at Radio Clinic when younger. Josh was proud of how our dad ran the business, his work as a community leader, and that he brought young neighborhood people into the business and mentored them. But it was getting hard for my brother to square that person with the man who continually pulled him aside either in a panic about X issue or to talk about how things are going to dramatically change for the better once he implements Y. Part of asking advice from someone who likes to dig into an issue is understanding that multiple follow-up questions are in your future. But Dad would mostly evade the follow-up questions and bristle when Josh pointed out the evasions. Many of Dad's ideas of the next thing he planned to implement that would turn things around for the business sounded like fantastical thinking. My brother's tolerance for fantastical thinking has always been minimal and he felt a growing friction between them when he didn't go along with Dad's line of thinking.

Both my brother and dad are problem solvers. But they each try to solve different types of problems and approach the problem-solving task very differently. I imagine Dad turned to Josh so often for advice because he respected his intelligence and trusted his opinion. I imagine that somewhere layered in there was that Dad would have liked his son to regard him the same way he regarded his Dad. Whatever the root of the reason, the fact that my dad rarely took my brother's advice, but kept asking for advice, was beginning to impact their relationship.

Maybe it's because I am the youngest, or the daughter, or not a problem solver, or lived hundreds of miles away, but it was easy for me to not be annoyed with Dad and his business decisions. No-one ever asked for my opinion.

Although we didn't talk that much on the phone, Dad did send me packages from the store. Every month or two, I would get a very securely packaged box filled with batteries and blank cassettes, with a short hand-written note on Radio Clinic letterhead from Dad tucked in it. These were welcome gifts since my obsession with making mixed cassettes was a little out of hand at the time. I made a mixed cassette for every possible mood. 'Love gone good' mixes for myself and friends at the start of new relationships, 'love gone bad' mixes for break-ups, driving mixes, running mixes, etc. I was on a tight budget in Ann Arbor, so I very much appreciated the cassettes Dad sent me. When I was in college I didn't think much of these packages, they were just one of the many random things that my slightly eccentric Dad did. But in our car ride out to Ann Arbor he told me how taking a few minutes to think about his kids helped ground him during an otherwise bleak day. His days at the store had become increasingly hard and long and he wasn't interested in talking about it.

During one visit home, Dad and Mike helped me buy my first car. Mike knew a guy who knew a guy that sold Toyota Tercels and could get me a good deal. So, the three of us drove out to Staten Island and after the salesmen did their bargaining dance I left with a very reasonably priced car. To thank Dad, I took him out for an expensive drink with a view at Windows on the World, at the top of the World Trade Center. Feeling very adult, I wanted to have an adult conversation with him. I wanted to form my own opinion about how he was doing, not relying on data points that were filtered by my mother and brother. As the evening wore on he described several minor crises at the store, going into excruciating detail about why this change he made recently would put the business in a healthier spot. Soon. His descriptions didn't align with how Mom and Josh described Radio Clinic's health, but I wasn't interested in that. None of his plans and expectations for the impact these plans could have on the business seemed plausible to me. But I wasn't really interested in talking about business strategies. At some point, I got frustrated and interrupted him to say, "I am interested in how you are doing, not how the store is doing." His response stuck with me. He said, "Telling you how Radio Clinic is doing is me telling you how I am doing."

In 1995 the lease for the 83rd Street store was going to expire and the landlord planned to raise the rent considerably. This was a moment of reckoning for Dad. While he continued to see the potential in the business, that many aspects of it were healthy and growing, he knew Radio Clinic couldn't absorb the rent increase of a new lease and continue business as usual. The fixed costs of doing business would be too high and Dad reluctantly came to the decision that he needed to close one of the two stores. Deciding which one felt like an impossible choice.

Ever since it opened in the mid-1940s, the 83rd Street store had more walk-in traffic, made more sales, and earned a significantly higher profit. Without these customers, my dad feared that the business would be in serious trouble. But he also feared it would also be in serious trouble without the 98th Street store basement. Without this vast warehouse, he would need to rent storage space for appliances, could no longer keep customer's air conditioners during the winter, or buy merchandise in large quantities to lower his costs. Neither store seemed optional. He needed both stores but could only afford one. The working assumption was that Radio Clinic would lose customers that lived below 90th Street if he closed the 83rd street store. Dad decided to test this theory before making any decision. He analyzed the delivery slips to where customers lived and which store they shopped in. Using 90th Street as a dividing line between the two stores, he went alphabetically through the delivery slips. By the time he got to M, he stopped because the findings were so consistent. Upper West Siders walked more than 10 blocks to do their shopping. Fifty percent of the deliveries to people who lived above 90th Street were purchased at the 83rd Street store, and 50 percent delivered below 90th Street were purchased at the 98th street store. The evidence showed that customers already walked more than 10 blocks to do their shopping and didn't only shop in the store closest to them. Reassured that he would not lose all his 83rd Street customers, he kept the warehouse and closed the 83rd Street store.

With just the one store, Charlie now managed the sales floor at the 98th Street store. The personnel of the store was changing too. Many of the salesmen that worked there when I was a kid had retired. Raymond had recently moved back down south and John E.[4] now had his job. John, a neighborhood teenager from 108th Street, started out as a stock boy, then was part of a delivery crew before helping Raymond run the warehouse in the year before he retired. It was clear to Dad that John was smart and he had the capability to run the warehouse; he just needed to be mentored. This was a perfect fit for Dad because he likes to mentor young people. And he took a great deal of satisfaction when a

---

4 I only used the first letter of his last name since I couldn't locate him to get permission to include his name in the book.

young employee grew into the job under his tutelage. I imagine if he could start his career over he would have incorporated coaching a high school soccer team when he was a younger man.

During our interview sessions, I realized that the more times Dad repeated a story, the closer that story got to some personality trait of his that he considered essential. And he had a favorite story about the early days of John running the warehouse. Dad told me that whenever there was a decision to make John would hand my dad the phone so he could make the decision. Dad said to him, "If you keep handing me the phone then I don't need you. Ask yourself, will this decision put Radio Clinic out of business? If yes, then hand me the phone. If not, then make your decision and we can discuss how it went later." When we were growing up, my brother and I didn't really get much of this first-hand guidance from Dad. He had more time and energy for the young people he worked with then he did for us, because he was with them all day, six days a week. But in his retirement, I saw him bring this quality of teaching to his relationship with my teenage son.

I stopped by Radio Clinic several times a year, whenever I was in the city visiting my family. Even though I was in my mid 20s, it was comforting to have the same ritual with Dad at the store that I had since I was a little kid. He would give me a twenty-dollar bill and I would go to the Korean deli on the adjacent corner to order our food. Then sitting on the 98th Street bench, we ate our roast beef and bologna sandwiches, until it was time to get back to work. During these visits, I met Solomon G[5], a newer salesman that Dad was excited to have working at Radio Clinic. Solomon brought many new customers to the store. In the same way that Russians came to shop in the store because of Grandpa in the 1950s, Ghanaians now came to shop in the store because of Solomon. From Accra, Ghana, Solomon was the regional head of his Ashanti tribe for the New York City metro area. He promoted commerce between Accra and New York City and enlisted Dad's support. When Radio Clinic's delivery crew dropped off new refrigerators for customers, they would remove the old refrigerator and need to dispose of it. For many years, Dad sold the old ones for scrap, but over time that market dried up. Solomon asked Dad if he could ship the used refrigerators to Ghana, where his tribe would recondition them and sell them for a profit. A few times a year, when there were enough refrigerators to make it worthwhile, Solomon arranged for a cargo container. Members of the Ashanti tribe from throughout Manhattan would stop by the store with clothing and household goods to cram into the refrigerators, for transport to their families at no cost. And many of them became customers.

5 I only used the first letter of his last name since I couldn't locate him to get permission to include his name in the book.

By now Dad was in his early sixties and started thinking about his eventual retirement. Without a pension and dwindling savings, he knew selling a healthy business to a younger entrepreneur was an important piece of his retirement plan. Perhaps the only piece. Since Radio Clinic's lease still had five years on it, he wanted to capitalize on it. His hope was that someone would want the chance to own a store in an increasingly thriving neighborhood and would buy him out of the business. While the rent was an increasing burden, locked into the 1980 agreement it was still lower than most comparable spaces in the neighborhood. Ideally he would like to help transition the business to a younger person, someone like Solomon. But he knew a young entrepreneur would have an impossible time taking over the business given the costs. From listening to fellow merchants, he knew many were in the same position as he was. Long-standing family businesses throughout the city had no one in the family wanting to take over the business and the aging merchants needed to get some money out of the business for their retirements. So Dad drafted a proposal for the city to finance what he called a small business transition plan.

Gail Brewer was now in the public advocate's office. Dad contacted her to pitch his plan. First he listed some things he knew to be true about New York City's small businesses. That government and politicians care and can help, but often do not understand the true workings and needs of city small businesses. That small businesses have a stabilizing effect upon their communities. And that creative programming requiring relatively little money can substantially help these businesses.

Before he got to the meat of the proposal, he stated his case.

You need a license to practice medicine, accounting law, etc—however, all you need to go into business is a store lease, a dream and guts. You do not have to prove that you are qualified to run a business. There are many programs designed to help small businesses get started. Their focus has been primarily on minorities and women. Recently, enterprise zones have been established to help entire communities rebound. This is all for the good, but my experience is that many of the small businesses that get started in these programs, and in other ones, will have a high fatality rate. This is because that under the best of circumstances, small business will fail.

It would have been much more difficult for me to run RCI if I had either started it from scratch or taken it over without any guidance from my father. It is probable that I would have gone out of business early on. One thing is for certain, I would not have started a retail business on my own for many reasons. However, if someone came to me and said, "I will teach you this business and when I retire you will take it over"—that would have been very attractive. This is the kind of opportunity I want to make available for a next generation of small business owners. I am now over 60 and will probably retire in 5 to 10 years. Instead of slowing down, I see so many opportunities for growth and expansion. What could be better than to share with a younger person (or persons) who can continue what my family started.

My dad's proposal was full of optimism and practical suggestions. He ended the proposal with this pitch: "It is the type of program that can get off the ground and work if we can get past the 'it has never been done' or 'it can't be done' phase." He understood how owning a small business had been good for his family. His father got some seed money from his brother Jack and then poured all his savings into opening Radio Clinic. My father and his sister went to college with the profits from the business. My grandparents used some of their money to buy bonds in my name when I was born. When I cashed the bonds in thirty years later, the proceeds helped with the down payment for the house I bought with my husband. The fact that my immigrant grandfather was able to open a small business had a positive ripple effect for the generations to follow. Dad's primary goal with the small business plan was certainly self-interest. He wanted to get out of the financial hole he was in. To leave the business with some money to show for it so he could have a comfortable retirement. But he also wanted to pass this opportunity to the next generation, give someone else, perhaps an immigrant, the type of opportunity he and his father had. But like many of Dad's favorite ideas, this program never came to fruition.

Meanwhile the time bomb kept ticking. Radio Clinic had good months and bad months. The store had plenty of customers. It was a popular neighborhood destination. Dad worked longer and longer days. The time bomb didn't really care, the fuse just kept getting shorter. My dad brought in a new business partner with good access to air conditioners, allowing the store to price them competitively. Tick. A strong relationship with Symphony Space brought new business to the store. Tick, tick. Dad closed the 83rd Street store to consolidate the business. Tick, tick, tick. He could streamline and get all the good publicity he wanted, but there was no getting around the inevitable. The 20 years on his lease were almost up.

14

That's All Folks

Is it not cruel to let our city die by degrees, stripped of all her proud monuments, until there will be nothing left of all her history and beauty to inspire our children? If they are not inspired by the past of our city, where will they find the strength to fight for her future?

—Jackie Kennedy Onassis in a letter to Mayor Beam, 1977

And you already know. Yeah, you already know how this will end.

—DeVotchKa

WHEN DAD SAT DOWN with Jack Weinreb in 2000 to negotiate lease terms, his family had been renting from the Weinreb family for many decades. Both men agreed that what had happened to commercial rents on Broadway in the last 15 years was crazy. Regardless, when the old lease ended, Radio Clinic's rent would increase from $6,000 to $14,000 a month, and given how rapidly the city raised property taxes, the monthly costs would rise even more significantly. In some ways, Dad was lucky that his landlord was a person, since many merchants were no longer dealing with an actual person but instead with the arm of a hedge fund. But that didn't change the reality that landlords charged what the market would allow, and the Upper West Side market would allow a great deal of rent increase. Dad argued with Weinreb that the space wasn't worth that much money. Weinreb agreed—but he knew someone would pay it.

Weinreb told my dad that he was not increasing the rent as much as he would for someone else and cautioned him to think hard before signing a new lease. He suggested that Dad take some time to ask himself if he really wanted to renew this lease and if the business could handle the rent burden. But Dad did not take the time to think. Instead, he signed a new 15-year lease.

This wasn't 1977 anymore. Keeping Radio Clinic open no matter the circumstances was bold and had elements of the heroic in 1977. In 2000, it looked a lot more like folly. But in truth it wasn't a straightforward decision for Dad. He had a good reason to be concerned about leaving the business in 2000. Selling the business, with a lease to go with it making it more attractive, was his retirement plan. He didn't own the building and had no pension. He had already invested personal savings in the business that he needed to get back. And closing the business would smoke out all the personal debt that Mom didn't know about, he had only partially disclosed the extent of it. He would have to pay a lot of money to retire and he didn't want to confront that. Losing the money would impact their retirement years and their marriage. As risky as renewing the lease was financially, it was also risky not to renew the lease. Dad knew that if he didn't renew the lease he would have no chance to get the money back. He would be left with less than nothing.

But the conditions in the neighborhood were unrelenting. The rising expense of doing business on the Upper West Side far outpaced the rate at which Dad could grow the business, no matter how many good ideas he had. He was having a hard-enough time making the business profitable before the rent increase. There was no way he could meet his monthly debt obligations. It was such a colossally bad idea that only a complicated mixture of fear, hubris, and misguided optimism allowed Dad to make the decision to sign a new lease. He didn't take his own advice from *Rubin's Rules of Survival* when he warned that one's ego can cloud judgment and allow you to rationalize a decision. And he certainly didn't listen to what he told the people with clipboards years earlier, that businesses could not survive the rent increases and they should follow the lease.

During our interviews, I kept circling back to this decision. I wanted to know precisely what he was thinking when he made this decision, what he thinks about it now and in hindsight does he see what he could have done differently. It took many interviews, Dad was understandably guarded about this decision, but we eventually got to an answer that made sense to me. He told me that he wished that instead of renewing the lease, he had asked for a nine-month extension on the lease. At the time, he still had a basement full of air conditioners. Nine months would have given the landlord time to find a new tenant and would have given Dad one more air conditioner season to clear out the inventory, pay off some debts, and then close the store. But he didn't' see it this clearly at the time. For years, he ran Radio Clinic in crisis mode, and it is hard to step back and fully assess a situation when in crisis. Dad felt he had gotten Radio Clinic through many obstacles and he could get it through the high rent obstacle too. He didn't listen to his gut, which told him it was time to get out, and he didn't listen to Mom who worried about where this was heading. The same determination and optimism that helped him save the business after the blackout was the very thing that made it hard for him to see that it was time to close it.

In the years right after Dad signed the new lease, the city become even more inhospitable to small businesses. Elected in 2002, Mayor Bloomberg seemed as disinterested in the plight of the small business owner as Mayor Koch had been in the 1980s. City Hall never decided that small businesses were in the city's public interest. New York City never put its thumb on the scales to add just a bit of weight in the direction of its small businesses. Commercial rent stabilization, small business successorship and explicit tax policy to protect existing small business never happened. There could have been an alternative narrative to the slow death of NYC's small businesses, but there wasn't.

The August of 2003 I loaded my husband, children, dog, bikes and seventeen hours worth of snacks into our minivan and headed east from Madison, Wisconsin, where I now live, to spend a couple of weeks with my family on the east coast. My kids were three and five, old enough that I felt ready to spend those many hours in the car with them. We stopped half way in Cleveland and spent the night at our friends Amy and Mark's house. We arrived on a brutally hot day where it was impossible to do anything ambitious, so we planned a low-key night. The power in the house and throughout the block went out soon after we got there. We sweated through half an hour to see if the power would return, and eventually learned from the car radio that the power outage extended beyond the neighborhood to all of Cleveland, all of Ohio, and most of the Northeast corridor, including New York City.

A power outage has a time-warp quality to it, since it forces us back to a pre-electric time. We abandoned our plans as we figured out how to cope without refrigeration, light, air conditioning, fans, and the possible loss of water. Once we realized the extent of the power outage and that it wouldn't be resolved quickly, Amy called for a house meeting to make sure the kids understood the implications of the blackout. Only two years removed from the terrorist and anthrax attacks of 2001, Amy wasn't convinced this was a benign power outage and wanted the kids to be prepared to quickly follow any urgent directions from a parent. So the adults and four children under the age of six sat down to hear Amy tell us the known facts of the blackout as it applied to us: no trip to the ice cream store, no barbeque since the grill was in the garage which can only be opened electrically, no air-conditioned rooms for sleeping and uncertainty about cause and duration. Later the adults sat in the car listening to the radio when we noticed Max, Amy's five-year-old son, on his bike pedaling as fast as he could with his helmeted head tilted down as he rammed his head full speed into the garage door to free the grill. Max's young mind had sorted through the information he was given, heard the parental anxiety, and reached his own conclusion: he would free the grill and then we could have dinner as planned and all would be okay.

The next day we continued our drive east and hoped that the power would be on in New York City when we arrived. I wondered if it was wise to drive onto the island of Manhattan during a blackout since we could be driving into looting and violence. The last citywide blackout hadn't gone so well for New York. When I was finally able to get in touch with Mom during our long drive, I learned that the power was back on and there was no looting. I also learned that Dad had done his version of trying to ram his bike through a locked garage door. He spent the night at Radio Clinic hand-pumping water out of the basement warehouse to protect the elevator motor and still had not left his post to come home.

I couldn't believe Con Edison had another multi-state blackout on its hands. Back in 1977 the Mayor had put together a blackout commission that placed blame squarely with Con Ed and the government regulatory agencies that didn't hold Con Ed's feet to the fire to make critical upgrades. At the time, the commission feared that the information and recommendations from their four months of intensive investigation would be ignored. The chair of the commission said, "We hope our work is not to be relegated to a file cabinet or some dusty shelf, to be brought out and reviewed the next time there is a blackout." A few days after the 2003 massive blackout, a reporter found that the committee was right to be cynical - the 1977 report was found on a dusty shelf in the city archives.

But even more than history repeating itself, I couldn't believe my almost 70-year-old Dad worked the hand pump for so many hours. It was hard to imagine that the entire time I was eating dinner, talking with friends, sleeping, and driving across I-80, Dad was pumping water in Radio Clinic's basement to save the electric motor of the elevator. I thought of Max's attempt to physically ram his way into the garage and knew my dad could relate to his stress-induced adrenaline surge. As far back as I can remember Dad had always been a bundle of nervous energy. When he applied his nervous energy to one of Radio Clinic's minor crises, he went at it full tilt until it was resolved or there was nothing else to be done to remedy it. Saving the elevator motor in the middle of an unrelenting heat wave was not a trivial matter for Radio Clinic. If the elevator motor shorted out he would lose air conditioner sales. In 2003, despite Dad's efforts, the store was barely treading water. I imagine Dad had enough adrenaline pumping through his body that he could ram himself and a bike through a locked garage door if it would help save the basement elevator.

Chain Stores like Crazy Eddy and The Wiz might have grown fast and flamed out, but they had something going for them that Radio Clinic did not have. Layers of staff. Owners of chain stores and department stores didn't need to be everywhere and do everything. Between the physical demands and the emotional strain, the burdens of the business were too much to be on 70-year-old shoulders. For the rest of the car ride I was anxious that I would get a call from Mom saying Dad suffered a heart attack in Radio Clinic's basement warehouse. I was equal parts worried for him and angry with him. Why was he still in the store contending with water that could short out the warehouse elevator at his age? He shouldn't have the physical demands of dealing with the radiator pumps and lifting heavy boxes. It was 2003 not 1977. He shouldn't still own Radio Clinic. No one other than Dad thought it was a good idea to sign a new lease in 2000. The business struggled to pay its rent. How could it handle damage incurred from another blackout? This shouldn't be his headache anymore. If he had closed the business in 2000, he wouldn't be trying to yet again ward off disaster. Yet here he was.

If anything, the city seemed determined to make life as hard as possible for Radio Clinic. Taxes, fees, and fines imposed on small businesses were higher now than they had ever been. Property taxes were staggeringly high, and the city became increasingly aggressive with issuing fines. Radio Clinic's delivery trucks often found a ticket under their wiper blades when they parked outside the store while loading the large appliances from the elevator into the truck. It wasn't like Radio Clinic had a parking lot or any kind of reserved parking spot it could use to load refrigerators and air conditioners into a delivery truck. But the city wasn't interested in the practical realities of its small businesses, but rather the income it could generate by enforcing these small business violations. As a result, the blitz of parking tickets was ongoing; Dad had to roll these tickets for the delivery vans into his regular cost of business. With this and other additional city regulations that were impossible for small businesses to meet, it seemed to Dad that the city was even more uncompromising and unsympathetic.

Large chain stores, in particular drug stores and banks, now dominated the neighborhood. The city had never put any reins on real estate developers and with Bloomberg as mayor the city was hyper-gentrifying. Building owners preferred renting to chains since smaller merchants often struggled with the rents. Gail Brewer, now the council member for the Upper West Side, called it the 'bankization" of the Upper West Side. In 2007, the blocks from 54th street to 96th street had 63 banks. It is hard to imagine that all 63 bank branches were successful, but if a corporation is large enough it can absorb an underperforming branch.

The problems that plagued Radio Clinic amplified after 2000. Dad was consumed by business worries and rarely took a day off. Keeping Radio Clinic out of the red became more and more impossible. He thought about it all the time, even when he wasn't there. We all worried about him having a stress-induced stroke or heart attack. And he still needed a way to pay his monthly expenses. So, he doubled down on his invested money and continued to put more money into the business, "Just to get over this hump". It took a toll on my parents' marriage. To Mom, it seemed like Dad was more committed to the business than the family. From her childhood, she knew how hard it could be not to have much money. Her mom was a seamstress in a factory, her dad was a day laborer and as a kid she often had to go without. She didn't want to be without money in her retirement years and felt it would have been better for him to take a lower-paying job at someone else's store than put their money into a failing business. It was hard for any of us to see how this invested money could be anything other than a temporary Band-Aid. But Dad always wanted to roll the dice one more time.

With my young kids, I continued to visit my parents a few times a year. I made a point to stop by the store with the kids, both to get a visual on how Radio Clinic was doing and to spend a little time with Dad. But he rarely felt he could leave the store, so no quick trip to get dumplings, donuts or eat deli sandwiches with the grandkids. The interior of the store looked very different than it did when I was my kids ages. While the switch to large appliances made practical sense for the business, it wasn't the fun house I experienced as a kid. A store full of stoves and refrigerators was not as interesting as a stereo sound room. The wall filled with televisions that riveted my attention as a kid and the shelves stacked with Boomboxes and videogames were no longer there. After making sure I said hi to everyone in the store, and more importantly that they saw his grandchildren, Dad would walk a block or two with us, give me some ice cream money and hustle back to the store.

Managing a business on the brink and being continually tense didn't bring out the best in my dad. He was so preoccupied with the business that he couldn't focus on anything else. There was no socializing with him because he fell asleep within minutes of sitting down. Even when he was with us he was absent. He was quick to snap at people. I had a hard time reconciling this tense man, a man who often fell asleep while I was talking to him, with the salesman from my youth. Living in the Midwest, I didn't have as much time to spend with my parents as I would like and I didn't want spend the hours Dad was not at the store talking about the store. I didn't want to confront him on the troubling stories I heard from my mother and brother or the panicked business decisions that were putting my parents' future retirement money in danger. I didn't want to spend our brief time together discussing something that wasn't exactly my business.

Dad worked 12-hour days, at least six days a week. What seemed clear to all of us, including eventually my dad, was that his health wouldn't survive him staying in the business much longer. He couldn't will the store to a better economic position. Hard work wouldn't solve this problem, and it wasn't going to resolve itself. I don't understand what specifically made the switch flip for him, but he must have remembered that he was a reasonable man. One day, Dad decided enough was enough, and started looking for a way out of the business. The last word of advice he listed on his 'rules for survival' was "relax." He wanted the business students to know that a problem will seem important at the time but that unless your health is in jeopardy it isn't worth getting upset about it. But at the bottom of that index card he also wrote, "easy to say—hard to do."

As tough as it was for Dad to decide to walk away from the business, the actual walking away wasn't going to be much easier. He still had a significant amount of personal money invested, and he was responsible for the business debt. What he needed was for someone to buy the business. The small business transfer plan he had pitched to the city more than 10 years prior would have been perfect, but that had been a no-go. But even without an official transfer plan, he was still hoping to enter into a mutually beneficial arrangement with a young entrepreneur that would like the opportunity to own Radio Clinic. The Upper West Side was no longer a place a regular person could open a business. A landlord wasn't going to simply trust your signature the way one did when my grandfather was starting out. To start a business in the 2000s on the Upper West Side, you needed to share your net worth and have a significant security deposit and backing. Transferring an existing business to someone else was one avenue to give another person a similar chance.

Dad let his contacts know he was looking to find a buyer for the store. A young salesman who often stopped by Radio Clinic to sell Dad the small appliances his company manufactured was interested in purchasing the business. And he thought he had a potential partner to buy the business with him. The young salesman was friendly with a merchant who had owned a small shop in Chinatown for the past 10 years. This merchant hadn't been able to take any days off of work other than Chinese New Year for several years, and liked the idea of having a business partner to share responsibilities. It sounded good on paper. An older man looking to retire from a well-established business and two younger men looking to own their own business and not wanting to start from scratch. All that needed to be figured out were the details of the deal.

There were definite pros and cons to taking over the business. The lease was both a pro and a con. On the one hand, the rents were absurdly high and an enormous burden. It seemed impossible to run a viable business selling appliances with this burden. No doubt about that. But the lease terms were locked in at the market rate levels that applied in the year 2000 and would stay locked in until 2015. Each year the rents rose at a breakneck pace and there seemed to be no ceiling to what the market would allow. As a result, the 2000 rent levels were much preferable to what they would pay if they were starting from scratch with a new lease. Radio Clinic had other strengths. It came with merchandise, a basement warehouse, and an increasingly affluent neighborhood in which to do business. But there was no denying it had its weaknesses. The business was in debt. With the strain of the rents, there wasn't a clear path to maintaining a profit and getting out of debt. What needed to be determined was how much Radio Clinic was worth. How much was the name of a long-standing respected business, a good location, and a solid customer base worth?

By this point, Josh was a lawyer working for the City of New York. While his focus was policy, his knowledge of the law was useful and Dad continued to call Josh with questions. It seemed to my brother that Dad could not see a path out of the business because of all the debt the store was carrying. Worried that he would keep doubling down on the debt and never retire, Josh put a lot of energy into advising Dad. He strongly advised him to hire his own lawyer and not to rely on Radio Clinic's longtime lawyer, and recommended one to contact. Not that his business lawyer wasn't trustworthy, but since Dad was leaving the business, his self-interest and Radio Clinic's best interest weren't necessarily aligned. It was good advice, and my dad took it. He had two major problems to contend with before he could retire. One was the personal savings he poured into the business. Could he recoup any of that? The other was the business debt he owed suppliers. Since Dad purchased merchandise on a floor plan, he owed money and until Radio Clinic sold the merchandise, he didn't have the ability to repay. This new lawyer helped Dad figure out what debts he could get out of and how to take a more aggressive negotiating position with some of his creditors.

Dad's biggest fear, the one that kept him up at night for years, was that if the business closed he would be personally responsible for all the business debt. He would need to liquidate his personal assets to repay the debt. This would have been catastrophic both for his retirement and his marriage. He needed to clear out the business debt before anyone would consider taking on ownership of Radio Clinic. Together with his lawyer, Dad was able to negotiate a major reduction in the debt as Radio Clinic settled with each creditor.

I don't fully understand what mathematical gymnastics were performed, and what agreements were eventually reached, but the two younger salesmen took over the business. I know there were complicated negotiations between the men with lawyers that left each of them feeling like they didn't get enough of what they asked for, but that they got enough to be willing to complete the sale. Why they took over the business has always been unclear to me. Dad and his lawyer were transparent about the problems that plagued the business. The untenable rents were self-evident. I still don't understand what made this look like a good idea to them, but in my mind I attribute it, at least in part, to the hubris of youth. These two men, already established with their own connections, probably looked at my 71-year-old dad and decided they could do it better. The young often think this about the old. And sometimes they are right, but sometimes they are wrong.

Dad came out okay financially. And by okay I mean he lost all the retirement money he invested but was not responsible for any of the personal guarantees he had on the merchandise. So not as good as he and Mom hoped, but better than we all feared.

I know my parents see the story of Radio Clinic as a story specific to them. It was my dad that made the business decisions that put their personal finances in jeopardy. It was my dad that stayed in the business too long. The closest I came to abandoning this book project was when it, belatedly, occurred to me that the book might require a judgment from me about how Dad ran the business. Each member of my nuclear family had very strong and conflicting opinions about what could and should have been the store's trajectory, and I didn't want to stir up trouble that was finally dormant. But ultimately, to me, it seemed straight-forward. Like my dad, I like a good story. I am a skilled storyteller, teach storytelling workshops and co-produce a Moth StorySlam in Madison. My favorite stories are the ones that give the listener an idea of the context behind the story, since no story exists in a vacuum. Even though the details about Radio Clinic are Radio Clinic's alone, the essential elements of its story were much bigger than Radio Clinic and were repeated over and over again throughout the Upper West Side since the 1980s. Sure, there were factors that were unique to Dad's personality, but the success and failure of small merchants were also intertwined with larger societal forces. Would Dad getting grants, or even loans with better interest rates, after the 1977 blackout have made a difference in Radio Clinic's overall fiscal health after 2000? Hard to say. Would Radio Clinic have closed before it could even get to 2000 and the momentous lease renewal decision if Dad hadn't put in personal money? Most likely. Dad was personally well regarded in the neighborhood, but could someone else have run the business better? Perhaps. But each small business shared the same central external question they'd been asking themselves since the early 1980s: How do we survive the rents?

Between my grandfather and my dad, the Rubin family had owned Radio Clinic for over 75 years. It had provided the rungs on the ladder that my immigrant grandfather climbed to pull his family into the middle class; it offered stable footing for my dad to remain in the middle class and to launch his kids into the middle class. But starting with the 1977 blackout and accelerating with gentrification, it became harder and harder to keep the store open. The rungs were getting increasingly slippery. Dad's signing of the new lease in 2000 seemed like an ugly moment of truth. The rest of us couldn't see how he would be able to retire without bankrupting his personal finances. It had been such a long and tortured road to get to the place where he agreed to retire and then found people to buy the business that we all felt a sense of relief when it was done. We didn't even stop to mark the occasion that the end of an era had occurred—that Radio Clinic was no longer my family's business.

15

Retirement

The world spins. We stumble on. It is enough.

—Colum McCann

Tell me, what is it you plan to do with your one wild and precious life?

—Mary Oliver

As a kindergartener, my daughter joined a recreational soccer team. She enjoyed wearing a uniform and running in the grass, but it was hard to get her off the monkey bars and onto the field during games. She wasn't particularly interested in kicking the ball. By the end of first grade, I was not surprised when she hung up her sneakers and shin guards. In fifth grade, when she learned that the recreational club was forming girls only teams, she decided to come out of her soccer retirement. Two girls' teams were formed. The A team included the girls who had been playing soccer for years, and the B team was for the rest of the girls. Since a coach was needed for the B team, my husband Matt, who had coached my son's team for a few years, also came out of retirement. He had a difficult time finding someone on the team willing to play goalie because, being on the weaker team, the goalie took a lot of shots, and didn't really have the skills to stop them. My daughter was one of the few girls that didn't complain about playing the goalie position, so she spent half of each game in the goal.

163

Anyone who has spent more than a few hours with my dad will have a passing idea of what a goalie needs to think about during a game. Dad has been a proselytizer for the game of soccer since as long as I can remember, and his purest devotion has always been for the position of goalie. He was a goalie for his high school team and at Lehigh University in the 1950s. After college, he played with mostly European and South American immigrants for a club team based out of Pennsylvania. When I was younger, I sometimes accompanied him to watch the New York Cosmos play. It doesn't matter if you shared his interest in soccer; if you spent time with my dad, you'd learn something about the game. When his grandkids started playing soccer, he liked to videotape international soccer games and during our visits watch highlights of a game with them. He always narrated the action based on the goalie's perspective. After she had a tough game in goal, I suggested she call her grandpa and ask him for some advice. If nothing else, I knew he would be happy to hear from her.

A few hours later, Dad calls me to tell me he will be arriving in Madison this coming Thursday and would I be available to pick him up at the airport. I had no idea what he was talking about. He told me that my daughter called him to say that she was now a goalie and needed his help. So he searched for a cheap airfare and booked a flight. He would be in Madison for three days and planned to run an informal goalie clinic for any interested kids. At this point, in 2010, Dad was two years into retirement. Retirement suited him.

By the time Dad retired from Radio Clinic in 2008, Mom had been retired for a year. In the 20-plus years Mom had worked, she had built up a decent pension but not enough to deal with the high costs of living in New York City. Finances were part of the reason they decided to move out of the city. While the rising real estate prices crushed Radio Clinic, my parent's Upper West Side apartment was an increasingly potent asset. It was now worth a great deal more money than it was when they bought it 20 years earlier. So, they sold the apartment, rented for a while in Brooklyn and then Manhattan, and eventually moved three hours north to the Berkshires. My mom moved first while Dad transitioned out of the business. He lived with Josh and his family four days a week in Brooklyn. They were renovating a home and together they lived in a small rental without hot water and Dad slept on an air mattress in the living room. The rest of the week he lived with Mom in their new home in Massachusetts. Being a very urban person, Mom wasn't sure how she felt about living so far away from the city. But she knew she didn't want to spend her retirement years within walking distance of Radio Clinic. It took a long time to get my dad to leave the business. Radio Clinic had been the third party in their marriage since its early days. And Dad was not a man that lets go easily. She worried that even in retirement he would remain deeply invested with Radio Clinic if he could easily pop into the store each day and offer his unsolicited advice. It wasn't hard to imagine him remaining engrossed in the business even when he didn't own it.

When Dad closed Radio Clinic, he had no interest in nostalgia or to mourn what was lost. Extricating himself from the business was too fraught. For over a decade, money worries kept him up at night. He had panic attacks about the very real possibility that he had irreversibly sunk the money he and Mom had saved for retirement into the business and there would be no getting it back. He worried about his employees. He had a one-track mind, and that track was Radio Clinic. It took him awhile to unclench after years of tense days spent just barely pulling the business back from the brink of collapse. Over time he relaxed into his retirement projects. He took classes, organized a history club, volunteered with a small business incubator, mentored young entrepreneurs starting out with new businesses, and helped out as a soccer goalie coach for the local high school. His version of relaxed was still fairly intense. It wasn't easy to pull him away from his computer and his projects. His enthusiasm for his projects still looked a lot like dogged determination. But the stakes were low. Whether or not his retirement projects panned out didn't really matter to anyone but him.

As the 2000s ticked on, the Upper West Side continued to be a tough place to own a small business. The number of small independent businesses that remained was dwindling. Hundreds of small businesses on the Upper West Side were replaced with chain stores. In 2014, there were 2,807 chain stores in Manhattan. When broken up by zip codes, the Upper West Side had 153 chain stores within its boundaries, and the zip code the Upper West Side shared with the Morningside Heights neighborhood had 91 additional chains. When I walked on Broadway from 80th to 100th Streets, I walked by significantly fewer stores than the 500 that existed in 1934. Radio Clinic remained on its 98th Street corner, but Dad thought its new owners were struggling. He kept in touch with them, stopping in the store whenever he was in New York City to visit my brother. His sense was that they were barely limping along. Unless something changed, he didn't see how they would make it past the lease renewal in 2015.

In October of 2014, I got an email from the publisher of the West Side Rag, the neighborhood's online newspaper, wondering if I knew that Radio Clinic had abruptly announced it was closing in a few weeks' time. I hadn't and neither had Dad. Neighbors noticed a large orange sign with large black lettering posted on the window that read: "To our valued customers. RCI is moving to Queens, NY! Due to loss of lease. All phone #, fax, email, and website will remain the same. Looking forward to your continued business." The *West Side Rag* ran an article, "Radio Clinic set to close after 80 years on the Upper West Side."

I was very glad the publisher had contacted me since both Dad and I were heading to New York in a few days for a family funeral. Since the store would remain opened for a few more weeks, we would have a chance to stop in to the store both to commiserate with the current owners and say goodbye to the store.

There was a long list of comments from *West Side Rag* readers. Some commenters bemoaned the demise of small businesses and loss of neighborhood control:

> I moved to the UWS in 1977. Thirty-seven years later, I am sick about the loss of our mom and pop stores. People like your father helped make it a neighborhood. It was manageable, human size. Now all our small businesses are being driven out, not by the small looters, but by the big ones, like the Duane Reade's and the CVS's. How many of them do we need? How many do we want? Why do we no longer have any say about what happens in our neighborhoods? What happened to the block associations? Everyone I talk to agrees, but we can't seem to be able to do anything about it.

There were comments of people who shopped in the store and would miss it:

> I was always afraid of this one going. I bought my first fridge, stove & dishwasher here. Truly a loss for the 'hood.'

There was the comments about the store's excellent customer service, which was only slightly mitigated by two other comments criticizing the store as an unfriendly place:

> This breaks my heart. When I moved to 80th St. and was beginning my real estate career in NY, RCI sold me scratch and dent specials with warranties to help me keep AC in my apt. They bent over backwards with every purchase I made there. It was obvious they truly cared. I never paid more there. They made sure of that. From vacuum cleaners to ovens to AC units at my subsequent.

But my favorite comment was a purely practical one:

> This is sad; I have many great years and memories with them. But they still have both of my air conditioners. How do I get them back??? The number is no longer in service. Any help would be appreciated.

I was more depressed about Radio Clinic's closing than I thought I would be. In 2008 I had been so relieved Dad had extracted himself from the business that I didn't really think about it. Somehow it seemed like Radio Clinic would always be there.

Since I was going to be in town and planned to travel to the Upper West Side to visit the store, I made an appointment to interview Ethel Sheffer at the

Alan in front of Radio Clinic   Jen in front of Radio Clinic

Metro diner, one block from Radio Clinic. The day before I left for New York City, I learned that the store had abruptly closed. It hadn't even made it a full week after the owners put up their announcement. Dad and I still wanted to take pictures of the store, both the interior and the exterior. He called Weinreb, the landlord, to see if he could let us in for about ten minutes so I could take some pictures. Weinreb wasn't willing to let us in the store. I don't know if it was just laziness on his part; maybe he simply didn't want to walk the four blocks from his office to the store. Or maybe it was a principled position of some sort on his part, but either way, many decades of my family paying his family rent didn't warrant ten minutes in the now-empty store.

We still wanted some exterior photos, so Dad and I took the subway from Brooklyn to the Upper West Side. We took the same IRT subway line and got off at the same, albeit renovated, 96th Street station that has been there since 1904, the inaugural date of New York's subway system. As we walked the two blocks to 98th Street, we passed by the Broadway malls that have been on the median strips for more than a century. We enjoyed the spacious sidewalks that were first widened in 1869, in part to make the property more attractive and in part to hire the workers laid off after the completion of Central Park. A couple of people recognized Dad and shouted out a "Hello Mr. RCI" as they passed us on the street. We walked by the impressive buildings of The Wilmington, The Borchardt, The Arragon, and The Gramont, several of the great apartment hotels whose ground floors had housed countless small businesses since they were first built at the turn of the twentieth century.

As we walked the two and a half blocks on the west side of the street, we passed a Chase Bank, a vacant storefront, T-Web, Cohen's Optical, 7-11, Housing Works, a dessert store, Jade Nails, Walgreens, the Texas Grill, a dry cleaners, the Green Café, a barbershop, and the Westside Market. Even though we knew what we would find when we got to the store, it was still a shock to see the same sign that had been haunting the Upper West Side for decades. Instead of "We Are Staying," the storefront window now read, "Lost Our Lease." The doors of Radio Clinic had been shuttered for two days.

Since we couldn't get inside for our last look around, we instead stopped to read the announcement of the store closing. Dad posed while I took photos next to the still existing storefront and Radio Clinic sign. People passing by recognized Dad and stopped to commiserate and wonder about the store's fate in Queens.

When Ethel Sheffer joined us in our booth at the Metro Diner she told Dad that she was surprised to see that Radio Clinic had closed and wondered what he knew about it. Before we got started on the interview, we talked about its closing and whether the store would open in Queens. And she really wanted to know about her air conditioner. She had started storing her air conditioners in Radio Clinic's warehouse about 20 years earlier. The delivery guys had just picked up her air conditioner two weeks before and she was incredulous that they never mentioned the possibility that the store might close. Like the commenter in the *West Side Rag*, she wanted to get her air conditioners back. She asked Dad if he could call Weinreb to ask him what would happen to her air conditioner.

What. About. The. Air. Conditioners. Air conditioners had been a major theme in my dad's life for most of my life. It was his fear that a shorted-out freight elevator would make it impossible to deliver air conditioners that impelled Dad to walk over to the store in time to see it looted. During a cool July, with depressed air conditioner sales, it was Dad's concern about what the weather meant for his cash flow that had him unbearably tense. He rarely took a day off in the summer because he might be able to negotiate a good deal on additional scratch and dent air conditioners to give Radio Clinic an advantage over competitors. It was the fear of missing a hot summer day that elicited Dad's first comment when I told him I was getting married on June 29th to ask whether I could change the date to sometime in September. He had been worrying about air conditioners for much of his adult life. He had no idea what Weinreb did with the air conditioners once the store closed. Six years into his retirement, on a sunny fall day enjoying a piece of chocolate cake with his daughter in a neighborhood diner, air conditioners were no longer his problem.

Postscript

Talk about a dream, try to make it real.

—Bruce Springsteen

THE FIRST BOOK I read while doing research for this book was *Blackout* by James Goodman. I was pleasantly surprised to find my dad quoted a couple of times in the book. Since this was very early in my research, I didn't yet know that Dad was the 'Where's Waldo' of Upper West Side small business owners, popping up in article after article between 1977 and the early 1990s. I called Dad, excited to tell him that he was quoted in a book. But this wasn't news to him. He remembered the interview well and the conversations he had with the author. Turns out there was only one degree of separation between them. James was the son of Dad's sister's best childhood friend, and he had known my aunt.

I asked Dad what he thought of Goodman's book, and he said, "He's a good kid but he missed the mark." I asked him what he meant because I had enjoyed the thoroughness of the book and its oral history approach to the blackout. But for my dad it was simple. The book didn't talk about what came next for the devastated small businesses, and for him that was an important story. Perhaps *the* story. Once the television cameras pack up and go home and the politicians move on to the next thing, what happens to the people that remain? It's a question that plays out again and again in the wake of other natural and man-made disasters, and Dad doesn't think it is ever sufficiently considered or answered.

When I started this project in 2012, I had a different emphasis in mind for the book. I had just been laid off from my job and decided to use this as the push I needed to write a book. Radio Clinic has always loomed large in my imagination. All that time I spent in Radio Clinic as a kid is probably why I am such a big cheerleader for small businesses today. I have long been incredulous at how dispensable our government considers its small businesses. It's not like small businesses are trying to radically remake our capitalist economy. If anything, small businesses are integral to the American imagination. The social mobility and economic opportunity that can come from owning one's own business is the stuff of rags to riches tales. Many people hang their ambitions on the notion that if they couple hard work with a dream, some chutzpa, and the first month's rent, then they too could have a successful business and comfortably move into (or remain in) the middle class.

Every president of the modern era has talked about the importance of our nation's small businesses. Some get quite poetic about it. Words like backbone, small business and economy, often end up together in their speeches. But in Radio Clinic's experience, the rhetoric doesn't mirror government policies. A tax break here. A deduction on real estate loan interest there. And before you know it the vast majority of tax breaks and subsidies support only big businesses. At every level, our government has tilted the playing field toward mega stores and away from small ones. So, they continue to close.

My initial intent with this book was to make a case for small businesses. I am not an economist. I am not an urban planner. I am someone who sees the value of having locally owned small businesses in my community. Through telling the autobiography of Radio Clinic I wanted to remind readers that small businesses are important to their communities and that their viability is ignored to our collective detriment. I believe that most people would like to shop where they live. This might be particularly true in a walking city like New York, but in cities and towns across the country people want to be able to buy their basic necessities without needing to spend the better part of an hour just getting to the store. In my mind Radio Clinic was the protagonist of this book. Radio Clinic witnessed and dealt with many pivotal moments in history. It was impacted by the uncontrollable economic forces of the twentieth century. My grandfather and Harry Baum opened Radio Clinic in the midst of the great Depression. FDR's fireside chats and news during WWII made owning a radio essential for every household. Manufacturing during World War II and the post war consumerism changed how people shopped and the merchandise Radio Clinic sold. Urban renewal policies of the 1950s and the subsequent displacement changed where people lived in cities and led to overcrowding and crumbling infrastructure in the blocks surrounding Radio Clinic. These blocks further deteriorated with the near economic collapse of New York City in the 1960s and 1970s. Government indifference made it very difficult for Radio Clinic to recover from the blackout and looting of 1977. And the gentrification of the Upper West Side created a seismic shift in the neighborhood. It pushed up rents which hammered small businesses and forced Radio Clinic to close.

From the day I started this project I knew I wanted to open the book with the 1977 blackout. While I changed most things in my approach to this book in my many drafts, I didn't waver on this decision. I saw the looting and Dad's decision to keep the store open as a defining moment. Both for Radio Clinic and my dad. Deciding to keep the business open meant that almost to the day of Dad being the sole owner of Radio Clinic, he needed to operate in crisis mode. This decision set the tone for what came next. In the months after the blackout, the survival of Radio Clinic was a hard-fought, in-the-trenches, kind of battle. But even after navigating that recovery effort, the store was never fully in the clear. What was threatening its survival changed over time, but there was always something. Lingering debt to creditors from the blackout, indifferent bureaucrats, hostile bank managers, chain stores, cold summers, and the rents all posed a danger. Crisis became normalized for Dad. Since he managed his way through so many of them he thought he could manage his way through whatever came next. Even the crazy rent.

But I kept circling back to Dad's comment about James Goodman's book. That he wanted him to talk about "what happened next." What happened next for Radio Clinic was both the result of economic forces and Dad's human response to those forces. What happened next was different for each looted business and each devastated merchant. Almost no business on the Upper West Side that survived the looting also survived the rent hikes. What happened next for Radio Clinic after the blackout was that Dad devoted most of his time, energy, attention and savings to keep it going for thirty more years. Without these outsized efforts, it would have closed decades earlier. For my dad, and all family-owned businesses, the fate of the business is deeply personal. Mixed in with what you cannot control are the day-to-day decisions, the mistakes, the creativity, the sacrifices, the rewards, the pride, the long hours. It is hard to separate the personal from the political.

The more I worked on this book the more interested I became in the human story of Radio Clinic. I wanted to capture both what it was like for a family to run a long-standing small business as much as I wanted to highlight what a neighborhood loses when it loses one. So, Radio Clinic moved from being the main character in the book to a supporting one and the humans moved closer to center stage. And there was no getting around the fact that much of this particular story was Alan Rubin's story. Initially I wasn't sure how I felt about Dad being the heart of the story. Certainly, he has enough personality to fill a book. That wasn't the issue. But I was worried that I saw his weaknesses more clearly than I saw his strengths. The last 15 years of Radio Clinic were tough ones and his compulsive optimism and seemingly willful blind spots were more present to me than his scrappiness and open heartedness. But I had under-estimated him. It just took one interview for the sheer force of his personality to win me over. Sure my dad, arguably the hero in this story, is a flawed man. But where's the fun in rooting for a perfect hero?

I decided to write this book in February of 2012. Interviewed Dad a few times over the phone in March. And in April met up with him at Josh's home in Brooklyn for Passover. This trip set the tone for the rest of the book project. First, ever the appliance salesman, he bought me a good hand recorder so I wouldn't need to rely on my aging iPhone voice memos for interviews. And true to form I never really figured out how to use it. He suggested I get in touch with Ruth Messinger and Gail Brewer to interview them about the fight for commercial rent control. Messinger had been the Manhattan Bureau President in the 1980s and was the Executive Director of Jewish Women International (JWI) in 2012. It was a big job and she was a busy woman. I emailed her to ask for an interview and her assistant set up a meeting at JWI headquarters. She greeted me and quickly let me know that it was because of her respect for my dad that she was making time to talk to me. And that I had one hour. Gail Brewer, now the Manhattan Bureau President and also a busy woman, also made time to talk to me. When Dad walked me in and out of the stores on Broadway to interview the longtime merchants, they all made time to talk. On our walk to the Metro Diner to meet up with Matt Baum, several years after Dad retired and moved out of the city, people on the street smiled when they saw him and greeted 'Mr. RCI.'

Seeing the respect that everyone had for Dad took me back to when I was a kid spending my days at the store. Before I started this project, it had been a long time since I talked about Radio Clinic with my mom or brother with anything other than a sense of dread of what was actually happening with the business and what might happen next. But now I was looking through Dad's clipping files and reading all the articles that were written about him. Now that I was interviewing him for a book, I let him talk as long as he wanted about any random memory about the store instead of trying to shut down stories I had heard before. I thought I had heard all the stories there were to hear, but I learned something new every time we talked. Josh and I reminisced about working in the store when we were younger and how proud we were as kids to be part of it. And while we could both compile quite a list of why we never wanted to own Radio Clinic and decisions we wish Dad never made, we both respected his community-minded approach to anchoring the neighborhood and recognized his impact on our approach to community building.

I knew I had a story to tell, but had a hard time convincing others of that fact. The first round of rejections from publishers and literary agents derailed me for about a year. I tend to believe complete strangers when they tell me something I have done, or created, isn't any good. Two years later, my second round of rejections made me angry.

By this time, I felt confident that my book was worth publishing. I had done my due diligence researching the literary agents interested in this genre of book, but they had all said no. By 2017, I started to feel like the clock ticking. My dad was 82 and while he could live another 15 years, he also might not. He was a big part of this project; we had plans to do book talks together, but first I needed to publish it.

I am usually more comfortable not pursuing ambitious goals than trying and failing. I am more comfortable championing other people's projects than my own. And as a result, I have under-achieved professionally. But over the past six years, I've been reminded of the lessons from my grandfather and father. I am the granddaughter of a man who used all of his savings, took a leap of faith, and opened Radio Clinic during the Great Depression. And I am the daughter of a man who declared, *We Are Staying*, and against a lot of odds, made those three words come true. Surely I could do this far simpler and much less risky thing.

It occurred to me there could be a publishing company that didn't care that I was an unknown author without a large social media platform—my own. Turns out I too wanted to work around institutional gatekeepers. I created *Carb House*, my own tiny press. I hired an editor and cover designer and published this book. I think of myself as more of a problem identifier than a problem solver, so I am inordinately pleased with myself for solving this problem—and seeing this book to fruition. Two-thirds of the way through writing *We Are Staying*, I realized that in writing this book I wrote a better ending for Radio Clinic. Now that the project is complete I think I wrote a better next chapter for myself too.

The Thank Yous

IF I COULD, I WOULD live my entire life by committee. Whenever logistically feasible I rely on my smart friends and family to weigh in before I make life decisions. There is no decision too small that I don't want input from my trusted advisors. This book was no exception. In 2012 I was unexpectedly laid off from my job. I had been kicking this book idea around in my head for years and decided to use this sudden unemployment as the push I needed to start writing it. I figured I would find some part-time work, research for 3 months, write for 9 months and then by the end of the year I would have some semblance of a book. Instead I embarked on a six-year exercise in self-doubt, picking up and putting down the book multiple times. During these six years, a great many people in my life offered sage advice, concrete editing skills, song suggestions and general motivational support to help me get this book to the finish line. Thanking people is a risky undertaking, since I am sure to leave people out. So, consider this a blanket thank you to anyone I know who wished me well in any capacity in the writing and completing of *We Are Staying*.

First the cheerleaders

Six years was a long time to stay committed to a project. In the busy day to day of life it is easy to forget about the creative projects friends are chipping away at. It was meaningful to me that these people made a point to often (*but not too often*) ask me how the book was going, were confident that I would finish it, and that it would be a good book. So, thanks, in alphabetical order to: Iyobosa

Ahonkhai, Char Braxton, Susan Calvert, Christy Clancy, Sally DeBroux, Jennifer Hay, Jill Jacklitz, Barbara June, Susan Kaye, Ruth Kraut, Dana Maya, Katie McGlenn, Susan Ramspacher, Philippa Rappaport, Tor Roessler, Lara Sutherlin, George Vecsey, and Kimberly Wasserman.

Word smiths of the highest order

I am not a concise person. My informal motto is why use 40 words when 400 will suffice. I count myself as immeasurably lucky to have Laura Dresser and Amy Hanauer, two smart and funny women that traffic in words all day long, in my life. Both were willing to take breaks from what they were doing when I emailed them, and moved some words around to make my descriptions a bit pithier.

The informal editors

I am fortunate to have many people in my life who are good editors. Both in terms of giving useful structural feedback and simply being more attentive than I am to the conventions of English grammar. Cat Cappellero, Judy Davidoff, Araceli Esparza, Kevin Mullen, Jonathan Rosenblum, and Bethanne Yeager were particularly helpful.

The taskmaster

My (mostly) monthly meetings with Marybeth Collins to make sure our creative projects were moving forward helped keep me moving forward.

The professionals

This book is only self-published in the sense that I paid for the publishing of it myself. A few professionals helped with editing, cover design and lay-out of the book. I enjoyed working with Diana Boger, Carrie Kilman, Matt Rothschild and Jane Rosenman. Heidi LaMarr Rudd took my photo for the author picture. Sharon Bjryd painted a great rendition of Radio Clinic for the book cover but I ultimately decided to go with the photograph for the cover. (Although her painting is hanging in my living room and I encourage you to find her online and buy some of her paintings.)

People I interviewed

Special thanks to Matt Baum, Kevin Baker, Gail A. Brewer, Ruth Messinger, Ethel Sheffer and the many Upper West Side small business owners that took the time to talk to me.

The blurb writers
Whenever I felt like there was simply too much to figure out to self-publish this book and my energy for it started to flag, I would re-read the blurb that John Nichols wrote for my book. John is a generous friend and an optimistic man who wrote a lovely book description. I mean who isn't encouraged when a well-regarded writer has this to say about your book, "...but what makes this book so brilliant, and so necessary..." Thanks also to Jenifer Hixon—who I think of as the story whisperer—, Kevin Baker and Gail A. Brewer.

The Wisconsin Historical Society Press colleagues
Kristin Gilpatrick, Sara Philipps, Kate Thompson, and Liz Wykoff kindly offered their cover design expertise to help me settle on the cover for this book. Special thanks to Kristin for her marketing input.

Clutch photographer
Jay Rappaport walked to the corner of 98th Street and Broadway several times to get just the right photo of the corner street sign for the back cover.

The children
Eli and Tamar growing into busy teenagers with their own interests, launching into their adult lives, gave me the time to devote to this project. Tamar was particularly helpful in showing me how to make a Spotify playlist. I still prefer a mixed CD (well actually a mixed cassette but who has a Sony Walkman anymore?), but having a Spotify playlist for each chapter makes me happy.

The spouse
Matt Calvert's consistent encouragement of this project, even though it seemingly came out of the blue in 2012, is a large part of why I was able to complete it. If he had only provided emotional support. Dayenu[6]. If he had only convinced me it was ok to just work part-time so I could finally finish this project. Dayenu. If he had only done a careful final grammar edit and made sure I was consistent with the Oxford Comma. Dayenu. And if he had only kept me nourished with his homemade sourdough bread and citrus cocktails. Dayenu.

6 It would have been enough, the refrain from my favorite Passover song.

The brother

Josh Rubin lived up to his wise older brother billing these past six years. He was a renaissance man with his help, no question he couldn't handle. Whether it was as small as the name of the guy who inspected all the Upper West Side elevators in the 1980s, as complicated as Upper West Side politics or as tricky as how to navigate rehashing thorny business and financial decisions with my parents, his advice was sage. Plus, he can wordsmith with the best of them and his song suggestions were always perfect.

The mother

Sandra Rubin's support and pride in my writing a book was unflagging, even though she might have told this particular story differently. And her impeccable memory for family history came in handy.

The father

I will forever be grateful at the trust Alan Rubin had in me to write this book about Radio Clinic. A book where he is essentially the main character. I covered an expanse of years and described some of his happiest moments and some of his absolute worst. Through this book we both had the pleasure of getting to know each other better and learned that there actually is a limit to how many times my dad wants to repeat the same story.

Appendix I

The store listings

Radio Clinic was located on Broadway between 97th and 98th street. For most chapters I listed what stores were on Radio Clinic's block during the time period described in the chapter. Since the events described in chapter 7 and chapter 8 took place the same year as chapter 1, I didn't list the 1977 stores again. I put chapter 9 and chapter 10 together since the events described in both chapters took place around 1980. The phone book archives were only available until 1993 so I couldn't list the stores on the block for chapters 13 and 14. In 2018 I walked up and down the block to record what stores are there now, and was able to include that list for the final chapter.

The books and articles I read

These books, newspaper articles and videos expanded my understanding of New York City, the Upper West Side, the 1977 Blackout, and the various economic forces that impacted the store over an 80 year period. For each chapter I list the sources that informed my understanding of the time period described in the chapter.

The soundtrack

I make a soundtrack for myself for almost everything I do. I can get obsessive about it. I have stayed in relationships longer than was advised because of how much the boyfriends in question liked the mixes I made them. I particularly like the challenge of themed mixes. While writing the book, I put together a mix of songs for each chapter that either fit the theme of the chapter, the time period covered in the chapter, had the right words in the title or in some way made complete sense to me as relevant for the chapter. You can find these playlists on Spotify (playlist titles below) or on my website, rubinjen.com.

(Covers are indicated with an * and songs that are not in the Spotify library are indicated with an **.)

Chapter 1
The Blackout

Stores on Broadway from 97th street to 98th street:
(*from the 1977 phonebook*)

2576: Eastern Craft Center

2578: Stationary

2580: Pathe (cleaners and dyers)

2581: Steinberg Moses (Rabbi)

2582: Oppenheimer meats; E.C Drug Discount Corp

2585: Mary & Tony Flower Shop; Joyeria La Pulsera (jewelry)

2586: Ab's Outlet Inc.

2587: Riverside Cleaners; Aquino shoe repair

2588: West Side Music Center; Blue Star Fashions

2589: Sloane's Supermarket, Inc.

2590: Variety Store

2592: Ernel Hosiery Center Inc.

2596: Spring Garden Restaurant; House of Siam Restaurant

2597: Riverside Pizza

2598: S.C.S. Discount Center

2599: Radio Clinic, Inc.

Books and Articles I read for this chapter

- Baker, Kevin. "Welcome to Fear City." *The Guardian.* May 18, 2015.
- Blackout History Project archive, retrieved from http://blackout.gmu.edu/archive/a_1977.html.
- Curvin, Robert & Porter, Bruce. *Blackout Looting!*, The Ford Foundation Report, 1979.
- Goodman, James. *Blackout.* North Point Press, 2003.
- Impact Assessment of the 1977 New York City Blackout, report commissioned by the Department of Energy, 1978.

- Jackson, Kenneth, editor. *Encyclopedia of New York City, Second Edition,* Yale University Press, 2010.
- New York City phonebooks, microfiche from New York City Public Library, 1934.
- Witten, M. and Mass, J. Blackout!, 1977. (*from a newspaper clipping in my dad's clipping folder with the title of the paper cut out, so not sure what newspaper*)

Songs I listened to while writing this chapter:
Spotify playlist: WeAreStaying_Chapter1
- Bad Luck, *Neko Case*
- Heatwave, *Martha and the Vandellas*
- Hot Fun in the Summertime, *Sly and the Family Stone*
- Hot In Herre, *Nelly*
- In The Dark, *Nina Simone*
- New York Blackout, *Soul Asylum*
- New York Blackout '77, *Mighty Sparrow*
- Simple Twist of Fate, *Jeff Tweedy**
- Summertime, *Janis Joplin**
- Summer in the City, *Regina Spektor*
- The Night the Lights Went Out, *The Trammps*

Chapter 2
From Russia with Love

Stores on Broadway from 97th street to 98th street:
(*from the 1929 phonebook*)
2576: Mutual Project Coupon Corporation (premium station);
    A. Schutte (cigars)
2577: Huyler's Confectionary & Teas Room
2578: Ben Fishman fruits; Hudson Fruit & Produce market; Franco Bros
    (shoe repair); Androvick (florist)
2580: Blau Brothers (dairy); Francois (hair dresser)
2581: Maurice Ackerman (dentist); Hudson Dyer & Company
    branch office; Nedick's Orange Juice
2582: Kramers Juvenile Boot shop; Daniel Reeves Inc. (branch)
2583: Snappy Dress & Waist Shop
2584: Epicure Food Stores Corp; S & B Delctsn Inc.

2585: Bright Painting Co.; Chock Full O' Nuts Co (shelled nuts store);
      Solon Cohn (real estate); Theodore Kriloff, (real estate), Milady
      Hat Shop, Mrs. Moir (gowns)
2586: Margarita Beauty Parlor (hairdresser)
2587: Dr. Frederick Baer (chrpdst); Franco Bros. (shoe repair); H & K Cigar Co
2588: Jules Bauer's (cleaner/dyr); Bauer's Sanitary Shop; West End Tailoring
      & Cleaning; Claire Specialty Shoppe, Robert Soffer (hosiery)
2589: Fleischer's Restaurant; French lingerie Shop; Riverdale Restaurant
2590: Gartenberg (house furnishings)
2592: D Piciulo (shoe repair)
2593: Arch Preserver Shoe Shop; Charles Markell
2595: Adelphi Dairy
2596: Irvings Dairy and Appetizing store; Trauts Realty Corp
2597: Schwartz & Forger (branch)
2598: Borchard Affiliations; S Bishop Marks (lawyer)
2599: Davega Inc. (sporting goods and radio store)

Books and Articles I read for this chapter

- A Timeline of Ellis Island. Retrieved from http://www.libertyellisfoundation.org/ellistimeline.
- Brotherhood of Sleeping Car Porters. Retrieved from: http://www.blackpast.org/aah/brotherhoodsleepingcarporters19251978.
- Cassette recording from 1969 when my cousin interviewed my grandfather.
- Cassette recording from 1978 when my brother interviewed my Uncle Jack.
- Gray, Christopher. "A History of New York Traffic Lights." *New York Times* May 16, 2014.
- History of Jewish Communities in Ukraine. Retrieved from: http://jewua.org/berdichev/.
- Jackson, Kenneth, editor. *Encyclopedia of New York City, Second Edition*, Yale University Press, 2010.
- Kaminer, Ariel. "College Ends Free Tuition, and an Era." *New York Times*, April 23, 2013.
- Kroessler, Jeffrey. *New York Year by Year*. New York University Press, 2002.
- Radio in 1936: Retrieved from: https://www.flickr.com/photos/70118259@N00/5490100800/in/set72157626051208969/lightbox/.
- Trager, James. *The New York Chronology*, Collins Reference, 2003.

Songs I listened to while writing this chapter

Spotify playlist: WeAreStaying_Chapter2

- Anatevka, *Fiddler on the Roof*
- Another Hundred People, *Stephen Sondheim*

- Anthem of Belarus, *Don Cossack Choir* (*my grandfather's favorite musicians*)
- Empire State of Mind (Part II) *Alicia Keyes*
- First Day in New York, *Nitin Sawhney*
- Immigrant, *Sade*
- Immigrant Eyes, *Guy Clark*
- Immigrants (We Get the Job Done), *K'naan, Riz Ahmed, Snow Tha Product, Residente, and Riz MC*
- In the Beginning, *K'naan*
- New York, New York, *Frank Sinatra*
- Statue of Liberty, *XTC*

Chapter 3
A Dream, Some Chutzpah, and the First Month's Rent

Stores on Broadway between 97th and 98th street:
(*from the 1934 phonebook*)

2576: A Schulte (cigars)

2577: Huyler's confectionary & tea rooms

2578: Geo Andlovick (florist); Central Florist Co; John Mazza (fruit); Rex Fruit Market

2580: Blau Brothers (dairy); Radio Clinic

2581: Chisholm & Chapman (brokers); Nedick's; Rosedust Beauty Studio; Wright Laundry

2582: Kramers Juvenile Boot Shop; Daniel Reeves Inc.

2584: New Yorker Delicatessen Stores

2585: Dave's Dairy; Thrift Hosiery Shop; L A Youdelman

2586: Louis Beauty Salon

2587: Dr. Frederick Baer (chrodst); Elkwood Bake Shops

2588: Orange Cleaners & Dyers; Phillip Appelbaum; Nancy Hat Shoppe

2589: Park Lane Drug Co; Coburn Delicatessen Inc.

2590: S Gartenberg (house furnishings)

2592: C. H. Shoe Repair Shop

2593: Arch Preserver Shoe Shop

2594: Riverside Bedding Shop Inc.

2595: A Leider & Son (stationary)

2597: Levan Dairy

2598: Borchard Affiliations Inc.; Melville Greencwald (attorney); Max Segal (attorney); Jos Morse (attorney)

2599: Davega City Radio Inc. (radio & sporting goods)

Books and Articles I read for this chapter

- Browning, Judith. *NYC Yesterday and Today.* Corsair Publications, 1990.
- Burrows, Edwin & Wallace, Mike. *Gotham: A History of New York City to 1898,* Oxford University Press, 1999.
- Collins Brown, Henry. *Valentine's City of New York: A Guide Book.* Valentines Manual, Inc., 1920.
- Federal Writers Project. *The WPA Guide to New York City.* Pantheon, 1939.
- Footner, Hulbert. *New York: City of Cities.* Lippincott, 1937.
- Jackson, Kenneth, editor. *Encyclopedia of New York City, Second Edition,* Yale University Press, 2010.
- James, Rian. *All About New York.* The John Day Guides, The John Day Company, 1931.
- La France, Ernest. "In 35 years, Subways Have Greatly Changed the City, and the Citizens as Well." *New York Times* November 26, 1939.
- Lockwood, Charles. *Bricks and Brownstone: The New York Row House, 1783–1929.* Rizzoli, 2003.
- New York City phonebooks, microfiche from New York City Public Library.
- Parker Chase, W. *New York: The Wonder City 1932,* New York Bound, 1984.
- Pileggi, Nicholas. "Renaissance of the Upper West Side." *New York Magazine.* June 30, 1969.
- Radio in 1936: Retrieved from: https://www.flickr.com/photos/70118259@N00/5490100800/in/set72157626051208969/lightbox/.
- Salwen, Peter. *Upper West Side Story: A History and Guide.* Abbeville Press,1989.
- "Seek to Beautify Upper Broadway." *New York Times* May 6, 1931.
- Trager, James. *West of Fifth: The Rise and Fall and Rise of Manhattan's West Side.* Scribner, 1987.
- "Settling the West Side." *New York Times,* September 11, 1886.
- "Clean up Drive Started in Upper Broadway Area." *New York Times,* March 28, 1937.
- The United States 1940 Census.
- 16th Census of the U.S. 1940 Retail Trade: 1939 Part 1.

Songs I listened to while writing this chapter

Spotify playlist: WeAreStaying_Chapter3

- Blue Skies, *Joséphine Baker* *
- Fairytale Of New York, *The Pogues and Kirsty MacColl*
- It Started Out So Nice, *Rodriguez*
- My Shot, (*The Roots, featuring Busta Rhymes, Joell Ortiz & Nate Ruess*)
- New York Town, *Woody Guthrie*
- Salt of the Earth, *Rolling Stones*

- Salt of the Earth, *Bettye LaVette**
- The Perfect Life, *Moby featuring Wayne Coyne*
- Tiger Woods, *Dan Bern*
- What a Wonderful World, *Joey Ramone**

Chapter 4
The Golden Age of Radio

Stores on Broadway between 97th and 98th street:
(*from the 1940 phonebook*)

2576: Endicott Restaurant

2577: Riviera theater

2578: A S Hoffman (stationary)

2580: Jean Pathe (cleaners and dyers); Radio Clinic; Riviera Barber Shop

2581: Chisholm & Chapman (brokers); Kanarek & Sladowski (furriers);
      Nedick's; Wright Laundry

2582: Daniel Reeves Inc.

2584: New Yorker Delicatessen Stores

2585: Gabriel & Wollman (dairy); Liebert Gaston Madison Ave Inc.;
      Louis & Murray (dairy); Thrift Hosiery Shop

2586: Louis Beauty Salon

2587: Riverside Cleaners; Frederick Bauer (podiatrist); Your Beauty Parlor

2588: Max's Millinery

2590: William Steinberg (bedding); Riverside Bedding Shop

2591: Blau Bros (dairy)

2593: Harvest Produce (fruits)

2595: A Leider (stationary)

2596: Renee (corsetiere)

2597: Philip Ermann (butcher)

2598: Borchard Affiliations Inc.; Borchard Management Corp;
      William Harrington (broker)

2599: Davega City Radio Inc. (radio & sporting goods)

Books and Articles I read for this chapter
- Ancestry: The United States 1930 Census.
- Ancestry: The United States 1940 Census.
- Federal Writers Project. *The WPA Guide to New York City.* Pantheon, 1939.
- Gray, Christopher. "Streetscapes: Central Park's 'Hooverville';
  Life Along 'Depression Street.'" *New York Times*, August 29, 1993.

- Jackson, Kenneth, editor. *Encyclopedia of New York City, Second Edition,* Yale University Press, 2010.
- New York City phonebooks, microfiche from New York City Public Library.
- Pileggi, Nicholas. "Renaissance of the Upper West Side." *New York Magazine.* June 30, 1969.
- Plumb, Stephan. *The Streets Where They Lived: A Walking Guide to the Residences of Famous New Yorkers.* MarLor Press, 1989.
- Radio in 1936: Retrieved from: https://www.flickr.com/photos/70118259@N00/5490100800/in/set72157626051208969/lightbox/.
- Salwen, Peter. *Upper West Side Story: A History and Guide.* Abbeville Press, 1989.
- Simon, Jordan. "The History of "Radio Row. NYC's First Electronics District." *The Gothamist,* July 25, 2016.
- The City of New York: Economic, Historical and Descriptive Facts, Chamber of Commerce of the State of New York, 1939.
- Trager, James. *West of Fifth: The Rise and Fall and Rise of Manhattan's West Side.* Scribner,1987.
- "Welcome to 1940s New York, New York City Market Analysis." *News Syndicate Co., The New York Times Co., Daily Mirror and Hearst Consolidated Publications, Inc,* 1943.

Songs I listened to while writing this chapter
Spotify playlist: WeAreStaying_Chapter4
- Golden, *Jill Scott*
- I Can't Live Without My Radio, *LL Cool J*
- King of the New York Streets, *Dion*
- Native New Yorker, *Odyssey*
- New York, *St. Vincent*
- On the Radio, *Donna Summer*
- Radio Daze, *The Roots, featuring Blue, P.O.R.N & Dice Raw*
- Step Right Up, *Tom Waits*
- Take the "A" Train, *Duke Ellington*

Chapter 5
The Post World War II Bust

Stores on Broadway between 97th and 98th street:
(*from the 1950 phonebook*)
2576: The Greenery (fruits & veggies)

2577: Riviera Theater

2578: Toby Rosenthal (stationary)

2580: Link's Infants & children's wear; Jean Pathe (cleaners & dyers);
      Jack Stranger (barber)

2581: Nedick's; Andres Oliveri (florist)

2582: A & P Flower Garden

2583: Jos & Son Trauring (jeweler)

2584: Gruenebaum Bros Inc. (meat market)

2585: Seymour Hoodack (dairy); Thrift Hosiery Shop;
      Wright Laundry; Youdelman L A

2586: Francois Labs; Louis Beauty Salon

2587: Riverside Cleaners

2588: Renee (corsetiere); Max's (millinery)

2590: Strand Café

2591: Blau Brothers (grocery); Essen Delicatessen; Sherlip & Vinnick (dairy)

2592: National Council of American Soviet Friendship; West Side Community

2593: Harvest Produce (fruits)

2594: Advanced Fine Arts Co.; Oscar Krasner (picture frames);
      Uptown Art Shop

2595: M Koutsavlis (luncheonette)

2596: Nelson Furriers

2597: Al Ermann (butcher)

2598: Borchard Management Corp; Max Segal (attorney)

2599: Radio Clinic

Books and Articles I read for this chapter

- Browning, Judith. *NYC Yesterday and Today.* Corsair Publications, 1990.
- Curvin, Robert & Porter, Bruce. *Blackout Looting!,*
  The Ford Foundation Report, 1979.
- Grutzner, Charles. "City Gives Plan to Rehabilitate Upper West Side."
  New York Times, Oct 6, 1955.
- Hevesi, Dennis. "Upper Broadway Loses Last of its Fur Trade."
  New York Times, July 25, 1990.
- Hourigan, Michael. "Small Businesses Now and Then." Retrieved from:
  blog.shoeboxed.com/smallbusinessthenandnow/.
- Jackson, Kenneth, editor. *Encyclopedia of New York City, Second Edition,*
  Yale University Press, 2010.
- Koenig, Peter. "The Problem That Can't Be Tranquilized."
  New York Times, May 21, 1978.
- Lyford, Jospeh P. *The Airtight Cage: A Study Of New York's West Side.*
  Harper Colophon Books, 1968.

- "Manhattan's Two Worst Blocks in the 1960s." *Ephemeral New York,* April 20, 2011.
- New York City phonebooks, microfiche from New York City public library
- Pileggi, Nicholas. "Renaissance of the Upper West Side." *New York Magazine.* June 30, 1969.
- Porter, Russell. "Our Changing City: Along Manhattan's West Side." *New York Times,* July 4, 1955.
- "Preliminary Plan: West Side Urban Renewal Area". *The New York Urban Renewal Board,* 1959.
- Salwen, Peter. *Upper West Side Story: A History and Guide.* Abbeville Press, 1989.
- Schweber, Nate. "A Community Erased by Slum Clearance is Reunited." New York Times, October 9, 2011.
- Television: Retrieved from: http://www.livinghistoryfarm.org/farmingin the50s/life_17.html.
- "The Tragedy of Urban Renewal: The destruction and survival of a New York City Neighborhood." *Reason TV,* September 28, 2011.
- Trager, James. *West of Fifth: The Rise and Fall and Rise of Manhattan's West Side.* Scribner, 1987.

Songs I listened to while writing this chapter
Spotify playlist: WeAreStaying_Chapter5
- Autumn in New York, *Ella Fitzgerald & Louis Armstrong**
- Flower, *Moby*
- New York City, *LeadBelly*
- Nueva York, *Santana*
- Open Letter (To a Landlord), *Living Colour*
- Oye Como Va, *Tito Puente*
- Television Rules the Nation, *Daft Punk*
- The Boy From New York City, *The Ad Libs*
- When Will I Get to be Called a Man, *Big Bill Broonzy*
- You Better Mind, *Bessie Jones (Alan Lomax Archive)***

Chapter 6
The Hornet's Nest

Stores on Broadway between 97th and 98th street:
(*from the 1965 phonebook*)
2576: DaiIch Sho Ten; Eastern Craft Center Inc.
2577: Riviera Theater

2578: Leonard Henigson (stationary)

2580: Jean Pathe (cleaners & dyers); Richard's Jewelry; Philip Vottiero

2581: Nedick's; Rabbi Moses Steinberg

2582: A & P Flower Market; Gruenebaum Co (meats)

2584: Gourmet Treats

2585: Joyeria La Pulsera (jewelry); Mary & Tony Flower Shops;
    Rafael Grocery Store

2586: Ab's Outlet Inc.

2587: R Feria (shoe repair); Moshe Lemberg Cleaners; Riverside Cleaners

2588: Dave Kramer (launderette)

2589: Sloan's Supermarket, Inc.

2590: Strand Café

2594: Gabriel Yagid (cotton goods)

2595: Promot Cleaners

2597: Al Ermann (butcher)

2599: Radio Clinic

Books and Articles I read for this chapter

- Aileron. "The Facts of Family Business." *Forbes Magazine*. July 31, 2013.
- Curvin, Robert & Porter, Bruce. *Blackout Looting!*, The Ford Foundation Report, 1979.
- Darton, John. "96th and Broadway Typifies Essence of a Changing City." *New York Times*, May 29, 1972.
- Gupte, Pranay. "Derelicts Vex Residents Along Upper Broadway." *New York Times*, July 17, 1973.
- Horsley, Carter. "The Columbia, 275 West 96th Street." *City Realty*.
- Jackson, Kenneth, editor. *Encyclopedia of New York City, Second Edition*, Yale University Press, 2010.
- Koenig, Peter. "The Problem That Can't Be Tranquilized." *New York Times*, May 21, 1978.
- Pileggi, Nicholas. "Renaissance of the Upper West Side." *New York Magazine*. June 30, 1969.
- "Preliminary Plan: West Side Urban Renewal Area". *The New York Urban Renewal Board*, 1959.
- Prial, Frank. "Sanitation Men to Spur Cleanup of Broadway from 72nd to 116th." *New York Times*, September 29, 1976.

Songs I listened to while writing this chapter:

Spotify playlist: WeAreStaying_Chapter6
- Crazy Mary, *Victoria Williams*
- Don't Forget Me, *Neko Case*

- I Happen to Like New York, *Judy Garland*
- Keep Me in Your Heart, *Warren Zevon*
- Living for the City, *Stevie Wonder*
- My Little Corner of the World, *Yo La Tengo*
- My Shot, *Lin Manuel Miranda*
- New Generation, *Washington Squares*
- Sons and Daughters, *The Decemberists*
- Talkin' Big Apple '75, *Loudon Wainwright III**
- The Magic Number, *De La Soul*
- Wipe the Clock, *Uncle Tupelo*

Chapter 7
The Looting

Books and Articles I read for this chapter

- Amsterdam News Editorial Staff. "Black Opinion Mixed on Looting; Merchants, Politicians Outraged." *New York Amsterdam News*, July 23, 1977.
- "Blackout." *Newsweek*, July 25, 1977.
- "Blackout Reactions." *New York Amsterdam News*, July 23, 1977.
- "Blackout '77, Once More, With Looting." *Time Magazine*, July 25, 1977.
- Cockburn, Alexander & Ridgeway, James. "God Gets a Bum Rap." *Village Voice*, July 25, 1977.
- Curvin, Robert & Porter, Bruce. *Blackout Looting!*, The Ford Foundation Report, 1979.
- Fricke, Jim. *Yes Yes Y'all: The Experience Music Project Oral History Of HipHop's First Decade*. Da Capo Press, 2002.
- Goodman, James. *Blackout*. North Point Press, 2003.
- Greenberg, David. "Where Have All the Looters Gone?" *Slate Magazine*, August 15, 2003.
- Impact Assessment of the 1977 New York City Blackout, report commissioned by the Department of Energy, 1978.
- Jackson, Kenneth, editor. *Encyclopedia of New York City, Second Edition*, Yale University Press, 2010.
- Lescaze, Lee. "The Most Talked About Paper in N.Y Isn't Tedious, but Also Isn't Ad Fat." *The Washington Post*, November 19, 1977.
- Rosen, Jody. "Scratch the Historical Record and Hear HipHop's Past." *New York Times*, February 13, 2006.
- Witten, M. and Mass, J. Blackout!, 1977. (*from a newspaper clipping in my dad's clipping folder with the title of the paper cut out, so not sure what newspaper*)

Songs I listened to while writing this chapter
Spotify playlist: WeAreStaying_Chapter7
- Accident Waiting to Happen, *Billy Bragg*
- Benny's Dispatch, *LinManuel Miranda*
- Controversy, *Prince*
- Don't Stop 'Til You Get Enough, *Michael Jackson*
- Embrace The Chaos, *Ozomatli*
- One Chance, *Modest Mouse*
- The Message, *Grandmaster Flash and the Furious Five*
- When a Fire Starts to Burn, *Disclosure*

Chapter 8
Better than a Kick in the Head

Books and Articles I read for this chapter
- Cummings, Judith. "Aid in Looting is Near Completion." *New York Times*, September 2, 1977.
- Curvin, Robert & Porter, Bruce. *Blackout Looting!*, The Ford Foundation Report, 1979.
- Gupte, Pranay. "Vivid Scars of '77 blackout Remain in the City." *New York Times*, July 13 1978.
- Impact Assessment of the 1977 New York City Blackout, report commissioned by the Department of Energy, 1978.
- Kempton, Murray. "Pride of the 44th." *New York Post*, July 15, 1977.
- Kihss, Peter. "Theft Damage Cost in Blackout put at 135 Million." *New York Times*, July 22, 1977.
- Kleiman, Dena. "New York is Denied Disaster Status Aid." *New York Times*, July 31, 1977.
- Rubin, Alan. "The Blackout Legacy, Op Ed." *New York Times*, July 12, 1980.

Songs I listened to while writing this chapter
Spotify playlist: WeAreStaying_Chapter8
- I Will Survive, *Gloria Gaynor*
- Reason to Believe, *Bruce Springsteen*
- Seven Nation Army, *The White Stripes*
- Stronger, *Kanye West*
- The Long Road, *Nusrat Fateh Ali Khan & Eddie Vedder*
- This Mess We're In, *PJ Harvey Featuring Thom Yorke*
- Under Pressure, *Queen* and *David Bowie*

Chapter 9
An Occasion Worth Remembering
Chapter 10
Aftershocks

Stores on Broadway between 97th and 98th street
(*from the 1980 phone books*)

2576: Broadway Army & Navy; Ialdo Japanese Sword Technique;
      Jodo Japanese Four Foot Staff Technique

2578: Li Long Chon (stationary)

2580: Jean Pathe (cleaners & dyers)

2582: E C Drug Discount Corp.

2585: LaDichosa #2; Mella Grocery

2586: Ab's Outlet Inc.

2587: Riverside Cleaners; Aquino (shoe repair)

2588: West Side Music Center

2589: Sloan's Supermarkets Inc

2590: Your Gift Shop

2592: Ernel Hosiery Center Inc.

2596: Hunan Balcony Restaurant

2597: Riverside Pizza

2599: Radio Clinic; RCI Discount Appliances

Books and Articles I read for this chapter

- Breen, Victoria. "Profile of Courage." *The West Side TR Shopper,*
  July 1420, 1979.
- New York City phonebooks, microfiche from New York City Public Library.
- Schulz, Dana. "The History of Symphony Space: From the Astor Market to
  the Leonard Nimoy Thalia." *6sqft,* March 4, 2015.
- "Transcript of Address Delivered by Mayor Koch at Inauguration
  Ceremony." *New York Times,* January 2, 1982.
- Weinbrenner, Don. "Applies New Angle to Appliance Sales." *Daily News,*
  May 11, 1980.

Songs I listened to while writing this chapter:

Spotify playlist: WeAreStaying_Chapter9

- Chariots of Fire theme song
- Dog Days are Over, *Florence and the Machine*
- Everything is Everything, *Lauryn Hill*
- Here Comes the Sun, *Richie Havens**
- Mona Lisas and Mad Hatters, *Elton John*

- New York Groove, *Ace Frehley*
- The Stoop, *Little Jackie*
- 8 Million Stories, *Kurtis Blow*

Chapter 11
Follow the Lease

Stores on Broadway between 97th and 98th street
(*from the 1986 phone books*)
2578: Salah Candy & Grocery Store
2579: The Wiz Distributors Inc.
2581: Empire Szechuan Restaurant; Fotorush Incorporated; J's
2585: A & M Discounts
2586: Ab's Outlet Inc.
2587: Aquino (shoe repair); Riverside Cleaners
2588: Friends
2589: Sloan's Supermarkets Inc.
2590: Your Gift Shop
2592: Amore Nails
2596: Hunan Balcony Restaurant
2597: Riverside Pizza
2599: RCI Discount Appliances

Books and Articles I read for this chapter
- "Building Banking Relationships." *New York Times*, April 25, 1982.
- Morrisroe, Patricia. "The Yupper West Side." *New York Magazine*, May 13, 1985.
- Rubin, Alan. "The Blackout Legacy, Op Ed." *New York Times*, July 12, 1980.

Songs I listened to while writing this chapter
Spotify playlist: WeAreStaying_Chapter11
- Guess I'm Doing Fine, *Beck*
- Follow the Money, *The Proclaimers*
- New York, I Love You but You're Bringing Me Down, *LCD Soundsystem*
- Sign of the Times, *Harry Styles*
- Stand Up, *Flobots*
- The Underdog, *Spoon*
- Trump, *Cindy Lee Berryhill*
- Wake Up, *Arcade Fire*

Chapter 12
Air Conditioners

Stores on Broadway between 97th and 98th street (*from the 1993 phone books*)

2578: Alpine Sound; Blimpie's; Café Viva; Salah Candy &
      Grocery Store; World of Nuts & Chocolate

2579: The Wiz Distributors Inc.

2580: Little Leepers Inc.

2581: Fotorush Incorporated; J's Restaurant

2586: Dramatics for Hair

2578: Tasti D Lite

2589: Red Apple Supermarket; Sloan's Supermarket

2590: MSC Variety and Gift

2596: Hunan Balcony

2599: RCI Discount Appliances

Songs I listened to while writing this chapter:
Spotify playlist: WeAreStaying_Chapter12
- Empire State of Mind, *Jay-Z, featuring Alicia Keys*
- Everybody Ona Move, *Michael Franti*
- Go Your Own Way, *Cranberries**
- New York State of Mind, *Billy Joel*
- Too Hot, *Kool & The Gang*

Chapter 13
The Time Bomb

Books and Articles I read for this chapter
- Gottlieb, Martin. "Trump Set to Buy Lincoln West Site."
  New York Times, December 1, 1984.
- Gutis, Philip. "Upper West Side Attracting New Settlers."
  New York Times, March 9 1986.
- Horsley, Carter. "The Columbia, 275 West 96th Street." *CityRealty.*
- Morrisroe, Patricia. "The Yupper West Side." *New York Magazine*,
  May 13,1985.
- New York Times Editorial. "Businesses Don't Need Rent control."
  New York Times, Nov 28, 1987.

- Powers, John J. "New York Debates Commercial Rent Control: Designer Ice Cream Stores Versus the Corner Grocer." *Fordham University Law School,* 1987.
- Purnick, Joyce. "Koch Panel Opposes Commercial Rent Controls." *New York Times,* June 5, 1986.
- Smolowe, Jill. "Plan for Housing Revives Dispute Over 96th St. Site." *New York Times,* Oct 16, 1980.
- Wedemeyer, Dee. "Debate on Rent Control Crackles." *New York Times,* March 18, 1984.

Songs I listened to while writing this chapter
Spotify playlist: WeAreStaying_Chapter13
- An Open Letter To NYC, *Beastie Boys*
- The Gambler, *Kenny Rogers*
- Hard Times in New York Town, *Bob Dylan*
- Have a Little Faith in Me, *John Hiatt*
- Hold On, *Alabama Shakes*
- Livin' in America, *Black 47*
- Lose Yourself, *Hans Nayna**
- My City Was Gone, *The Pretenders*
- New York Is Killing Me, *Gil Scott-Heron*
- Our Song, *Joe Henry*
- Strugglin' Blues, *T-Bone Walker*
- Where Do the Children Play, *Yusuf/Cat Stevens*
- Worrisome Years, *Greg Brown*

Chapter 14
That's All Folks

Books and Articles I read for this chapter
- Saul, Michael. "'77 Outage Report Was Left in the Dark." *New York Daily News,* Aug 21, 2003.
- Gonzalez Rivera, Christian. "State of the Chains." *Center for an Urban Future,* 2015.

Songs I listened to while writing this chapter:
Spotify playlist: WeAreStaying_Chapter14
- Are You Alright?, *Lucinda Williams*
- End of the Movie, *CAKE*

- How It Ends, *DeVotchKa*
- Looking For A Way Out, *Uncle Tupelo*
- New York City Serenade, *Bruce Springsteen*
- On Your Way, *Alabama Shakes*
- Pursuit of Happiness, *Kid Cudi*
- Rouse Yourself, *JC Brooks and the Uptown Sound*
- There's a Starbucks (Where the Starbucks Used to Be), *John Wesley Harding*
- Til I Collapse, *Eminem*
- You Can't Always Get What You Want, *Rolling Stones*

Chapter 15
Retirement

Stores on Broadway between 97th and 98th street (*from walking up and down Broadway, 2018*)
2576: Tobacco Shop
2578: Global Copy; Value Cub Pharmacy; Café Viva
2581: Texas Rotisserie Grill
2583: Tower West Cleaners
2586: The Jewel Boutique
2587: Upper West Cuts, (barbershop)
2588: Awadh restaurant
2589: West Side Market
2590: The Oasis Nail Spa
2592: Mono Cleaners
2599: (vacant bank branch coming soon)

Books and Articles I read for this chapter
- Gonzalez Rivera, Christian. "State of the Chains." *Center for an Urban Future*, 2015.

New York City songs I listened to while writing this chapter
Spotify playlist: WeAreStaying_Chapter15
- Astral Plane, *Valerie June*
- Blue Skies, *Willie Nelson**
- Dodge, *Dog's Eye View**
- Feeling Good, *Nina Simone*

- Here Comes the Sun, *Richie Havens**
- I Can See Clearly Now, *Johnny Nash*
- I Can See Clearly Now, *Holly Cole**
- I'll be There, *Jackson Five*
- Let's be Still, *The Head and the Heart*
- One Day/Reckoning Song, *Asaf Avidan & the Mojos*
- Redemption Song, *Johnny Cash and Joe Strummer**
- Redemption Song, *Bob Marley and The Wailers*

Appendix II

Tributes Radio Clinic received from people who lived in the neighborhood

The West Side Rag published an excerpt of the book in April, 2014. *Weekend History: How One Store Fought to Survive the Blackout and Looting of '77*. Below are some comments posted after the article.

> I remember the blackout, I had to walk home from 116 & Broadway to 89 & Amsterdam. It was certainly a crazy night. RCI was where my dad brought the AC for my room, and I brought my boom box. I remember AMC, I had a few friends that worked there Henry D., Bradley D. and a few others, West side camera, Berman twins all truly family owned stores. That was what made the UWS what it truly was. Now it's chain stores that need to cover their rents by selling $5k outfits.. miss the old times.

> I grew up on 99th Street around the corner from Radio Clinic, we shopped there all the time (for air conditioners, of course) and I remember that blackout well. It still survives today, in an era of big box stores and online next day delivery. Nice to hear more of the back story to the family that owns it.

I moved to the UWS in 1977. 37 years later, I am sick about the loss of our mom and pop stores. People like your father helped make it a neighborhood. It was manageable, human size. Now all our small businesses are being driven out, not by the small looters, but by the big ones, like the Duane Reade's and the CVS's. How many of them do we need? How many do we want? Why do we no longer have any say so about what happens in our neighborhoods. What happened to the block associations? Everyone I talk to agrees, but we can't seem to be able to do anything about it.

Beautiful memories interlaced with memories of a not so beautiful episode. Nevertheless, the UWS won't be same without RCI on the corner. I don't know anybody in the neighborhood who didn't buy something from RCI. The real problem is there is no cap on commercial real estate. It forces out all the small businesses, which is a shame. The UWS has become a wasteland of banks, drug stores and highend markets. Truthfully, the UWS has lost its charm, and its bohemian type neighborhood atmosphere.

The West Side Rag announced that Radio Clinic was closing in October, 2014. *RCI Appliances Set to Close After 80 Years on the Upper West Side.* Below are some comments posted after the article.

Growing up, I remember a Radio Clinic on Broadway and 83rd....I think where Artie's is now....my dad was a friend of Mr. Rubin...he not only repaired radios, but in those early days I think we got our first TV and air conditioner there....he was a true pioneer!!!

As I've commented before, you never had to leave 79th to 86th on Broadway for ANYTHING! A self contained village. Will they sit around the campfire one day reminiscing about Duane Reade and TD Bank???

I was always afraid of this one going. I bought my first fridge, stove & dishwasher here. Truly a loss for the 'hood.

Really sad about this. I always went there first because I trusted the staff. They were knowledgeable, friendly and the service was always great. I can't stand what this neighborhood is becoming because of greedy landlords.

A neighborhood is defined by local businesses like this one. You could write a sad song with the names of the departed and sorely missed, starting with Harry Oppenheimer's great meat store. Kudos to RCI for sticking around so long, and good luck to them in Queens!

This breaks my heart. When I moved to 80th St. and was beginning my real estate career in NY, RCI sold me scratch and dent specials with warranties to help me keep AC in my apt. They bent over backwards with every purchase I made there. It was obvious they truly cared. I never paid more there. They made sure of that. From vacuum cleaners to ovens to AC units at my subsequent purchase of an apt in Inwood, they were truly my neighborhood store. I hope they become the same for their new neighborhood in Queens.

I checked on the Internet to see if I was right after all remembering a Radio Clinic also at 83rd and Broadway. (#2390). I was!!! There are old ads for both stores. When did that one close???

The Rubin family left a wonderful and heartwarming legacy.... The West Side of those days are memories that never tarnish...

I was heartbroken when I went there yesterday and saw the sign. I have the exact same experience with RCI that others above have had. Try to get such personal treatment at a "superstore."

We—meaning the residents of NYC—CAN do something about this ongoing demolition of small businesses. We can find a way to REGULATE landlords so that the rent increases to commercial tenants are reasonable and within bounds. They do it in London. Why can't we do it in NY?

I went by RCI yesterday and was shocked to see the sign! What a loss for the neighborhood! I could always count on them for what I needed. They were a true "neighborhood" store dealing with some difficult delivery problems, etc. I will miss them. I hope things go well for them in Queens.

Jesus, that was one of the staples that set above 96th street apart from the rest of the Upper West Side. Now that that last little stretch is going away, I mourn the neighborhood I knew.

Appendix III

Alan Rubin's NYT op-ed about the blackout in 1980

On the evening of July 13, 1977, the day of New York City's last blackout, I stood on the sidewalk at Broadway and 98th Street contemplating the ruins of what, just a few hours earlier, had been one of my appliance stores. Less than an hour after the lights went out in Manhattan, the looters arrived, forced open the steel gate protecting the store, shattered the glass storefront, and pillaged the store. Like many other owners of small businesses on the West Side, that night I considered moving my business out of the city.

The West Side Chamber of Commerce's figures show that a total of 41 West Side stores were looted during that night. Mine was one of the 12 stores that were completely gutted. Five small West Side businesses that were looted and vandalized have never reopened their doors.

The looting crystalized in one night what, in fact, has happened over the last decade to small businesses in New York City, and, further, it provided a dramatic, condensed example of the difficulties that are encountered by small-businessmen here who seek help in the forms of loans or tax rebates.

Encouragement provided by my neighbors, both shopkeepers and apartment dwellers, reinforced my determination to stay.

Broadway and 98th Street is in one of those marginal areas that all-too-common in the city. You find one good block where there are shopkeepers and apartment dwellers who care about property and community life, and it is juxtaposed with blocks filled with vacant, garbage-strewn storefronts besmirched with graffiti.

It was those caring New Yorkers who came to tell me that it is stores such as ours that help to maintain stability on the Upper West Side. If we were to leave, my neighbors said, another gutted, deserted building would be added to the neighborhood and to New York City. I had to stay.

And then came the efforts to rebuild. Funding to repair damage and replace inventory was my top priority.

I began making the wearying rounds of city and state agencies, such as the Office of Economic Development of the City of New York. At each, I was listened to courteously and was given expressions of sympathy and apology. But I received no financial aid.

The hastily set up Emergency Aid Commission was able to grant me only $1,800—despite the fact that my losses were in excess of $100,000.

A United States Government-funded Small Business Administration loan that would take me the next 20 years to repay did not arrive until Jan.5, 1978—more than five months after the disaster.

Now, there is a 16-month waiting list for Small Business Administration loans. Today, loans can be obtained for expansion but not for working capital.

I had to use my own working capital to start on repairs, and this put additional pressures on the business.

The faith of my suppliers was the major asset during this difficult and trying time.

Local legislators are currently seeking an expanded Small Business Administration appropriation for New York City together with a reduction in the discount rate for small businesses.

But small-businessmen must also contend with leases that double or triple rents at expiration time, and many of them contain clauses that are tagged to the Consumer Price Index, which do not reflect true costs.

I made over 100 telephone calls to officials in trying to arrange an interest-free loan, a grant, a moratorium on taxes—anything that would help get me on my feet again all without success.

Ironically, by staying in business, I was saving 19 jobs, which prevented 19 people from going on unemployment. Not only were unemployment funds being saved for New York City and for the state, but also each year these employees contribute to the city's and state's coffers, both from their taxes and their spending.

An estimated sum in excess of $200,000 each year in taxes from my employees' wage packets and from the sales tax on goods sold in my stores goes to the city and state from my small business alone. Multiply this by 10 similar businesses and that is $2 million.

I can't help but think that the Chrysler Corporation is being rescued from its own bad judgment by the same United States Government that will not come to the aid of tax-paying small-businessmen when they are the victims of criminal acts.

It is this policy that has cost New York City as many jobs and taxpayers over the years as would be lost if the Chrysler Corporation went bankrupt.

The small-businessman is always being praised for begin the backbone of the economy and for providing stability for the community. And yet the small-businessman is in the same position as the victim of a crime who never regains all that he has lost. So, too, with New York City.

Alan Rubin, a proprietor of two appliance stores, is a member of the board of directors of the West Side Chamber of Commerce.

Jen Rubin's NYT op-ed about the 40th anniversary of the blackout

On the morning of July 14, 1977, my dad stood on the sidewalk at Broadway and 98th Street staring through the shattered windows of his store, Radio Clinic. A lightning bolt had led to a cascading power failure that had plunged New York City into darkness. By the time the power came back on, 25 hours later, more than 1,600 stores had been looted. With its shelves of stereo equipment, televisions, boomboxes (remember those?) and other electronics, Radio Clinic had been an irresistible target.

The Upper West Side was one of the hardest hit sections of Manhattan, with 61 stores looted between 63rd and 110th Street. Looters tore off iron security gates by hand, or with chains attached to cars. New Yorkers feared that the blackout was proof that the social order and perhaps the city itself was in an irreversible decline. Many small-business owners, and even more residents, decided it was time to get out.

While my dad and his employees cleaned up the store, neighbors streamed in to ask if Radio Clinic was shutting down, too. The store had been on the block since 1934, when my grandfather set up shop and sat in the store front window in a white lab coat fixing broken radios. My dad had worked there since he was a teenager. I was only 11, but I already spent my weekends there sticking prices on film and demonstrating the new Atari arcade game to people as they passed by the store. My dad had no intention of abandoning Radio Clinic.

So finally he put up a sign in one of the few remaining windows. Thick black marker on white poster board read: "WE ARE STAYING." Neighbors saw the sign and came in offering thanks, flowers and hugs. They were relieved that this business was not giving up.

The sign also drew reporters' attention. "I'm responsible for 25 families — the families of people that work for me," my dad told a Time magazine reporter. "What's going to happen to them if I pull out? As bad as I got hit, there are other guys that got wiped out. What's going to happen if they can't reopen? What can the city and the government do to keep people like us from leaving these neighborhoods?"

My dad knew he needed help from the city to rebuild his business. Just two years earlier, New York the city had been on the verge of bankruptcy, and it wasn't too big a leap to think it would now put some muscle into keeping the looted businesses from boarding up their windows, if only to stabilize neighborhoods (and tax revenues).

My dad began making the wearying rounds of city agencies. He was full of ideas on how the city could help looted businesses, from offering interest-free loans to waiving July taxes. At each meeting, he was offered plenty of sympathy. But in the end he received very minimal financial aid — $1,800 — an amount so negligible he considered it only "slightly better than a kick in the head." He was so frustrated he wrote his own Op-Ed for this newspaper about the experience. As far as my dad was concerned, the city had failed to protect its small businesses during the blackout, and now it was abandoning them in its aftermath.

He managed to keep the store afloat, however, eventually renaming it R.C.I. A few years later, it turned out that his vote of confidence in the city had been prescient. By the 1980s, the Upper West Side was experiencing a real estate boom and was gentrifying quickly. But the small businesses like my dad's that anchored the neighborhood were now victims of their own success. As property values went up, storefront rents became untenable. "Lost our lease" signs popped up all over.

My dad got involved in lobbying for rent stabilization for small businesses. Mayor Ed Koch acknowledged that rents were a problem but opposed any rent controls. He felt confident that the free market was the most effective mechanism for determining what type of store a neighborhood needed. Mayor after mayor, City Hall never decided that small businesses were in the city's public interest. As the rents continued to rise through the 1980s, 1990s and 2000s, small family-owned stores continued to close. It was increasingly clear that one thing the market couldn't bear was small businesses.

My dad retired in 2006. R.C.I. hung on until 2014, when it, too, finally closed.

In 1977 my dad asked a reporter what the city could do to keep stores like his in business. In the 40 years since, the city has been indifferent to this question. As a result, many neighborhood stores, in business at the same locations for decades, are gone forever, replaced by a revolving cast of chain stores that do not sink deep roots into the neighborhoods they serve. The next time the city is down, facing hard times, will there be anyone left who will put up a sign that says "WE ARE STAYING"?

"What can the city and the government do to keep people like us from leaving these neighborhoods?" It is still a good question.

About the Author

Jen Rubin is a former New Yorker living in Madison, WI. An obsessive maker of mixed tapes and quite possibly the best challah baker in town, she has worked for social change throughout her career. Jen leads storytelling workshops around Madison and teaches the occasional social policy class at the University of Wisconsin. Jen likes to tell a good story and hear a good story and coproduces the Moth StorySlam in Madison.

http://www.rubinjen.com

Made in the USA
Columbia, SC
22 October 2018